THOMAS HARDY

THOMAS HARDY

BY

EDMUND BLUNDEN

" By love of truth
Urged on, or haply by intense delight
In feeding thought, wherever thought could feed,
I did not rank with those . . .
Who, in this frame of human life, perceive
An object whereunto their souls are tied
In discontented wedlock ; nor did e'er,
From me, those dark impervious shades, that hang
Upon the region whither we are bound,
Exclude a power to enjoy the vital beams
Of present sunshine."

WORDSWORTH'S *Excursion*

MACMILLAN
London · Melbourne · Toronto

ST MARTIN'S PRESS
New York
1967

PR
4754
B5
1967

—

First Edition 1942
Macmillan's Pocket Library 1951
Reprinted 1954, 1958, 1962
Reprinted in Pocket Papermacs 1967

MACMILLAN AND COMPANY LIMITED
Little Essex Street London WC2
also Bombay Calcutta Madras Melbourne

THE MACMILLAN COMPANY OF CANADA LIMITED
70 Bond Street Toronto 2

ST MARTIN'S PRESS INC
175 Fifth Avenue New York NY 10010

PRINTED IN GREAT BRITAIN

PREFACE

In these pages some account of Hardy's life, and especially his literary life, is given, within which, as well as in the remaining chapters, a personal impression of his nature and his writings is attempted. The usual sources of information, such as Hardy's own prose and verse, including essays, articles and speeches, and Mrs. Hardy's two volumes of biography, have been kept in view. The two volumes of Dr. W. R. Rutland have been appreciatively read and referred to, and while the book was approaching its final stages Dr. Carl J. Weber's equally agreeable and instructive *Hardy of Wessex* came to hand. Let me say, however, that for such similarities as may be found in passages of information, or of critical surmise or conclusion, I have not been drawing upon the works of others, except when the specific acknowledgment is made. All who examine Hardy's life and work closely will inevitably often found their views on the same things, and their views will often be of a kind.

A great deal of hunting has been done in outlying places for this new study—in memoirs, critical surveys, topographies, in magazines, newspapers and printed odds and ends beginning to be of some antiquity. Old interviews and letters to the press have been sought for, with some success, though the war has made all such searches increasingly troublesome. In this and other labours necessary to the occasion Miss Sylva Norman has given me noble help. Indeed I am indebted to many friends for assistance, a useful hint here and there, sometimes on a point of available information, sometimes on a probable characteristic of our author. The list of these obligations would be lengthy to complete here ; but I cannot omit the names of Siegfried Sassoon, Lt.-Col. C. H. Wilkinson, Sir Sydney Cockerell, Rupert Hart-Davis, A. E. Filmer, Thomas Hennell, F. A. Downing, H. W. Garrod, A. Stanton Whitfield, Amiya Chakravarty, E. J. Finch, A. Hayashi and Dr. Marie Stopes.

No one could accept an invitation to write a book about a man of Thomas Hardy's eminence and long experience without a deep sense of responsibility, and doubt of his own qualifications. It was so with me. But, whatever the measure of my success or failure in depicting Hardy and his work, the book represents the warm affection which I feel to this day for one of the kindest and brightest of men, one who received the youngest of us without the faintest shade of distance or inequality, and whose memory, even from days all too few of walks and talks, shines steadily through all decline and change.

E. B.

May 13th, 1941

CONTENTS

CONTENTS

I

ORIGIN AND UPBRINGING

WHEN Thomas Hardy was born, the deaths of Scott, Coleridge, Charles Lamb, even the earlier ones of Byron, Shelley and Keats, were fresh in memory. All these names were something more than names to him throughout his life. When he was a country boy going to school and discovering literature, Wordsworth, with whom he has been both bitterly and sympathetically compared, was ending his days as Poet Laureate and robust old gentleman. Thackeray's editorship of the *Cornhill*, the jubilee of which was observed in candid verses by Hardy in the fullness of time, was among the themes of sensible conversation in Hardy's early manhood. Charles Darwin's new book *The Origin of Species*, with the controversy ensuing, was another. Carlyle, whose cryings in the wilderness did not resound in vain for Hardy, might not have noticed any remarkable difference between his own epoch and that of his admirer, who was over forty years old when the Sage of Chelsea died. Thomas Hardy lived beyond the Victorian age to be the personal friend of many who had had their first experience of mature life as young soldiers in the War of 1914–1918 ; and it was not fancy or vanity in the Georgians which discerned that he read their literary productions—among many others—with no less zeal for any promising and creative evidence therein than he had brought formerly to the famous utterances of J. S. Mill, and Swinburne, and Trollope.

It would be inexact, by a large margin, to leave the preliminary note for an account of Hardy in this state of reference to authors and nobody else. This master of the written word, to the end of his days, was not by any means one of those whom Byron condemns as " all author " ; and the great ghosts who appealed to him were, some of them, persons of importance in Byron's extraordinary rhyming review *Don Juan*—men of action, dynasts of the early nineteenth century. Hardy's feeling for these figures was next door to actual experience and contact. As a child, he could and did hear of fantastic history, such as the retreat from Moscow, from those who had taken their small but intense part in it, and so when he spoke of Napoleon a hundred years after Napoleon's passing, to hear him was as though the flaming belfries of Moscow and the unshaven jowl of the thwarted Corsican were just outside the window. No melodrama mingled with this almost direct reporting : the forms of the time simply offered themselves in familiar imperishable colour to their quiet critic. Possibly he had been born too late, though he came only a generation after the zenith of Buonaparte and Byron.

In his carriage and his treatment of affairs Hardy had some manner of military ability, or at least his presence suggested the potential corps commander. Immensely peaceful as he was, thoroughly wise on the problem of force and bloodshed in international argument as he showed himself in speech and in writing, his being still kindled at the hint of heroic contest. He may not have known that distinctly. There were many things about himself that he did not know. Nevertheless, even in his ninth decade, he could flash out a reminder of the times when swords were bright in honour's cause ; he could give a martial rhythm to a sleepy summer moment. At such a time, it might be recalled that he would have read Tennyson's poem on the funeral of the Duke of Wellington with all the excitement of immediate news, being at that date a serious and race-conscious boy twelve years of age ; one should perhaps write kin-conscious, for all that Hardy felt and reasoned about mankind was founded in a particular appreciation of " local hearts and heads ". His absolutes (and who among his country's speculative masters has ever excelled him in attempting to set forth the mystery of things ?) were conjectured first and last from a profound submission to the diurnal visible microcosm of Wessex. Even that term, in this regard, may be too wide.

Who and what were his kinsmen, from what sort of people did he come ? The raising of the question would have pleased him. One of the problems which entertained his leisure for many years was the origin, never yet ascertained by biographers, of the family of John Keats. Having an acquaintance with some of that name, and tracing in them something of the poet's own liveliness and pugnacity, he willingly associated Keats with Dorset, much as he claimed Henry Fielding for another of the sons of Wessex. We may therefore in a spirit of equanimity indulge our ideas on the descent of Thomas Hardy. In offering an opinion on this point, possibly, the recollection of the man himself may be allowed as having a value. But, in reference to his especial work and experience, what value ? Is genius connected in any respect with ancestry ? Is race or class of any significance as touching the individual ? Let us be clear at once : Hardy was, for the greater part of his life, at something of a disadvantage in English society. He could not produce the proper seals and ratifications : he was not " county ". And this would not be difficult to negotiate, were it not the case that he was equally not " peasant ". His father was a stonemason, one who in his world " spoke with authority ". The position requires a subtle understanding of the English village community ; in justice to Hardy himself it is necessary to dwell on the point, for he was not so superhuman as to be unaffected by it, and his works are here and there related to it. As a novelist he was peculiarly worried by the idea that the artificial structure of society could and often must destroy true nature, or impede and injure high endeavour ; from that uneasiness he derived something of his best literary animation, and perhaps too the spectre of convention occasioned some of his weak and unconvincing satirical and sentimental moments.

If there was in him, at one time and another, a strain of resentment as of one excluded, unplaced, there was also a reticent pride, as of one with a lineage ; and indeed the Dorset Hardys were an ancient and interesting race, " formerly of influence ". Perhaps accurate investigation could have clarified his descent from that Clement Le Hardy who was lieutenant-governor of the island of Jersey in 1488.[1] Certainly he knew that his more recent ancestors had played their parts well and truly in the life of that honourable country world Wessex. Aristocracy of one kind might have been travelling byroads there, occupying fastnesses ; but the other kind was marching on, and through its constancy, strength and practical skill the land was mature, the public spirit high. Hardy could feel natural confidence and clearness of outlook by merely being in his native scenes and walking among those steady and unostentatious achievements acclaimed by his friend, the Rev. William Barnes, in verse—and in the Dorset dialect. That good man's poem " Our Fathers' Works " expresses an unalterable element in Hardy's attitude to the fabric of English tradition :

> They clear'd the groun' vor grass to teäke
> The pleäce that bore the bremble breäke,
> An' drain'd the fen where water spread,
> A-lyen dead, a beäne to men ;
> An' built the mill, where still the wheel
> Do grind our meal, below the hill ;
> An' turn'd the bridge, wi' arch aspread,
> Below a road, vor us to tread.

One may also catch something like the very speech of Mr. Hardy, though he did not use dialect in speaking, in the better-known piece by the same excellent hand, called " Praise o' Dorset " :

> We Do'set, though we mid be hwomely,
> Be'n't asheäm'd to own our pleäce ;
> An' we've some women not uncomely ;
> Nor asheäm'd to show their feäce.

Yet his entire personality was not long confined within

[1] A genealogical chart in Professor Carl J. Weber's *Hardy of Wessex* begins with John Hardy, whose will is dated May 8th, 1704.

these happy limits, and from early years he stood in a degree of detachment from the thing he loved. He could not be a second William Barnes even, devoting a subtle literary talent to expression of the assumed character of " husbandman or hamleteer ". He had a larger command.

On June 2nd, 1840, Thomas Hardy was born at Higher Bockhampton in the parish of Stinsford (with about fifty houses and under three hundred inhabitants) near Dorchester—" the capital of Dorset, a town of great antiquity on the Frome ", $119\frac{1}{2}$ miles from Hyde Park Corner and $15\frac{1}{4}$ from Bridport. As yet the railway had not reached these country places : it came when Hardy was six or seven years old, but the coaches still continued to run for a time even then. Dorchester, known widely for its excellent ale, was already proud of possessing " the most perfect Roman amphitheatre in the kingdom ". Its streets were " neatly paved, and the houses in general built regularly of stone ". Vast flocks of sheep grazed on the wide meadows and downlands round about. Another celebrated place " of considerable antiquity " thereabouts was Weymouth, well established as a seaside resort, with a population of only 2669, and picturesque memories of George the Third and other royal holiday-makers. Among the country seats pointed out by the road-book for the London-Bridport road was " Stinsford House, Lady Susan O'Brien ". At that house Hardy's father practised violin-playing. A great and public-spirited family in Dorchester was that of the Pitts.

According to current method, here should appear some bioscopic impression of the world in 1840 into which the subject of this volume arrived. At least, Hardy himself would not be displeased by the indication of a few circumstances of that year. Queen Victoria married Prince Albert in February; an attempt to shoot them both as their carriage was going up Constitution Hill in June was made by a pot-boy named Edward Oxford. A penny postage envelope, designed by Mulready, and ridiculed by the ungrateful, marked the new era in postal business. War broke or crept out against China, though it was not from Japan. Prince Louis Napoleon, in a Thames steamer, invaded Boulogne, but failed and was sentenced to perpetual imprisonment. The foundation stone of the Nelson Monument in Trafalgar Square was laid. The second funeral of the Emperor Napoleon occurred at the Invalides, Paris. There was a war in Afghanistan. Fanny Burney died aged eighty-eight, Mary Shelley revisited Italy, Robert Browning published *Sordello*, and Dickens *Master Humphrey's Clock*. More might be said, but life at Bockhampton went on much as usual.

The old photographs of Hardy's parents published by Florence Hardy in the *Early Life* of her husband tell us something to the purpose. The father appears a tolerant, humorous, probably indolent man, of an absolute integrity and general friendliness. He obviously deserved his son's comparison of him to Hamlet's Horatio. The mother's looks show one determined, critical, far-seeing, capable of sharp comment, but ever essentially kind to human realities. Thomas Hardy the elder, had he been more worldly, would have obeyed his wife's judgment and transferred his business and builder's yard, and four children, into some more conspicuous and profitable place than Stinsford, but he never did—and Mrs. Hardy could understand it, though she would have had things otherwise. In any case, there was enough to keep the business going and to employ several men. Times were serene and homely. We hear of Father Hardy giving his little boy a toy accordion and teaching him to fiddle and prepare himself music-books. Of Jemima Hardy and her son (and it is known that the quality of the relationship remained much the same through many years) the significant picture is drawn in Hardy's poem on the Roman Road across his native heath ; yet it is improbable that he was deliberately characterizing her as a Roman matron—

> But no tall brass-helmed legionnaire
> Haunts it for me. Uprises there
> A mother's form upon my ken,
> Guiding my infant steps, as when
> We walked that ancient thoroughfare,
> 　　The Roman Road.

Besides Thomas Hardy, the children were Mary, Henry and Kate ; the last two survived the author.

Naturally, when the urgency of an education for the boy Tom was arriving it was his mother who dealt with it. The character of a scholar, so profoundly marked in all the career of this man, though he would never have claimed the name, was originally impressed by her zeal. In truth, Hardy had small schooling by comparison with later conventions, and maybe his parents were a little puzzled by the educational problem. His mother hoped at one time, as he himself recalled, to obtain for him a presentation to Christ's Hospital, London,—this would have been about the year 1848,—but, the Governor through whom this admission should have come happening to die, the opportunity was lost. Had it chanced otherwise, we should have seen in all likelihood a great classical scholar and an eminent divine named Thomas Hardy ; but there must have been some works of imagination over the same name or a neat pseudonym nevertheless. In his village, he was set to work on the usual simple plan and with school-books of ancient style, *Walkingame's Arithmetic*, *The Tutor's Assistant* and the like ; and he took some pains with these. But his chief ability led towards classical reading, and his mother, as if signalizing a certainty so soon, gave him a useful copy of Dryden's *Virgil* at this period. Passing on to a school in Dorchester, the boy was put through the " venerable Etonian *Introduction to the Latin Tongue* ", and laid the foundations of that grammatical mastery which in later days even brilliant classical men do not always display. Ahead of him, in a way only to be fully perceived by those who went to rural schools before the world changed its mind, there shone a misty dream of learning's attainments, of advancements, of " academic institution "—but Hardy, like Charles Lamb, was to be defrauded of that even in its plainer realities, and to notice the difference throughout life.

While he was occasionally fancying that his Latin would pave the upward way for him into holy orders, another path and a nearer one was opened. In 1856 his father had some conference with John Hicks, the ecclesiastical architect to whose designs he sometimes worked, on the subject of Tom's getting into the world ; and the boy became Hicks's pupil, leaving the old British School at Dorchester and the strict discipline of Isaac Last with regret but with his usual good-will. Within a very short time, in his new employment, Hardy prepared a " notebook exquisitely written and with neat diagrams of architectural structure ", which is now kept among the Hardy treasures at Dorchester Museum—those including also a book with his musical studies and annotations. In Hicks's office the talk was good, and professional tasks were not allowed to prevent other studies ; the dream of a quiet paradise of learning stayed and charmed the boy who " in his walks to and from the town often caught himself soliloquizing in Latin on his various projects ". Besides, next door was the school of that wonderful scholar Mr. Barnes, the pride of the country, and it was easy enough to get him talking on the wellsprings and beauties of philology and literature. Hardy was soon finding his way into Greek as well as Latin, and inevitably in that day and that particular office a notion of theology was involved with the rest. The Greek Testament edited by Griesbach, which Hardy acquired in February 1860, was not bought for caprice, but for the exact discussion of matters like Paedobaptism. His fifth edition of Liddell and Scott (1851) was a favourite great book. One may hardly say of him what he said of William Barnes, " A more notable instance of self-help has seldom been recorded ", for Hicks and the young men who came to him were all contributors to Hardy's education ; but the picture of the earnest youth in this phase is exceedingly touching and pleasing, and it may well be outlined in Hardy's later comment that round the year 1860 for him, " the professional life, the scholar's life, and the rustic life, combined in the twenty-four hours of one day ". I have seen similar instances, and wish them more numerous.

For indeed his country world was so far his greatest education. There stayed his canon of life, of beauty, of merit; thence without effort he drew from fountains that had run clear for his forefathers, and still flowed in sun and shade with eternal attraction, variousness and blessing. As yet his heart was light,—reflection had not become more than immediate response,—his old home was his " without intervals ", and, it is clear, his father was a good companion. The countryside lived not on farming and building and weaving and baking and brewing only, but on plenty of merry occasions, dancing and music-making and social interchange between parish and parish; the Hardys were familiar figures and valued musicians at these. The future novelist was interested in the natural and kindly way of that community, in everybody who was of it, from the clothes each wore to the loves each had; there went playing through all that moving frieze of old and young the spirit of humour, which some observers of country life miss through habitual sorrows or high themes of their own. Hardy, however his later experience and accumulation of evidences on destiny affected what he wrote, never lost in himself the ready, innocent cheerfulness which was the world he lived in as a young man; and again, in his age, he was locally celebrated, apart from his greater fame, as one who abounded in anecdote mainly of an amusing kind. With much else that delighted him as the gift of those years of childhood and youth, one thing is always striking: it was then that he formed his inward gallery of the beauty of women. It was as though he could paint their portraits for himself, and house them quietly and gladly within his heart, much as the actual artists of the day, Etty, Maclise, Collins, were doing with solid pigments and canvas; and far on in his course he could still name many and many a woman who was blossoming when he was Tom Hardy of Bockhampton, and still could eagerly identify the especial appearance and the individual music of each one. The dance of life, the ardent and yet the shy faces passing round in rhythm, the light hearts and melody of words, the wit of beauty and the supremacy of frankness, these he had known and these never wholly failed him; his most enshaded pages are ever revisited by them, and behind the ominous lead-hued storm you see him, to quote the poet whom he largely resembles, " standing on the top of golden hours " in those Dorset revels of almost a century since.

I have borrowed Wordsworth's Shakespearean phrase to sum up Hardy in his home and his first manhood, and it is to Wordsworth that Mrs. Hardy has ascribed something in the tenor of the earliest poem from his pen that she could find, " written between 1857 and 1860 ". Appropriately, its subject is his birthplace, and its Latin title, " Domicilium ", commemorates his Latin studies and inaugurates that long series of classical titles to be seen as one turns the pages of his poetical works. It is questionable whether the influence upon the composition of these calm and delicate blank-verse lines was Wordsworth so much as Coleridge, who had meditated so agreeably on " our pretty Cot " and with more of imaginative control in " Frost at Midnight ". Venturing into poetry, Thomas Hardy came with obvious reverence for an art so lovely in its placid strength, and so well exemplified in England by the accomplished genius of many seers. The time would come when his feelings and thinkings would compel the development of a stranger, a more strenuous and more explorative versecraft, but for that young hour there was no need beyond usual words and cadences; and one may wish, without grudging at what he has left us, that circumstance had granted him more impulses to play this quiet and haunting tune. It has its sadness, too, for he is recording not only the house he knew, but the house that had gone even before his time with the years, the deep personality of the scene which his father's mother could still defend for a space from oblivion:

> Our house stood quite alone, and those tall firs
> And beeches were not planted. Snakes and efts
> Swarmed in the summer days, and nightly bats
> Would fly about our bedrooms. Heathcroppers
> Lived on the hills, and were our only friends;
> So wild it was when first we settled here.

This poem, in all probability the survivor of a group of juvenilia, accords with Hardy's reiterated statement (not always treated with much respect) that he set forth in literature not as a novelist but as a poet. He would frequently and gratefully mention an early friend whose example and conversation in matters of literature affected him considerably as a beginner. The pages of fame do not include the name of Horace Moule, classical scholar and critic, but in Hardy's retrospect that name was honoured. Horace Moule, " rich in manifold gifts ", was one of the sons of the vicar of Fordington, then a village and now united with Dorchester. The vicarage must have been a delightful place in every way, and enchanting to Hardy in its resources of conversation and enlightenment. Besides, Hardy's mother had long been an admiring member of the vicar's congregations. Moule, as Mrs. Hardy has recorded, was responsible for giving his young friend the advice not to concentrate upon Greek literature at the expense of his training as an architect. That training proceeded well, since in truth the character of Thomas Hardy was such that he could do nothing slackly; and in that work were problems and methods and materials to which he came naturally, acquainted with them as he was in essence from his earliest recollections. Besides, the period was that in which the quantity of church restoration, and the general applicability of, or passion to apply, the ecclesiastical touch in architecture, offered the initiate so steady a livelihood that to throw it aside without strong reasons would have been remarkably like recklessness. Moule, a natural leader, did not recommend in preference to it the visions of a university, a parsonage, a connection like his own with the literary press; and Thomas Hardy accepted the considered verdict for the time.

And now, enlarging his horizon through the interchange of ideas with Moule and others, Hardy realized that the arguments in the architect's office on points of theological doctrine were minor matters compared with an intellectual force working through the whole world of religious and philosophic thought. How early he considered what *On the Origin of Species by Means of Natural Selection* (1859) would mean to the place of the Bible in the interpretation of man, I cannot find noted; but there is no doubt about his quick access to the volume of *Essays and Reviews*, published in 1860, and republished very rapidly—the seventh edition is dated 1861. Such a statement, the achievement of several hands working independently, is often glowingly promised but rarely found fulfilled in substance : the book is a masterpiece, now seldom remembered in a day of coarser controversies, but soon proving itself when it is met with. The point of it was the reasoned counsel that the friends of Christianity should accept with lively hope the findings of modern science, not as threatening but as reanimating faith. Here was Benjamin Jowett, urging in italics *Interpret the Scripture like any other book*. Here Frederick Temple declared, " If geology proves to us that we must not interpret the first chapters of Genesis literally ; if historical investigations shall show us that inspiration, however it may protect the doctrine, yet was not empowered to protect the narrative of the inspired writers from occasional inaccuracy ; if careful criticism shall prove that there have been occasionally interpolations and forgeries in that Book, as in many others ; the results should still be welcome. Even the mistakes of careful and reverent students are more valuable now than truth held in unthinking acquiescence." But indeed throughout these *Essays and Reviews* there may be read sentences as couragcous in their meaning—particularly at that juncture—as they are eloquent in their form ; and this book, it is easily seen, is associated with the mental coming of age of Thomas Hardy. As the freedom of the ideas suited him, so did the elegance and decorum of the utterance. Let it be duly added that he was not an excessively solemn young seeker after truth ; for, not long after this publication appeared, he strung his entertaining rhymes on the Higher Criticism as it might be supposed to visit the Respectable Burgher, and send him off in alarm " to read that moderate man Voltaire ".

As this episode belongs to the period when the Cambridge scholar Horace Moule was conspicuously valuable to the progress of the unknown and striving Thomas Hardy, it may be concluded with a brief sketch of Moule's personal brilliance, and that I gladly take from a choice little book of memories by Handley Moule, Bishop of Durham. " My dear brother Horace ", he writes, " had a hundred charming ways of interesting and teaching me, alike in scholarship and in classical history. He would walk with me through the springing corn, translating Hesiod to me. He would draw a plan of ancient Rome with lines of pebbles on the lawn. . . . Wonderful was his subtle faculty for imparting, along with all due care for grammatical precision, a living interest in the subject matter, and for shedding an indefinable glamour of the ideal over all we read."

While he was still articled to John Hicks, Hardy was much employed in measuring and examining details of such churches in the county as had incurred the doom of being restored. This work gave him occasion, more than he would have found otherwise, to attend services and hear still some of the old church bands and choirs in which his family history gave him so affectionate an interest. " But they were going." The American organ was coming. The last of those once famous and important little companies, with its clarinet, flute and violoncello (" Ye mid burn the old bass-viol that I set such value by "), accepted its fate in the nineties. In Hardy's private world their tunes and minds and manners went on for his time if not for all time ; his pastoral tales of course do honour to their talent and feeling and personal oddity, but something yet deeper moved him in his reminiscence of these faithful musicians. To them and their devotion, it was discernible, he was bound by a link that was like no other. In the short poem " A Church Romance (Mellstock : *circa* 1835) " he has exquisitely conjectured the moment when his mother, somewhat to her surprise, fell in love with his father, then looking forth from the singers' gallery at Stinsford, gladly busy

> As minstrel, ardent, young and trim,
> Bowing " New Sabbath " or " Mount Ephraim ".

It had been so ; his mother never forgot that unexpected and momentous first regard. And the very names of those tunes were the son's lifelong treasure and mystery.

II

THE GREAT CITY

FEW people think of Thomas Hardy as a Londoner, and his spirit will scarcely choose to haunt the great city in preference to the valleys and knaps of his first and last years; but now, in 1862, he was to begin a long acquaintance with the metropolis—an acquaintance closed in 1920, which he was unwilling in after times to see casually denied. How carefully and happily he spent his time in crowded streets can be seen not only in his contemporary letters to his home but even better in an address which he gave in 1908, happy to share his knowledge with the rising generation. " For clearness ", he said, " let us imagine ourselves in the situation of a young man just arrived in London from Dorsetshire, with a half-formed intention of making the capital the scene of his life's endeavours, and a probability of finding there his home and his interests, possibly his grave. . . . He pauses, maybe, on Waterloo Bridge, and, Dorset people being impressionable, he experiences as he gazes at the picture before him a vivid sense of his own insignificance in it, his isolation and loneliness. He feels himself among strangers and strange things. Being, however, though impressionable, also a very thorough sort of person, he means to explore the town, and leaning against the parapet of the bridge he looks at his new map to find out his bearings." And then Hardy set before his listeners a masterly compilation of all the Dorset names and edifices and illustrious associations which were to be discovered and enjoyed in London by his friends from Wessex. He recommended them to continue with " this line of inquiry, for ", he concluded, " I think— at any rate I hope—that the investigation will tend to lessen that feeling of gloomy isolation to which young men of Dorset stock are peculiarly liable in an atmosphere not altogether exhilarating after their own air— say in days of fog, when the south-west country is known to be flooded with sunshine, or in those days of piercing rawness from the eastern marshes, that seem to eat into the bones, a rawness seldom or never felt in their own shire. They may gradually learn to take these inclemencies philosophically, and to decide, as those noted predecessors of theirs, good and bad, probably decided, that their true locality and anchorage is where what they can do best can best be done."

These passages have the ring of autobiography, and tell us plainly enough the moods and conflicting emotions of young Thomas Hardy when he arrived all alone in the town in April 1862 to find out what Architecture at headquarters might want of him. Without much delay he was given an opening (as " a young Gothic draughtsman who could restore and design churches and rectory houses ") in the offices of A. W. Blomfield, whose reputation stood high already and was to be recognized with a knighthood later. Under this athletic, clever and friendly master Hardy worked for five years, and although he is said to have been

dreamy in the office and inclined to hold up business
with discussions of literature as often as possible, he
took his profession seriously. He competed for, and
won, two architectural prizes at this stage, but it is
remarked that the chief of these successes—the R.I.B.A.
Essay prize in 1862—" had its literary aspect ". All
the same, the subject was " The Application of Coloured
Bricks and Terra Cotta in Modern Architecture ".
The other honour won by Hardy was the Sir William
Tite prize, 1863. For the amusement of his companions he produced a prose sketch called " How I
Built Myself a House "—gentle jesting, done with an
ease which makes one wish he could have continued
in the vein ; and this light satire on his profession and
Victorian improvements has the distinction of being
the earliest published piece by Thomas Hardy traced
by bibliographers. It came out in *Chambers's Journal*
for March 18th, 1865. While he was studying design
with Blomfield, Hardy was also a student of modern
languages at King's College. London University may
presumably claim him as an alumnus.

If there was in Hardy some inborn tendency towards
a more sinister and un-Victorian humour than his first
publication expresses, his duties were occasionally of
a kind to strengthen it. Mrs. Hardy has drawn the
picture of the young man assisting in a work of super-
vision at Old St. Pancras Churchyard when its re-
cumbent occupants were being removed to let the
Midland Railway in. Winter nights, high hoardings
around, flare-lamps, old coffins upheaved and new
ones stacked near by in case the old went to bits, the
mechanical procession of remains from this ground to
another—it would all have been shabby and melancholy

enough without special contributions, like the coffin
which did go to pieces and disclosed one skeleton but
two skulls. Even in country churches, where there
had been no such desperate call for the migration of
the dead, Hardy as restorer was to happen upon queer
ironical facts—time's transference (for example) of
mural tablets, leaving " the stone of the theatrical
couple over the solitary divine, and that of the latter
over the pair from the stage ". In the end, shocked
as he was at the " facetious carelessness ", Hardy
attuned such deeds of time and chance to his whole
theme, which permits the comic spirit to appear even
in the midst of

> Sands, ignoble things
> Dropt from the ruin'd sides of kings,

but does not finally permit ; for the supreme voice
attested by Hardy there is that enthrallingly noble
eloquence of " very gods' composure " in the poem
" Friends Beyond ".

At the period of Hardy's working in Adelphi Ter-
race, and lodging sedately in Kilburn or Bayswater,
some uncommonly good things were happening in the
world of literature : to select a few, George Eliot's
Romola, Trollope's *Small House at Allington*, Browning's *Dramatis Personae*, Swinburne's *Atalanta in
Calydon*, Newman's *Apologia pro Vita Sua*, Dickens's
Our Mutual Friend, Meredith's *Rhoda Fleming*,
Matthew Arnold's *New Poems*, Ruskin's *Sesame and
Lilies* all appeared between 1863 and 1866. Periodical
literature was in a flourishing condition, and space
was increasingly devoted by its proprietors to intellectual debate. The worship of great men, and
notably of those who were leaders of philosophic

movement and scientific speculation, besides the celebrated novelists and poets, was one of the activities
of London. Hardy found all this agreeable and exciting, though he was of a character not to let an
excitement run away with him. He surveyed the land
with the deliberateness of one who came from an un-
hurried and long-living race. If he was to alter his
course, it would be done at the proper time. He
shared in the many evening recreations of the Londoner, but there was nothing of Cruikshank's Mr.
Lambkin about him : and with regard to the competition for literary or dramatic eminence his sense of
his own powers was free from the usual weaknesses
of egotism. " Thomas Hardy " was not the question.
The said individual might be one of the exponents of
humanity to itself, but only the exposition and the
result would matter.

We see him still, beyond the dubious arts of sympathetic guessing, a small, neat, rather French-style
citizen, observing the mind of his age with a reserved
intensity ; two representations of this unassuming but
sharply real action are well known. One is of the
year 1865, the date of the " general release " of *Atalanta
in Calydon*, and the delineation is that made by Hardy
himself in 1910, upon a visit to Swinburne's grave at
Bonchurch :

> O that far morning of a summer day
> When, down a terraced street whose pavements lay
> Glassing the sunshine into my bent eyes,
> I walked and read with a quick glad surprise
> New words, in classic guise. . . .

And, if this assurance may be accompanied with
a surmise, can Hardy not have read with deepest

emotion, and (as he told Swinburne) risk from passing traffic, the address to Aphrodite :

> Was there not evil enough,
>   Mother, and anguish on earth
>   Born with a man at his birth, . . .
> That thou, having wings as a dove,
>   Being girt with desire for a girth,
>   That thou must come after these,
>   That thou must lay on him love ?

Such an indignation, or at least such a perplexity, was soon to be the directing influence of this newcomer's picture of life's inquietude.

The other inevitable reference at this point is the name John Stuart Mill, and again the date concerned is 1865. Hardy set down his impression of this man, whom he had watched making a speech as a parliamentary candidate, forty years later. He says that the treatise on Liberty was known to youthful students like himself " almost by heart ". In 1865 Mill on Utilitarianism was equally interesting, and, in comparison with a mighty though laconic roar from Hardy later on, Mill's conclusion there is worth recalling : " Justice remains the appropriate name for certain social utilities which are vastly more important, and therefore more absolute and imperative, than any others are as a class (though not more so than others may be in particular cases) ; and which, therefore, ought to be, as well as naturally are, guarded by a sentiment not only different in degree, but also in kind ; distinguished from the milder feeling which attaches to the mere idea of promoting human pleasure or convenience, at once by the more definite nature of its commands, and by the sterner character of its sanctions ".

The man who was one day to present *Tess* was less anxious to be in complete agreement than to be assailed by the daemon of thinking; and in bringing his centenary tribute to Mill, Hardy styled him " one of the profoundest thinkers of the last century ", and worded the lasting vision of the man, like a modern Saint Paul or Donne, standing up to arouse the market-place. " The religious sincerity of his speech was jarred on by his environment—a group on the hustings who, with few exceptions, did not care to understand him fully, and a crowd below who could not. He stood bare-headed, and his vast pale brow, so thin-skinned as to show the blue veins, sloped back like a stretching upland, and conveyed to the observer a curious sense of perilous exposure. . . . The cameo clearness of his face chanced to be in relief against the blue shadow of a church, which, on its tran-scendental side, his doctrines antagonized. But it would not be right to say that the throng was absolutely unimpressed by his words; it felt that they were weighty, though it did not quite know why."

The architectural student who was one of Mill's auditory that day had been a thinker from a boy, and the age favoured that serious type. Perhaps there has been no more tremendous time for Hardy's kind of man since Christ challenged selfishness as one of those lies which must abdicate and let life triumph. A glance back at men of genius, beloved by Hardy, flourishing well within the memory of men known to him, may help to illustrate the position. Coleridge was a being endowed with as victorious an intellect as anyone in English story, yet his reasoning strength was chiefly spent on " the constitution of church and state "; that is to say, he worked along the same lines as Bacon or Milton might have done, taking it for granted that the bases of our conduct were arranged by a revealed Deity. Wordsworth allowed that we might draw mystical enlightenment from " Nature " (and so we may to the end), but on the whole it was our duty to follow rules refined by the Church of England and to leave other points, left unmanaged by those, to look after themselves. Keats, whose poetic paganism made Wordsworth turn not quite " celestial rosy red ", saw men struggling with their anxieties and fevers, but expressed no clear suspicion that these pains might be partly conventional and artificial. Keats did not write a poem against the miseries of the world or in quest of their possible origins. Shelley did, but, to say it briefly, his world " had a mask like Castlereagh "; his greater daring was in the main rounded with futility, except in some astronomical or electrical ultimate, wherein Adonais should be made one with Nature. Shelley's rebellion was against a religious or a political creed ; was emotional rather than scientific, notwithstanding his pursuit of physical discoveries.

A quality of thinking which one may call more impersonal arrived with the Victorians. War broke out over it, of course, but we have seen and we see men in the centre of the battle devoted to something above the battle. The truth of praise or blame, of hate or love for the vicissitudes of mortal nature began to thin into irrelevance once the generous progress of all science had become really potent. Something of profounder mystery and fuller involution than a difference between Kentish men and Men of Kent was perceived to underlie and overwhelm society. What Milton

evaded, or was not at a point of time to see, FitzGerald
with far less energy of mind could not help facing :
we are zoological and not theological productions, and
the admixture of the theological test is (love it as we
may) a catch :

> O Thou, who man of baser earth didst make,
> And even with Paradise devise the snake—
> For all the sin wherewith the face of man
> Is blackened, man's forgiveness give—and take !

Darwin himself, who was not given to rhapsody,
extolled the enlargement of considerations on man and
his problem in such words as these : " In the distant
future I see open fields for far more important re-
searches. Psychology will be based on a new foundation, that of the necessary acquirement of each mental
power and capacity by gradation. Light will be thrown
on the origin of man and his history."

Coming to his strength as a critic of life when the
world was burning with the dawn of a new sort of
theory of its creator, Hardy, like other candid young
men, was at once exalted and humbled. Being a steady
man, he persisted in framing his notions as simply and
usefully as he could ; and he was sensible enough to
know that the life of the individual, usually, proceeds
without surrender to one cosmic vision or another. He
was confiding to his notebook, round the year 1865,
many aphorisms on people, manners and characteristics
which do not openly assert that the scheme of things
is illogical. But poetry was his freedom, and he was
not a long while after Meredith in avowing, and that
on a larger view,

> Ah, what a dusty answer gets the soul
> When hot for certainties in this our life !

Several items remain from his lucubrations about the years 1866 and 1867 to illustrate what he was enabled to advance in a newly starlit universe, where no friendly Puddletown band would play the music, no irruption into William Barnes's study elicit an unshakable answer. Of those expressions, struck out with a cold ferocity, a neutrality that looks like the neutrality of a shell before loading, " Hap ", dated 1866, is the most instant. It may have been retouched in later days, but the drive is original.

> If but some vengeful god would call to me
> From up the sky, and laugh : " Thou suffering thing,
> Know that thy sorrow is my ecstasy,
> That thy love's loss is my hate's profiting ! "
>
> Then would I bear it, clench myself, and die,
> Steeled by the sense of ire unmerited ;
> Half-eased in that a Powerfuller than I
> Had willed and meted me the tears I shed.
>
> But not so.   How arrives it joy lies slain,
> And why unblooms the best hope ever sown ?
> —Crass Casualty obstructs the sun and rain,
> And dicing Time for gladness casts a moan. . . .
> These purblind Doomsters had as readily strown
> Blisses about my pilgrimage as pain.

The voice of Nature cries above that of the analyst here.   What had happened to young, dance-loving, wit-playing Tom Hardy that he should be writing such condemnations of the world we live in ?   For the others, " At a Bridal ", " Postponement ", " Neutral Tones " and the rest, all beat like sad waves against unconscious rocks.   No one in comfortable employment, as Hardy was, with appreciative companions, whom he knew he had, ought really to be singing dirges only, however the philosophers of the day might be undermining his gaiety.   The answer is unknown, but " Neutral Tones "

is the kind of hint which is to be recollected here,
though Hardy's addiction to the dramatic lyric must
be allowed for. " Keen lessons that love deceives "
probably lent an edge to his cutting honesty under
the firmament, the Lucretian theatre of distance and
brilliance and infallibility ever appealing to man and
keeping him away. On his twenty-fifth birthday he
wrote, " Not very cheerful. Feel as if I had lived a
long time and done very little. Walked about by
moonlight in the evening. Wondered what woman,
if any, I should be thinking about in five years' time."
That signifies that in much less time there would have
been a woman in the case, or that there had been one
recently ; but the records are silent, except the few
poems which have escaped destruction, and they reflect
the obvious. Hardy, disciplined to a fault, cautious
perhaps to a fault, in spite of his excellence and outward
charm, was in love with someone who preferred other
approaches and, in those days it may be, another social
prospect. This is not mere biographical probing. The
writings of Thomas Hardy, the proportion of sun or
gloom in them, depended much upon his felicity or
frustration in finding a mate : it was an inherited, it
was an individual crisis. But he did not talk of this in
Blomfield's office.

From that office, under the pressure of illness and
upon a timely invitation, Hardy went back in July
1867 to the county town and assisted his old instructor
in ecclesiastical architecture, Mr. Hicks ; he had
abandoned a notion of becoming an art critic, but it
was now that he set about experiments in fiction, the
first of them being " The Poor Man and the Lady, by
the Poor Man." Some parts of this work were presently

transferred to other publications, and one episode was converted into a Browningesque poem " for preservation " ; but it is in the main identified with the short novel called " An Indiscretion in the Life of an Heiress ", printed in the *New Quarterly Review* for July 1878. The social dilemma round which it was constructed may be described in quotations : " The youthful schoolmaster . . . entered on rational considerations of what a vast gulf lay between that lady and himself, what a troublesome world it was to live in where such divisions could exist, and how painful was the evil when a man of his unequal history was possessed of a keen susceptibility ". As for the stately heiress (who, believe it or not, was no more than seventeen years old), " she was on the verge of committing the most horrible social sin—that of loving beneath her, and owning that she so loved ". Poetical passages served as chapter headings, revealing a keen taste in our English verse : they came from Shakespeare, Shelley, Waller, Browning, Tennyson and others. In the element of background worked from nature and village scene, the writer showed some special freshness. " The Poor Man and the Lady " was submitted to Mr. Alexander Macmillan in July 1868, and called forth an impressive letter from that great publisher, who protested that Hardy had treated the upper class with too unrelieved severity : " It seems to me that your black wash will not be recognized as anything more than ignorant misrepresentation " ; and who had the insight to address his new correspondent as a writer " at least potentially, of considerable mark, of power and purpose ". John Morley, whose recent book on Edmund Burke Hardy had not missed, was then consulted ; like

Macmillan he found the marks of novelty and energy, but on the whole was uncomfortable and indecisive over the question of publishing. And so, late in 1868, Hardy and his MS. were sent away with Macmillan's letter of introduction to Messrs. Chapman and Hall, and the business dragged on; but it produced in March 1869 a dignified interview between the young novelist and the publisher's reader, who afterwards was known to Hardy as George Meredith—" A handsome man with hair and beard not at all grey, and wearing a frock-coat buttoned at the waist and loose about ".

Meredith, referring to the young novelist's skirmishings against Society, advised worldly caution; urged Hardy to diminish his reforming zeal for the time being and compose a novel more as an artist, with a larger content of story. So Hardy used his manuscript as a source-book, or half forgot it, and began to piece together a new thing entitled *Desperate Remedies*. He could not yet give his full attention to these matters. At Dorchester and Weymouth he had plenty to do in making drawings for church restoration, and incidentally in recovering his health and watching the characteristics of the time. We have a glimpse of his enthusiasm for such shows in connection with the notorious tirades called " The Girl of the Period ", published during 1868 in the *Saturday Review*. The author was Mrs. Lynn Linton; but Hardy " was amongst those who never suspected the sex of the writer. He was much impressed by the articles ", so much so that thirty years later he could " point out the exact spot—a green slope in a pasture—where he first read them ".

Indeed, Hardy was at once magnetized towards and affronted or baffled by the womanhood of Bays-water and Belgravia, and an event of importance in his life was related to the mood he was in. Having given up his rooms, swimming and dancing at Weymouth so as to be at peace in Bockhampton, for the benefit of his novel, he received a letter from his employer dated February 11th, 1870, asking him to " go into Cornwall for me, to take a plan and particulars of a church I am about to rebuild there ". Accordingly he made his way to St. Juliot, near Boscastle, and was received at the Rectory by a young lady, the sister-in-law of the Rector. Her name was Emma Lavinia Gifford, and the reason why she was there was principally her busy share in the church affairs. She, among others, was deeply interested beforehand in the visit of the archi-tect to their remote village, and when this stranger came she was surprised, but not displeased, to find that " a blue paper sticking out of his pocket " was not an architectural but a poetical manuscript. She herself was something of a painter in water-colours.

Some feelings of satire have been expressed against the lady who was to become Hardy's first wife because (in biographical directories, for instance) she liked it to be made clear that she was a niece of Archdeacon Gifford,[1] of St. Paul's Cathedral. It has been assumed that, in the marriage, the attitude she favoured was that of the Lady towards the Poor Man. But this tone is not to be caught from the touching reminiscences

[1] Edwin Hamilton Gifford (1820–1905) was in 1865 chaplain to Francis Jeune, Bishop of Peterborough, whose daughter he married ; archdeacon of London and canon of St. Paul's, 1883 ; spent his last years in scholarly retirement at Oxford, where he is buried at Holywell.

of early acquaintance and sympathy which Emma
Hardy wrote down in 1911. " We grew much interested in each other. I found him a perfectly new
subject of study and delight and he found a ' mine '
in me, he said. He was quite unlike any other person
who came to see us, for they were slow of speech and
ideas." The romantic beauty and freedom of the place
were even more adorable when " my Architect " was
there ; and he on his part experienced what later years
bringing monotony and restraint could not rob of
enchantment. In the stanzas " When I set out for
Lyonnesse ", Hardy celebrates with fit brightness of
style the day of his first visit to St. Juliot, and " my
radiance rare and fathomless " marked by his friends
upon his returning thence. In several other retrospective poems, which are grouped as " Veteris
Vestigia Flammae ", he brings back from Beeny and
St. Juliot and Vallency in the spring of 1870, as though
in their original grace and joy, the love-encounters with
her of the

> Nut-coloured hair,
> And gray eyes, and rose-flush coming and going ;

there, with the Atlantic for chief scene, the girl-rider
emerged on his rather desultory years as a figure of
legend come true.

In April 1870, having received *Desperate Remedies*
back from Messrs. Macmillan, Hardy passed it on to
the less fastidious firm of Tinsley Brothers, and
eventually came to an arrangement with them for its
publication at his own risk. One of his ablest investi-
gators, Dr. W. R. Rutland, has set forth the indebtedness of Hardy in this novel to Wilkie Collins's recent
publications : and it is noteworthy that one at least

of those, *The Moonstone*, had the imprint of the Tinsleys. *Desperate Remedies*, published in the usual three volumes on March 25th, 1871, was equally praised and condemned, and occasioned a small money loss to the novelist, who did not remember the sting of that so much as a rather bewildering moral onslaught delivered by the *Spectator*. The reviewer approved of the author's anonymity because even a " *nom-de-plume* might," in such a connection, " at some future time, disgrace the family name ". And yet the same judge appreciated the quality which the example of George Crabbe had encouraged Hardy to express with confidence, a " talent of a remarkable kind—sensitiveness to scenic and atmospheric effects, and to their influence on the mind, and the power of rousing similar sensitiveness in his readers ". Indeed, some of the landscape painting in *Desperate Remedies*, even from the first few pages, and a sketch of a country house, a cider-making scene, a couch-grass-burning, and a description of an old mill, are still quite flourishing specimens of Hardy's genius in the kind. Other novels offered to the readers of 1871 included Lytton's Utopian extravaganza *The Coming Race*, Trollope's *Ralph the Heir*, James Payn's *Not Wooed, but Won*, George Meredith's *Adventures of Harry Richmond*, and *Ready-Money Mortiboy* by Besant and Rice ; George Eliot sent forth some of *Middlemarch* in five-shilling parts, and Lewis Carroll reappeared with *Through the Looking-Glass*. A comparatively unknown writer, William Black, who had also been thinking of becoming an art critic but turned to fiction, made a far more successful bid for fame than Hardy with his story *A Daughter of Heth*, excellently followed up a year later with

The Strange Adventures of a Phaeton. These two young novelists became friends.

Hardy did not continue the attempt at the sensational which had not saved *Desperate Remedies* from being sold off cheap, but perceiving that he had a strong chance of satisfying himself and others in his Dorset countryside and home scenery, he composed *Under the Greenwood Tree : a Rural Painting of the Dutch School.* It was first called " The Mellstock Quire ", but the change was natural to the period and the poetry-loving author. Tinsley published this pleasant book in May 1872, paying Hardy a small sum for the rights ; an illustrated edition was issued in 1876. The idyll was compared in some respects by Horace Moule, in the *Saturday Review,* to *Hermann und Dorothea,* and the tendency of Hardy to cultivate his own garden in fiction rather than improvise according to the patterns of others must have been much strengthened by that and other thoughtful reviews. Had Moule lived long, he would have proved even more valuable as an understanding critic of Hardy ; but in the autumn of 1873, after some memorable June days together in Cambridge, Hardy, home at Bockhampton, received news that his friend was dead. It was a tragic death, the interpretation of which Hardy offered in a poem printed over half a century later—a tribute to an utterly brave man.

As yet, whatever reason was behind it, Hardy's attention to his work as an architect was considerable though fluctuating. He could claim to have " gone personally from parish to parish through a considerable district, and compared existing churches there with records, traditions and memories of what they formerly were ". He observed all sorts of queer things happening in the name of restoration, but could not come to any conclusion except that generally " to do nothing, where to act on little knowledge is a dangerous thing, is to do most and best ". Those who have entered a church in Mr. Hardy's company may remember the immediate sense of his mastery of all its various material detail, as of its spiritual or emotional appeal, which his look and manner and movement showed. The training he had undergone meant an additional quickness and rightness in his observation as a general habit, which was so valuable a resource in his novels and his other writings ; the singularities and visible strange histories of ancient buildings impressed on him, still young, the analogous unexpectedness and incongruity of the fabric of human affairs.

It was not until September 1874 that Thomas Hardy and Emma Lavinia Gifford were married ; they had previously made numerous excursions together, in the teeth of any Victorianism there may have been round their path, a fact which suggests that the early photograph of Miss Gifford given in Mrs. Florence Hardy's first volume is no got-up study. It represents a young woman of eager vitality and fearlessness,—scepticism, at least,—and illustrates the important case that she was by nature intensely fond of her solitude ; so was he, and the years of union to come were characterized for both of them accordingly. Yet this does not mean that either of them repelled friendly society in its round, and the rising novelist was glad of many interesting contacts in London. Mrs. Procter, who about sixty years earlier had seen Keats, and who told Hardy little stories of another distinguished acquaintance, Charles

Lamb, not only sent him some of her famous candid letters (rejoicing over his works) but made the best of his company ; he was welcome at the house of Leslie Stephen, the editor of the *Cornhill*, and among others there met Miss Helen Paterson, the water-colourist, then known as an attractive illustrator of serial fiction. She was married to the poet William Allingham a little before the date of Hardy's own marriage. Miss Paterson was at the time illustrating a new novel by Hardy as it came out in Leslie Stephen's magazine, though without his name. Hardy, who could not easily produce eulogy in the course of polite conversation, told her that her illustrations were not at all bad, and that they showed how differently the same thing might be seen by different minds ; he afterwards described her as the best of his illustrators.

III

FEW persons in the story of English literature excel Leslie Stephen in the ability to propose the obvious and necessary. At the time when he enters the biography of Hardy, he had only occupied the post of editor of the *Cornhill* a year or so, and was beginning that series of literary judgments which may be said to have culminated in his task of directing the *Dictionary of National Biography*. Upon reading *Under the Greenwood Tree* [1] he sent Hardy (" in a remote part of the country ") a letter of appreciation with the object of getting a new story for his magazine : " Though I do not want a murder in every number, it is necessary to catch the attention of readers by some distinct and well-arranged plot ". This was at the end of 1872. But before Hardy could comply with the alluring request he had to complete a novel, now sufficiently well known, for *Tinsley's Magazine ; A Pair of Blue Eyes* was being delivered in instalments there. This sketchily beautiful and daringly contrivanced novel appeared as a separate book in May 1873. In scenes, though not in other respects, it was founded on Hardy's

---

[1] Frederick Greenwood held that he had been the real motive force. Attracted by his own name in the title of a novel on a bookstall, he had persuaded the proprietor of the *Cornhill* to ask its author for a serial, which would not cost so much as one by George Eliot or Charles Reade.

visits to Cornwall ; once again it had the aspect of being written for lovers of poetry in particular, for the chapter headings were principally lines or phrases from Shakespeare, Marlowe, Gray, Scott, Tennyson, Dryden and others, with occasional sentences from the Psalms. The persons of the tale, to anyone acquainted with the life of the novelist as we have traced it hitherto, might have seemed to betray lack of invention—the clergyman and his daughter, the church-restoring architect, the reviewer and essayist, the master mason ; nevertheless these were not servile copies of the people whom Hardy knew so well under their various styles. He had summoned up original characters. *A Pair of Blue Eyes* was well received. Tennyson liked it, Coventry Patmore wrote to Hardy praising him as a potential poet, reviewers were gracious. The heroine was all that a nice Girl of the Period should be, in spite of hazardous moments

But the real test of the novelist, perhaps, came when his next work was given prominence in the illustrious *Cornhill*, where *Far from the Madding Crowd* was printed between January and December 1874. It was a success from the first instalment, and its progress was attended with interest in the press month by month. The editor, author and some others were surprised in the early stages by critics who attributed the work to George Eliot (" because ", said Stephen, " you know the names of the stars ") ; when it came out in two volumes, Hardy's name for the first time found a place on the title-page of one of his novels. He had gained a recognizable position as " a vigorous exponent of the pastoral novel ", whose characteristic theme was " that, in these sequestered spots, great tragedies can be enacted, and strong loves and passions aroused, equally as much as in cities and in the busy haunts of men ". Even Edward FitzGerald, four years later, allowed this merit : " An incomprehensible novel, *Far from the Madding Crowd* (I tried it on the strength of the title), contains some good Country Life ". The second edition of *Far from the Madding Crowd* appeared in January 1875. Not long afterwards, a manuscript of Gray's " Elegy " coming up for sale at Sotheby's, the *Figaro* suggested, in view of Hardy's finding his title in that poem, that he should make a bid for it. From the same journal for June 12th, 1875, comes the following : " *Far from the Madding Crowd* was so attractive in the *Cornhill*, that we are not surprised to hear that its author is engaged to write another story for that magazine . . . called *The Hand of Ethelberta ; a Comedy in Chapters* ".

This concoction, called by Hardy " a satire on the fusion of classes ", although it must have had some reputation, being practically the only contemporary novel on Matthew Arnold's reading list for 1888, was never much liked and never will be. From the outset there is complication and patchwork, but of comedy little enough,—it was " hardly less doleful than most modern comedies in acts " ; and the characters, even the rustic brothers of the heroine, attain a remarkable pitch of dullness and sub-humanity. Still, it is recorded that " one experienced critic went so far as to write that it was the finest ideal comedy since the days of Shakespeare ". It was the last thing that Hardy did for Leslie Stephen's magazine, but friendly feelings survived between editor and contributor.

Two early criticisms of *The Hand of Ethelberta*

must have been examined by Hardy with respect if
not with full assent. In the *Saturday Review* it was
argued that he had tried to do in a novel what the stage,
whence he borrowed his sub-title, alone could. " The
characters often resemble figures who upon the stage
might come in and out, utter quaint sayings, amuse
an audience by their bewilderment at events to which
the spectator has the key, and by the aid of costume
and appearance make each for himself some kind of
individuality. These helps to identification are necessarily absent in the pages of a book. . . . The book is
full of faults, but their existence has not shaken the
belief which we have long entertained, that Mr. Hardy
is capable of making himself a place in the first rank
of novelists. Only to do that he must, it seems to us,
abandon such out-of-the-way subjects."

The *Athenaeum*, among other things, cautioned
Hardy about his own selection of language—and indeed
he, like Wordsworth in prose, was always oddly fond
of heavy, dressy expressions—and the speech of his
peasantry. " He twice uses ' transpire ' for ' happen.' "
But, graver charge to him, " he does not seem to
appreciate the exceeding scantiness of ideas in the
brain, and words in the mouth, of a modern rustic.
It is said that careful examination failed to detect 200
words in the vocabulary of a certain village in Cam-
bridgeshire ; is it possible that Somerset and Dorset
are so much more eloquent ? "

Perhaps the publication of " The Fire at Tranter
Sweatley's, a Wessex Ballad " in the *Gentleman's
Magazine* for November 1875, a piece with some
hints of the influence of Barnes, was of greater interest
to Hardy than his novel ; as poet he had begun, as

poet would end ; but the support he got on the occasion was insufficient to encourage him to communicate more of his verses just then. He tried to persuade Leslie Stephen to publish " some tragic poems " by way of relief from *The Hand of Ethelberta*, but " Stephen seemed disinclined, as editor, to take up the idea ". It has been supposed that Patmore's letter to Hardy dated March 29th, 1875, " regretting at almost every page " of the novels " that such almost unequalled beauty and power should not have assured themselves the immortality which would have been conferred upon them by the form of verse ", was the first cause for Hardy's tendency to write poetry. The error needs little attention now, and perhaps in 1875 the letter influenced Hardy in some measure. Ten years later, Hardy was represented for the first time in an anthology of poems—but it was one of *Songs from the Novelists*, edited by W. Davenport Adams.

Having travelled already a good deal in England, and being now clear that he was an author but an ex-architect, Hardy took occasion to visit the Continent with his wife, and with a great idea stirring in his mind. He had noted it down : " an Iliad of Europe from 1789 to 1815 ". It was present to him on the scene of the battle of Waterloo, it moved him to make a search for the house in Brussels where the Duchess of Richmond had given the ball before the battle. But that house guarded its secret. " Its site ", Hardy wrote thirty years later, " has not as yet been proven. Even Sir W. Fraser is not convincing. The event happened less than a century ago, but the spot is almost as phantasmal in its elusive mystery as towered Camelot, the palace of Priam, or the hill of Calvary."

Mr. and Mrs. Hardy first settled in a cottage at Sturminster Newton, an old market and manufacturing town on the Dorset Stour, and here he wrote one of his main-line novels, *The Return of the Native*, first published, in the fashion then prevailing, as a serial in *Belgravia* in 1878. It appeared there with illustrations by Arthur Hopkins, brother of the poet Gerard Manley Hopkins. Leslie Stephen, to whom the opening was shown, liked that but " feared that the relations between Eustacia, Wildeve and Thomasin might develop into something ' dangerous ' for a family magazine, and refused to have anything to do with it unless he could see the whole ". A singular literary truth is connected with the startling figure of the raddleman. Hardy might reasonably think that here was something new to literature, and yet—I owe the detail to Col. C. H. Wilkinson—he had been anticipated. A seventeenth-century poet, Nathaniel Whiting, in his whimsical " Pleasant Historie of Albino and Bellama ", 1638, disguises his hero :

> With raddle-crimson then, fit for his trade,
> He clothed his face.

A later line might have served as a motto for Hardy's novel,—

> But let the monks and tinker take their chances.
> We'll view the travels of our raddle-man.

It would have been strange if the magnificent portent of the opening chapter, the delineation of the mysterious presence Egdon Heath, had not been followed by a story of considerable stature ; but there was doubt among the critics. The evident struggle between Hardy's intellectual passion and the necessities of a set of emotional occasions, arranged for habitual novel-readers, worried some of them. The *Academy* detected in his work " a certain Hugoesque quality of insincerity ", and yet, how " earnest in all he does " the man was ! According him many merits, this critic found them all dogged by some artificiality ; " rare artist as he is, there is something wanting in his person-ality, and he is not quite a great man ". In the *Illus-trated London News* the notion that a novelist might inform his book with a kind of nature-worship was censured ; he should rely on his story, and Hardy's story did not satisfy. An uncommon book, but " though the descriptions are uncommonly good, the movement is uncommonly slow, the personages are uncommonly uninteresting, the action is uncommonly poor, the conclusion is uncommonly flat ". *Black-wood's* called Hardy " an original thinker and writer ", but alleged that he repeated himself and that his book " might have been a clever parody " of his earlier ones. The *Contemporary Review* was willing to have him with all his faults : " Mr. Hardy, one of the strongest of our novelists, if not the strongest, and a man between whom and Mr. Browning there are some affinities. Where else are we to look for anything like the same amount of rugged and fantastic power ; the same naturalness mingled with the same quaintness ? Lift out, by way of experiment, what is pleasingly wrong in the work, and then see how you will be baffled in any attempt to supply its place." But the enthusiast who wrote this was concerned that Hardy's representation of " Nature in her lonely greatness " accompanied, uneasily, figures of " men and women sordid and stunted, blundering and ignorant ".

Not very long afterwards Henry Holbeach (really
W. B. Rands), in the same review, published a paper
entitled " The New Fiction " which throws light on
the general feeling of that day about the novelist's
function as well as the reputations that were upper-
most. In a list of authors assembled for his purpose,
besides some earlier Victorians, the critic included
Meredith (*The Egoist*), William Black, George
MacDonald, Mrs. Oliphant and Hardy (*Far from the
Madding Crowd*). He claimed that between 1860 and
1880 the novel had developed astonishingly, and could
now be considered, as a principal means of expression,
alongside poetry and philosophy. It was true that to
some kinds of people this form still looked profane ;
Scott and Fenimore Cooper had offended them still,
and quite recently the bold Archbishop of York had
surprised some persons by publicly declaring that there
were novels which might be read with both pleasure
and profit. But works of fiction had truly gained
ground, notably through the example of Mrs. Gaskell.
" Novels go everywhere, more or less. The recent
revivals of the old-fashioned ' Evangelicism ' are against
them, but the victory will remain with the novelist."
The writer called the leading characteristic of progressive fiction then " Poetic Naturalism " ; this term
would link up Hardy's work in some parts with the
rest. His love of the poets might entitle him to it in
a special sense ; but in *The Return of the Native* he did
not strew quotations from themes freely as he had
done—he was working more passionately from his
deeper nature, and his reading of earth. The harmony
of the whole, which he had in mind before elaborating
his details, came from his Wessex scenes and seasons.

On a previous occasion the *Athenaeum*, that wonderful but magisterial weekly, had requested Hardy to reconsider the vocabulary he attributed to his rustics ; this time there was a fresh complaint, and Hardy defended himself in print. " An author may be said to fairly convey the spirit of intelligent peasant talk if he retains the idiom, compass and characteristic expressions, although he may not encumber the page with obsolete pronunciations of the purely English words, and with mispronunciations of those derived from Latin and Greek. In the printing of standard speech, hardly any phonetic principle at all is observed ; and if a writer attempts to exhibit on paper the precise accents of a rustic speaker, he disturbs the proper balance of a true representation by unduly insisting upon the grotesque element." Three years afterwards, Hardy reading his *Spectator* found himself indicated as one whose rustic conversations were " to the ordinary reader, nothing but a series of linguistic puzzles ", and again he defended himself, but when he had spoken of the useful compromise he practised in depicting dialect, he passed to something very near his heart. His friend Barnes must have approved. " It must, of course, be always a matter for regret that, in order to be understood, writers should be obliged thus slightingly to treat varieties of English which are intrinsically as genuine, grammatical and worthy of the royal title as is the all-prevailing competitor which bears it, whose only fault was that they happened not to be central and therefore were worsted in the struggle for existence, when a uniform tongue became a necessity among the advanced classes of the population." Long afterwards, Barnes being dead, Joseph Wright applied to Hardy for help, in respect of the Dorset Language, for his great *English Dialect Dictionary*, and Hardy duly figures on the list of correspondents in that work.

In March 1878, persuaded that the literary profession requires one's home to be in London, Hardy removed from " the Sturminster Newton idyll " to " just beyond Wandsworth Common ", or Upper Tooting. He was then able to attend imposing occasions and meet remarkable men and women, but otherwise the change was no gain. The eye of fancy and retrospect may dwell eagerly on one of the said occasions. Prince Louis Napoleon had been killed on a reconnaissance in the Zulu war ; his body was brought home to England and buried at Chislehurst on July 12th, 1879 ; Hardy went to the funeral. There he was fascinated by the profile of the great Napoleon's nephew, and in time this sight of the Buonaparte face was to haunt him and lead him through his finest work. No such result followed a meeting—in W. P. Frith's studio—with Sir Percy Florence Shelley, the poet's son, though Shelley's life and genius were beloved by Hardy to the end. The poet's son was an excellent and an ingenious man, but " not much given to literature ".

About this time a dining-club, called the Rabelais Club, was founded, and Hardy became a member. He was elected as representing strongly what the club stood for : " virility in literature ". There were no speeches but abundance of celebrities. Among the famous writers to whose rank he was approaching Hardy now met Robert Browning (whose character perplexed him), Matthew Arnold and Tennyson, as

well as J. R. Lowell from over the Atlantic. In connection with this last name, a sequel occurred in
1886 : " Thomas Hardy, our greatest novelist over
here, as I think, was very much wounded by what
Lowell was reported to have said about him. There
are circumstances in the case which would make the
sneer at Hardy's personal appearance singularly cruel.
I cannot myself believe that Lowell said all that—it is
quite in the Julian Hawthorne vein. Hardy, who has
always been a great supporter and admirer of Lowell,
is wretched at this supposed snub."

Steadily pursuing his profession, of which in his
old age he was apt not to speak with much pleasure,
Hardy supplied *Good Words* with *The Trumpet-Major*
by monthly instalments, " from hand to mouth as it
were ", through 1880. It cannot be that he did not
take pleasure in writing this novel, for it originated
in local history and topography which he prized, the
ghost of Napoleon walking in Wessex, and viewed by
him with ancestral sight. Looking back, Hardy remarked that he had a haphazard way with documents
at the time he wrote it ; " however, it was the writing
of that book which led to *The Dynasts*, the matter I
collected being five times as much as I required for
The Trumpet-Major, including what is now very
valuable to me . . . oral information on those times
from people who lived in them, which now could not
be got : *e.g.* the arrival of the regiments at camp, at
the beginning of the story, which was described to me
by eye-witnesses ". *The Trumpet-Major* also pleased
most of the reviewers, and drew from the *Athenaeum* the
compliment, " Mr. Hardy seems to be in the way to do
for rural life what Dickens did for that of the town ".

The next novel, *A Laodicean : or*, *The Castle of the De Stancys*, was the result of a contract with *Harper's Magazine* and had to be kept going number by number for many months, although Hardy was lying ill and believed it was his last illness. This must have been the novel alluded to by Hardy in a letter to the *Athenaeum* dated from the Savile Club, December 19th, 1882, defending Messrs. Harper against an attack made by W. Clark Russell. The allegation was that the firm was publishing Russell's novels in America without imparting to him " one single farthing ". Hardy's letter closes, " For my own part, I may state—not to mention the *bona fides* of the Messrs. Harper in ordinary transactions—that some time ago I agreed to supply them with the advance sheets of a novel for so much money, the said novel to be no shorter than a specified length while if longer there was to be no additional payment. When finished, the story, planned without reference to the agreement, turned out to be one-third longer than the guaranteed length ; and I was greatly surprised, and not less charmed, to receive from them the proportionate third above the price agreed on. It is said that other publishers delight in paying an author more than he expects to get, but I believe the excellent practice is not yet universal." In 1890, with Walter Besant and William Black, Hardy once again protested against the " sweeping condemnation " of Messrs. Harper which had appeared in the *Athenaeum*, this time in reference to a grievance of Rudyard Kipling's ; that produced an angry poem by Kipling, but Hardy won his friendship.

" *A Laodicean* ", as Hardy later on told William Lyon Phelps, " contained more of the facts of his own

life than anything else he had ever written." That
would seem probable from the first page, when we
encounter the tweed-clad figure of a young draughtsman, in sunset light, copying the chevroned doorway
of a village church tower, and apparently with all
technical dexterity ; but it might be difficult to extri-
cate the autobiography from the make-believe. At
least, this first page announced a novel which perhaps
only professional knowledge could make good. A
valuable essayist in the *Architect* (January 20th, 1928)
says what is necessary : " *A Laodicean*, published in
1881, finds Hardy still trailing his professional past ;
the hero is an architect, ' the second villain ' is an
architect, there is a competition and stolen plans and
a client heroine (eventually secured by the hero as
well as the commission !), and curious dated discussions
on architecture take place. The whole philosophy of
the newly founded ' Anti-scrape ' is stated at the
Society's foundation." The essay brings together
earlier and later instances of Hardy's use of his special
training for the benefit of his novels, distinguishing
him so clearly, as the Great Barn in *Far from the Madding Crowd*, the manor-house fallen on evil days in
the same book, a thatched cottage in *Under the Greenwood Tree*, and others. Even a single epithet is pointed
out as a sign of his unique power to realize architecture
in words : it is the one underlined in the following
allusion to St. Mary's Church, Oxford, " with the
Italian porch whose *helical* columns were heavily
draped with creepers ".

Upon his recovery, it was decided that the Hardys
should leave London and find a place in Dorset, whence
they could pass to town for a few months of each year ;

they settled at Wimborne, another market town on the
river Stour with fine country all around. Here Hardy
became a member of the Dorset Natural History and
Antiquarian Field Club. And duly the trade of fiction
was carried on. An incidental result was the production of "a New and Original Pastoral Drama, entitled
Far from the Madding Crowd, by Thomas Hardy and
Comyns Carr," at the Royal Globe Theatre in May
1882. It at least enabled Mrs Bernard-Beere to give a
glorious performance in Bathsheba Everdene; but it
caused a wordy dispute. A. W. Pinero's *The Squire*
at the St. James's was suspected of being drawn also
from Hardy's novel. In one of his unrivalled talks on
the Playhouses, in the *Illustrated London News*, George
Augustus Sala said, "I fail to discern any similarity. ...
It is the same scene, but the words at either theatre
are different." He found them "both exceedingly
clever plays," in spite of the appearance in either of
"a gang of garrulous, selfish, drunken hawbucks, full
of uncouth waggeries, and jabbering an archaic *argot*."

Two on a Tower, Hardy's next novel, was first
printed serially, in 1882, in the *Atlantic Monthly*, then
at its best. It may have surprised some of Hardy's
readers to find him mingling some astronomy with his
love story, but there had been previous signs of this
interest, as in *Far from the Madding Crowd*. Hardy
had now a more decided aim, setting "two infinitesimal
lives against the stupendous background of the stellar
universe", yet with the awareness that "of these contrasting magnitudes the smaller might be the greater"
in the human estimate. But, as he later remarked,
people did not worry much about "these high aims
of the author" when they could busy themselves with

protesting against his impropriety and his satire on
the Church of England. Not everyone was content
with such busying. An adventurous young medical
man, by name Havelock Ellis, had become so delighted a reader of Hardy that in order to write a critique
on the novels he had toured Dorset in 1881. His essay
appeared in the *Westminster Review* of April 1883, and
was not lost upon Hardy, who enjoyed it both for its
generous tribute and as a practical help. " If novelists
were a little less in the dark about the appearance of
their own works, what productions they might bring
forth ! but they are much in the position of the man
inside the hobby-horse at a Christmas masque, and
have no consciousness of the absurdity of its trot,
at times, in the spectator's eyes."

Edmund Gosse visited Hardy in Shirehall Lane,
Dorchester, during July 1883 ; for Hardy was now
beginning to build himself a house near the county
town, and meanwhile had taken a rambling old one
" of which a townsman said, ' He have but one window
and she do look into Gaol Lane ' ". As for the permanent abode, Hardy bought some land from the
Duchy of Cornwall, not far from the railway from
Dorchester to Wareham, and very near a tree-covered
mound called Conquer Barrow. That might have
been the name of the new red house, but Hardy eventually preferred Max Gate, the old name of the site on
which he was settling. " I was resolved ", he says,
" not to ruin myself in building a great house as so
many other literary men have done." Was he thinking
of Scott ? While the well and foundations of the house,
Max Gate, were being dug, some Romano-British
skeletons and relics were discovered, of which Hardy

wrote an account for the Dorset Field Club. It was not printed, however, until 1890, when it came out in their *Proceedings* and in a few offprints. Hardy found it useful, when interviewers were probing him about God and man, to deviate into this subject of the Roman legacy to Wessex.

A remarkable interest in rural affairs and village communities was stirring in England at the time when Hardy was forming his series of Wessex novels, and it touched him closely. He had a faith in agricultural life which extended beyond his pastoral fictions ; [1] he had a knowledge which, with a slight change of circumstance, would have made him a rival of his Wiltshire acquaintance Richard Jefferies, whose *Hodge and his Masters* appeared in 1880, or of the Rev. Augustus Jessopp, whose Norfolk is so genuine and explicit. Jefferies' title would have suited a little known but eloquent and eager study of " The Dorsetshire Labourer " published by Hardy in *Longman's Magazine* for July 1883. It opened with a few observations on the usual town ideas of the rustic : " the pitiable picture known as Hodge . . . a degraded being of uncouth manner and aspect, stolid understanding, and snail-like movement, [who] hangs his head or looks sheepish when spoken to, and thinks Lunnon a place paved with gold ". Against such caricatures, Hardy urged that the actual Hodge was " a number of dissimilar fellow-creatures, men of many minds, infinite

[1] Of the Wessex novels he wrote in 1911, " They have at least a humble supplementary quality. . . . At the dates represented in the various narrations things were like that in Wessex : the inhabitants lived in certain ways, engaged in certain occupations, kept alive certain customs, just as they are shown doing in these pages."

in difference ; some happy, many serene, a few depressed ; some clever even to genius, some stupid,
some wanton, some austere ; some mutely Miltonic,
some Cromwellian . . . each of whom walks in his
own way the road to dusty death ". The essayist
then offers some realistic pictures of these people in
their world, with a quantity of detail about their em-
ployments and wages, all presented with a balanced
mind, and as he goes he well describes a man whose
name still lingers with a fond light round it in the
memory of our countryside—the " agitator " Joseph
Arch. He had founded, in 1872, the National Agricultural Labourers Union.

For such portraits of people, even on a single encounter, Hardy had a delightful talent ; and it is not
inconvenient here to pass on to another instance. In
October 1886 he contributed to the *Athenaeum* a short
memoir of his old friend Barnes, and although the
opening paragraph has been transplanted more than
once, it is too valuable an example of Hardy's devoted
delight in human characteristics to be avoided on that
account. " Until within the last year or two there
were few figures more familiar to the eye in the county
town of Dorset on a market day than an aged clergyman, quaintly attired in caped cloak, knee-breeches and
buckled shoes, with leather satchel slung over his
shoulders, and a stout staff in his hand. He seemed
usually to prefer the middle of the street to the pavement, and to be thinking of matters which had nothing
to do with the scene before him. He plodded along
with a broad, firm tread, notwithstanding the slight
stoop occasioned by his years. Every Saturday morning he might have been seen thus trudging up the

narrow South Street, his shoes coated with mud or
dust according to the state of the roads between his
rural home and Dorchester, and a little grey dog at his
heels, till he reached the four cross-ways in the centre
of the town. Halting here, opposite the public clock,
he would pull his old-fashioned watch from its deep
fob, and set it with great precision to London time.
This, the invariable first act of his market visit, having
been completed to his satisfaction, he turned round
and methodically proceeded about his other business."
In such walking epitomes of a country tradition at
once simple and far-seeing Hardy found an inspiration.
This notice of Barnes drew from Edmund Gosse the
discerning praise, " It puts all others in the shade.
What a biographer was lost when nature stamped
Novelist on your brow ! "

But to return to Hardy's progress as a novelist.
Two on a Tower was published in book form by
Sampson Low on October 25th, 1882. Next came
*The Mayor of Casterbridge : The Life and Death of a
Man of Character*, first in the pages of the *Graphic*
and then in two volumes with the imprint of Smith,
Elder, in May 1886. Here, like old Mr. Barnes, he
considered gods and men from Dorchester as the
centre, with the Hardyan difference that, for literary
purposes, Dorchester was still a Roman as well as an
English capital. In this also, one finds a Thomas
Hardy who need not have been a novelist in order to
win fame as a writer ; the point may be supported by
reference to an equally pathetic and humorous sketch,
dated 1885, called " Ancient Earthworks at Casterbridge ", which was included with photographs of Mai-
Dun in the *English Illustrated Magazine* in 1893. Apart

from the plot, the piece shows Hardy's great ability for topographical and reflective composition,—the midnight ascent up the outer, the second and the final rampart is perfectly realized.

The reviewing of *The Mayor of Casterbridge*, which was certainly a bold attempt to identify character and fate, may be noted in a few words from the *Westminster Review* : " We can give no higher praise to Mr. Hardy's new book than to say it is a worthy successor of *Far from the Madding Crowd*. There is the same consummate art in describing persons and places, the same aptness and picturesqueness of expression, the same under-current of sly humour, which have gone far towards forming Mr. Hardy's charming *accent personnel*." But discussion, praise, blame were simplified in the author's own notebook : " I fear it will not be so good as I meant ". He was a true critic, but laconic wherever he could remain so. In 1883 he praised Mark Twain, in a conversation with W. D. Howells the novelist, with characteristic wisdom. " Why don't people understand that Mark Twain is not merely a great humorist ? He's a very remarkable fellow in a very different way." Hardy specified *Life on the Mississippi*, as indeed might have been expected : and Howells felt that " all the admiration I had ever felt for Hardy's books " was justified. But he did not seize the moment and persuade Hardy to write an essay on the true Mark Twain.

Writing to Robert Bridges on October 28th, 1886, the poet G. M. Hopkins made an interesting distinction : " In my judgment the amount of gift and genius which goes into novels in the English literature of this generation is perhaps not much inferior to what made the Elizabethan drama, and unhappily it is in great part wasted. How admirable are Blackmore and Hardy ! . . . Do you know the bonfire scene in the *Return of the Native* and still better the sword-exercise scene in the *Madding Crowd*, breathing epic ? or the wife-sale in *The Mayor of Casterbridge* (read by chance)? But these writers only rise to their great strokes ; they do not write continuously well ; now Stevenson is master of a consummate style and each phrase is finished as in poetry." A few months later another poet, Coventry Patmore, paid Hardy the tribute of a general appreciation of his novels (in the *St. James Gazette*) ; this was on the appearance of *The Woodlanders*. Patmore thought the novelist least happy in this work of all the series, and found it straining credibility too much when Hardy caused Grace Melbury to marry Fitzpiers and induced that " flippant profligate " to display " abiding repentance and amendment." The general argument was that " if the student of 1987 wants to know anything really about us " he will find it in our novelists, " feeling, as we do when we look at a portrait by Velasquez or Titian, that it must be like—nay, that it is the life itself " ; the class of novelists in his mind included of the recently dead, Thackeray, Trollope, George Eliot, Mrs. Gaskell ; and among the living, Hardy and Mrs. L. B. Walford. The article ended with an illustration of what Hopkins was watching, Hardy's failure in these novels to write continuously well. It must always be a source of disturbance to his readers. " Why ", says Patmore, " such a master of language should, in his latest work, have repeatedly indulged in such hateful modern slang as ' emotional ' and ' phenomenal ' (in the sense of

' extraordinary ' instead of ' apparent '), and in the equally detestable lingo of the drawing-room ' scientist', seems quite inexplicable." The fact is probably not unconnected with the sense of drudgery acknowledged by Hardy even in the composition of novels so rich in his especial opportunities as *The Woodlanders*. The book, Hardy noted on the last day of 1887, " enabled me to hold my own in fiction, whatever that may be worth."

Possibly the ablest of the reviews was that written for the *Academy* by William Wallace, the philosopher. He at least recognized the intellectual imagination which in the long run was separating Hardy's novels from those of contemporaries more skilful in some points of the art of a feigned narration. He said : " *The Woodlanders* is decidedly the best and most powerful work Mr. Hardy has produced since *Far from the Madding Crowd*. With the possible exception, also, of *Two on a Tower*, it will be regarded as his most disagreeable book not only by the ordinary clients of Mr. Mudie, who feel dissatisfied unless Virtue passes a Coercion Bill directed against Vice at the end of the third volume, but even by those of Mr. Hardy's own admirers who complain, as Mr. Morley complains of Emerson, that he is never ' shocked and driven into himself by the immoral thoughtlessness of men ', that ' the courses of nature and the prodigious injustices of man in society, affect him with neither horror nor awe '. . . . We have an entirely new creation in Marty South, the poor girl who ascends from the ridiculous in the first chapter, in which she loses her hero. . . . Mr. Hardy not only justifies—by reproducing—the Unfulfilled Intention ; he provides, in *The Woodlanders*, a strong plot, diversified rather than marred by whimsicalities of incident. . . . Even *Far from the Madding Crowd* does not contain more passages in which Mr. Hardy permits his readers, though not himself, to turn from contemplating the tragedy of the Unfulfilled Intention, in order to enjoy the pensive contentment of a Coleridgean sabbath of the soul."

In the spring of that Jubilee year the Hardys crossed the Channel once more, but this time for an Italian journey, some results of which are seen among the poems ; the best known of those were expressions of Hardy's devotion to the genius of Shelley and of Keats. He wrote, at the time, the pretty stanzas on " Shelley's Skylark " (for once his universe included benevolent fairies), and the daring and carved-out ode " At the Pyramid of Cestius "—

> —Say, then, he lived and died
> That stones which bear his name
> Should mark, through Time, where two immortal Shades
>   abide ;
> It is an ample fame.

And after passing Sirmione he attempted an "imitation" of " Catullus: XXXI ", which is remarkable for evading or obscuring all the familiar beauties of the original and for Hardy's retaining it in his collected works ; but it serves to remind us of his studious inclinations.

After his travels, which included something of Napoleonic associations, increasingly appealing to him, Hardy returned to his usual English round, based on his two headquarters, Max Gate and the Savile Club. He saw Browning more than once, met Matthew Arnold again, was a guest of persons of quality. He had a view of the Royal procession of June 21st, 1887,

from his club windows, and felt that such a jubilee
with so many royal visitors would not come to pass
again in our country. There is an agreeable glimpse
of Hardy himself at a literary party attended by
Katharine Tynan : she did not get a word with the
lady novelist specially honoured on the occasion, but
" was quite satisfied, for I talked with Thomas Hardy
. . . standing with his peculiar air of modesty, his
head down-bent ". And old Mrs. Lynn Linton was
equally happy when Hardy called on her at Queen
Anne's Mansions and managed to compliment her on
her handsome appearance. He contributed a short
story or two to magazines, and in 1888 put forth a
collection of five pieces of the kind, with the general
title *Wessex Tales*—a slight mystery is connected with
that. In the edition included in Messrs. Macmillan's
" Colonial Library " during the same year, the title
on the cover stands, " Wessex Tales, Strange, Lively,
and Fascinating "—on the title-page, instead of the
last of these epithets one sees " Commonplace ". Did
Hardy supply both descriptions ?

At this point there may be seen something of a
stage in the progress of Thomas Hardy the novelist.
To the ordinary readers he appeared to have established his name on a consistent group of tales, included
among Sampson Low's " Standard Novels ". In that
familiar list Hardy's run of titles stood among others
of reputation, but not excitement any longer : William
Black, R. D. Blackmore, W. Clark Russell, Mrs. Cashel
Hoey. Few of those who were enjoying such Standard
Novels in the Jubilee year would have forecast that
Hardy could develop in any other direction, or come
to represent a spirit of enquiry and protest far away

from the " jolly good book " of leisure hours. We
have already found critics, such as Havelock Ellis and
Patmore, inclined to consider his productions not
severally but as a whole, and to use each new one
as occasion for a general estimate ; but after *The
Woodlanders*, while Hardy paused for a few years
so far as publishing novels was concerned, the sense
of his massed achievement and comparative position
became emphatic. In a long article sub-titled " The
Historian of Wessex ", a young writer of growing
popularity, by name J. M. Barrie, discussed Hardy's
characteristics and performances in the *Contemporary
Review* for July 1889. Barrie was sure that Hardy,
attempting to find his field outside Wessex, had failed ;
that his sketches of London society and even of literary
types were silly ; but he saw this novelist making his
way to posterity by virtue of his provincial scenes and
psychologies. This article was in some sort an appeal
to Hardy to confine his energies within the home
boundaries : " As a ' stylist ' Mr. Hardy stands higher
than any contemporary novelist. His writing has not
always the air of distinction which sometimes catches
one's consciousness, and will henceforth, one may
hope, be exclusively devoted to adorning the Wessex
stories, of which the last, *The Woodlanders*, is a falling
away, but the second last *The Mayor of Casterbridge*
in some ways the most dramatic and powerful. A
further inducement to the author to continue this
memorable series, is that when treating of Wessex life
he is a humorist, and that his other novels have scarcely
a glimmer of humour from beginning to end." [1]

---

[1] Somebody had accused Rider Haggard of plagiarism from
Hardy : the scene where Sergeant Troy's sword encircles Bath-

What Barrie was saying chimed very well with " what the public wanted " of Hardy, and with the growth of a pilgrimage habit, which is the incidental reward of the " definite " novelist, who is not afraid to simplify characters and invent incident. " From London to the heart of Wessex, the land of Hardy's novels—of ' Bathsheba Everdene ', ' Clym Yeobright ' and ' Giles Winterborne '—seems far away enough, but it is only five hours from Waterloo, as a matter of fact." So opens an article on Hardy, typical of the interest in him and what he appeared to represent in or about the year 1890 and his own fiftieth year. The writer was inclined to assume that the pilgrim would not only wish to see Dorsetshire and the neighbouring regions but also Hardy himself at Max Gate : but, he observed, " the morning hours are held sacred by him to his literary creations ". As for the house that Mr. Hardy had built,—" There is a distinct and satisfying individuality about Max Gate, though it is not old. Standing where it does, near one of the up-lifted prehistoric barrows that are not uncommon in Dorsetshire, on a high and solitary spot, commanding well the surrounding country, it might claim to be remembering its master's outlook upon human affairs, the watch tower of Wessex : lucky the visitor to that ancient part of the world who may talk over the great human tragi-comedy, as localized there, with the watchman within his tower ! Still luckier to entice

sheba had, it was said, been copied in the whirling of Umslo-pogaas's axe round a cowardly Frenchman (in *Allan Quatermain*). Barrie rejected the charge : the scenes were essentially different—Hardy's a great moment, Haggard's a poor joke which made *Allan Quatermain* a book " that I, for one, would not put into Mr. Andrew Lang's hands ".

him to go out, to go exploring under his guidance the places where the viewless people of his fiction have lived, moved and had their being." Noting that Hardy appeared to have all Wessex topography and associations under his eye, as if he might one day need every item of them for his myth of these hills and vales, the writer passed on to summarize the steps by which he had already made his position as one of the two or three leading writers of novels, with an incidental comparison to " Tourgenief, who had also no want of philosophy behind his fiction ".

And naturally there was by this time a call for Hardy's own critical remarks on the art which he represented. He was always a keen but not a voluble judge of literary questions, and the typical article " The Profitable Reading of Fiction ", which was printed in the New York *Forum* for March 1888, was as clearly that one man's particular and determined production as any of his tales. It may have surprised the unwary by its many signs that Hardy commanded a variety of great literature of all ages, the notice of which reveals as well his confidence that his reader was a fully educated being ; he did not fear a dark age then, he trusted in that literate tradition which had called him among many others into the metropolis long before. The Victorian age had its points. Also, Hardy made it clear that whatever of pessimism might be attributed to him in matters of personal bliss or bale and the governing scheme of things, he was not at all Swiftian in his estimate of the prevailing morality of the race. The business of the novelist, in his opinion, was anything but coarse and clotted realism. Here is his doctrine : " Good fiction may be defined here as that kind of imaginative writing which lies nearest to the epic, dramatic, or narrative masterpieces of the past. One fact is certain : in fiction there can be no intrinsically new thing at this stage of the world's history. New methods and plans may arise and come into fashion, as we see them do ; but the general theme can neither be changed, nor (what is less obvious) can the relative importance of its various particulars be greatly interfered with. The higher passions must ever rank above the inferior—intellectual tendencies above animal, and moral above intellectual—whatever the treatment, realistic or ideal. Any system of inversion which should attach more importance to the delineation of man's appetites than to the delineation of his aspirations, affections, or humours, would condemn the old masters of imaginative creation from Aeschylus to Shakespeare. Whether we hold the arts which depict mankind to be, in the words of Mr. Matthew Arnold, a criticism of life, or, in those of Mr. Addington Symonds, a revelation of life, the material remains the same, with its sublimities, its beauties, its uglinesses, as the case may be. The finer manifestations must precede in importance the meaner, without such a radical change in human nature as we can hardly conceive as pertaining to an even remote future of decline, and certainly do not recognize now."

IV

THE NOVELIST COMPLETES HIS TASK

THIS sketch of Hardy's career now approaches a period with which he is seldom associated in the mention : the Nineties. In his volume of lively papers called *After Puritanism* Mr. Hugh Kingsmill defines Hardy's track amid the more exotic and fantastic coruscations of the day, such as Wilde and Beardsley displayed, with insight : " an attempt to return to a reasonable frankness was being made by Thomas Hardy, whom the confusing atmosphere of the age sometimes compelled to write like Hall Caine, and sometimes allowed to write like Shakespeare ". From the statement of principle quoted in the last chapter (in Hardy's address to novel-readers), it would be improbable that Hardy should ever play with slim gilt boys or golden girls or turn Max Gate into a modern Hell Fire Club, even found a new and weirder magazine in his passion for a bolder and freer kind of public thought: he could and did delight in Swinburne's pagan vista through the drabness of pretence, but he had not in himself that kind of rhapsodic excitement. Yet it was Hardy as much as anyone who during the Nineties declared the necessity of exploring in daylight the relationships and the complications which make up the history of men and women. It was he who offered a prologue

64

to his own full declaration, through the novel, on the subject when—in the *New Review* for January 1890— he published his opinions on " Candour in English Fiction ".

The *New Review* is not in the catalogue of periodicals with big circulations, and the effect of Hardy's article was limited accordingly.   Still, conscious of what it heralded, we may well refer to it with interest. Hardy was, at the time, weary of the long years he had spent in a literary compromise, the principal merit of which, from his point of view, was that it had brought him an income ;   he had toiled long enough in the factory of household reading, supplied in monthly or weekly rations by the magazines and in other forms by the circulating libraries, and now he would have a day off to release his natural indignation.   The bondage imposed upon imaginative writing was becoming intolerable ;   how could he, who saw as the real literary world the conditions which had produced for example " the Periclean and Elizabethan dramatist ", and who felt that there was ability and activity enough in his own age to create great achievements, refrain longer from declaring what was barring the way ?

In special, Hardy announced that prudery about the relations of the sexes was barring the way, but not that only.   " The crash of broken commandments is as necessary an accompaniment to the catastrophe of a tragedy as the noise of drum and cymbals to a triumphal march.   But the crash of broken commandments shall not be heard ;   or, if at all, but gently, like the roaring of Bottom. . . .   An arbitrary proclamation has gone forth that certain picked commandments of the ten shall be preserved intact—to wit, the first, third, and seventh ; that the ninth shall be infringed but gingerly ; the sixth only as much as necessary ; and the remainder alone as much as you please, in a genteel manner." Such a complaint might have caused the strait-laced or malicious to class Hardy with the de Kocks of his time ; and he went on in an effort to prevent any such persons in their doings, " Were the objections of the scrupulous limited to a prurient treatment of the relations of the sexes, or to any view of vice calculated to undermine the essential principles of social order, all honest lovers of literature would be in accord with them. All really true literature directly or indirectly sounds as its refrain the words in the *Agamemnon* : ' Chant Aelinon, Aelinon ! but may the good prevail '. But the writer may print the *not* of his broken commandment in capitals of flame ; it makes no difference. A question which should be wholly a question of treatment is confusedly regarded as a question of subject."

In this and other papers of Hardy, such ability of reasoning, such wealth of original comment appears that a wish springs up aside from the actual occasion. How fortunate for many readers it would have been if he had found time, in the season of his full energies and interests, to devote some volumes to his love of nature and country life, unmodified by the tactics of fiction ; and equally, what studies of literature, what critical surveys he might have sent forth ! Those which he has left us, few as they are, emerge from the mass of literary causerie in his age (and that is still agreeable) as specimens of powerful yet unforced grappling with the important and profound factors in the imaginative illustration of life. His career as a

popular novelist obscured this evidence of his independent intellectual value ; and for his part he seems
to have cared little to form up his observations into
any kind of challenge to the chair of criticism, leaving
Pater, Birrell, Lang, Dobson, Gosse, Saintsbury and
the others to take that as they would. The secret of
that apparent indifference was his lifelong purpose, not
even of triumphing over the embarrassments of the
Victorian novelist, but of striking for truth under the
intense sunshafts of philosophic poetry.

But, however it happened, that essay on " Candour
in English Fiction " came along at a moment when
Hardy was making a famous experiment, and when
the restraints and reactions of which he was already
too well aware in his endeavours as a serious visionary
uttering his knowledge in the form of novels were
becoming more than ever acute to him.

At what date Hardy first saw, with the feelings of
some watcher in the skies, the imagined life and death
of Tess of the d'Urbervilles, no record discloses ; but
we know from Mrs. Hardy's book that when he returned to Dorchester from his London summer in
1889 he was daily at work on the book throughout
August. That the central character existed in real
life, we know (unless he was misreported) on his own
authority, though he did not treat the matter very
solemnly. To an interviewer from the office of *Black
and White*, in 1892, he said : " Tess, I only once saw
in the flesh. I was walking along one evening and a
cart came along in which was seated my beautiful
heroine, who, I must confess, was urging her steed
along with rather unnecessary vehemence of language.
She coloured up very much when she saw me, but—

as a novelist—I fell in love with her at once and adopted her as my heroine."

Hardy continued in this vein of localisation : " Old Mr. Clare was a Dorsetshire parson whose name still lives enshrined in the hearts of thousands. ' Shepherd Oak ', in *Far from the Madding Crowd*, I knew well as a boy ; while ' Bathsheba Everdene ' is a reminiscence of one of my own aunts. Our family, you know, has lived here for centuries. ' Joseph Poorgrass ', ' Eustacia ', and ' Susan Nunsuch ' in *The Return of the Native*, were all well-known local characters. Girls resembling the three dairymaids in *Tess* used to get me to write their love-letters for them when I was a little boy. I suppose that unconsciously I absorbed a good deal of their mode of life and speech, and so I have been able to reproduce it in the dairy at ' Talbothays '." Elsewhere it is noted that Talbothays was one of his father's properties in the Vale of the dairies, and his brother and sisters at length lived there.

And as for the important element in Hardy's tragic tale, that Tess was of a formerly conspicuous family, reduced by time and change, the same interview produced an eager justification.[1] Hardy was always a stubborn defender of the probability of his coincidences and paradoxes, following Byron's aphorism,

> Truth is always strange—
> Stranger than fiction. If it could be told,
> How much would Novels gain by the exchange ?

[1] The d'Urberville situation in real life was not only found in Dorset. James Hogg, the Ettrick Shepherd, writes in *The Mountain Bard*, 1807 : " The Lintons were, in those days, and even till toward the beginning of the last century, the principal farmers in all the upper parts of Ettrick and Yarrow ; yet such a singular reverse of fortune have these opulent families experienced, that there is now rarely one of the name to be found above the rank of the meanest labourer ".

So, when the interviewer enquired about the d'Urber-villes, there was some activity. Mrs. Hardy brought out a sketch of the actual house where Tess's confession (on which the story's final movement depends) was said to have been made. " ' That is Woolbridge Manor House,' explained the host, ' one of the seats of the ———, the family to whom Tess belonged by right of her descent. In that house and on that same night, if you remember, she tried on the jewels that Clare gave her. I think I must tell you that that was an idea of Mrs. Hardy's.' . . . ' And, Mr. Hardy, is it no mere figment of your brain that Tess was of ancient lineage, and possessed of more old " skelingtons " than anyone else in the country ? ' ' Oh, no,' replied the author. ' It is an absolute fact. I will go and fetch you the genealogical tree of the actual family.' While he was out of the room, Mrs. Hardy told me of her over-hearing some labourer boasting to a friend of the vault of Bere Regis, which was full of the ' skelingtons ' of his family. It was a fact, she said, that this man was always addressed by an antiquarian clergyman as ' Sir John ', ' for ', said he, ' he is Sir John '." The inter-viewer mentioned a Northamptonshire village where he knew of a labourer, the last of a famous line, effigied in the church. " ' Exactly,' replied Mr. Hardy. ' There are many such cases about here. You will trace noble lineage in many a face, and there is a certain conscious pride about some of these people which differentiates them at once from middle-class cock-neyism or provincialism. And in another sense, the rather free and easy mode of life adopted by the squires of the last century has contributed to the ancient lineage, and to the fine features of many of the labouring

classes in this neighbourhood. A gentleman told me
the other day of a whole village to which he was related
through his grandfather. Here is the pedigree of Tess's
family,' said my host, as he placed an enormous volume
in my hand. And here I traced without a break, right
back to the Conquest, the records of this stately house.
' Woolbridge Manor House,' continued Mr. Hardy
after a while, ' as you can see by Mr. Moule's sketch,
is only a farmhouse now. The farmer's wife has lately
been much exercised as to what the many pilgrimages
to her house have meant. You will see on the stairs,
exactly as I have described, those two dreadful portraits of Tess's ancestresses ; and only a few weeks
ago a number of records of the family were discovered
hidden away amongst the rafters in the roof.' "

Resuming the history of the novel at its early stage,
we find Hardy completing it as a whole and with
intentness, leaving the task of sorting things out to
meet the exigencies of magazine publication until the
end. We also find him having some difficulty in
getting an editor to accept it as a practicable example
of household reading. First it came back unwanted
from *Murray's Magazine*—at least, the part of it which
was ready in October 1889 ; then from *Macmillan's*.
For a third trial, Hardy became ingenious. He detached, and he substituted, being determined to restore
his original version once the work of monthly instalments was over and the time for simple publication
came. The editor of *The Graphic*, Arthur Locker,
accepted the qualified and beatified novel, which he
published between July and December 1891. (In
The Graphic there also appeared part of Hardy's book
of that year entitled *A Group of Noble Dames*, which

took shape from that same curious scrutiny of Dorsetshire pedigrees as was at work in *Tess*. The *Group*
received no particular welcome, and offended one or
two people in the county for a while.)   As for the
amputated passages in *Tess*, some observers sounded
a note of protest, even at the time, that Hardy should
have had to deliver them, as it were, surreptitiously.
" Considering the whole," the *Pall Mall Gazette* said,
" one hardly wonders that editors should have hesi-
tated over presenting such strong fare to their gentle
readers ; but it is a singular commentary upon the
open chances of English fiction that the strongest
English novel of many years should have to be lopped
into pieces and adapted to three different periodicals
before it succeeded in finding a complete hearing."

Upon the appearance of *Tess of the d'Urbervilles* in
time for Christmas 1891, the reviewers of novels were
of one mind at least in this, that the occasion called for
plenty of comment.   Some of the vast numbers of
words then written were not at all friendly :   " Few
people ", according to the *Saturday Review*, would
" deny the terrible dreariness of this tale, which, except
during a few hours spent with cows, has not a gleam
of sunshine anywhere ".   The aged *Quarterly* too,
mindful of its lethal past, objected to the tale, the
manner of its telling and the " affectation " of the
writer who professed to be throwing light on moral
laws.   In the *National Review* Tess was ridiculed as
" A Prig in the Elysian Fields ".   Hardy found this
article " smart and amusing ", and ominous.   But in
the main the reviews were such as to show the sense
of the literary world to be that Thomas Hardy had
brought off a great piece of work, and several of them

might be mentioned as themselves masterly specimens of immediate criticism. In *The Star*, under the pseudonym " Log-Roller ", Richard le Gallienne was picturesque and keen ; he began with complaints against the intermittent gawkiness of Hardy's style—no new trouble. " It seems to come from sudden moments of self-consciousness in the midst of his creative flow, as also from the imperfect digestion of certain modern science of philosophy which is becoming somewhat too obtrusive through the apple-cheek outline of Mr. Hardy's work. For example a little boy talks to his sister ' rather for the pleasure of utterance than for audition '. . . . Think how absolutely out of colour in Arcadia are such words as dolorifuge—photosphere —concatenation. . . . Where indeed are such in colour ?—And Mr. Hardy further uses that horrid verb ' ecstasise '." In conclusion Mr. le Gallienne wrote, " So ' the woman pays '. Thus you see the plot is the plot of Mr. H. A. Jones, but the hand is the hand of Thomas Hardy. One would venture further and breathe ' Shakespearean ' concerning the women, but the adjective is so apt to be misunderstood." Hardy must have been unusually grateful for the opening notes of H. W. Massingham's salute in the *Daily Chronicle* : the " new novel is as pitiless and tragic in its intensity as the old Greek dramas. Not Aeschylus himself nor any of his brethren who so rigidly illustrated the doctrine of human fate, could have woven a web that should more completely enmesh a human soul than Mr. Hardy has done in the case of his heroine Tess." As for the allusion to Aeschylus, Dr. Walter Lock, the Warden of Keble College, told Hardy that his book was the *Agamemnon* without the remainder of the Oresteian trilogy. Hardy thought this inexact, though interesting.

Out of many other spirited appreciations, mention must be made of two : Miss Clementina Black in the *Illustrated London News* summed up : " [The book's] essence lies in the perception that a woman's moral worth is measurable not by any one deed, but by the whole aim and tendency of her life and nature. In regard to men the doctrine is no novelty ; the writers who have had eyes to see and courage to declare the same truth about women are few indeed ; and Mr. Hardy in this novel has shown himself to be one of that brave and clear-sighted minority." The *Academy* reviewer was William Watson, who was allowed four and a half columns and who used his space with high seriousness ; he was at that date a fine and eloquent critic ; he found elements of style and attitude to reprove within the general and ultimate impression that he was honouring " so great and terrible a conception ".

By way of variety, and indeed in strict retrospective justice, let us glance at *Punch* for February 27th, 1892. *Punch* stood up exceedingly well to the sociological dangers of the novel and was as pleased as anybody to acclaim the work as a masterpiece, but found (and it was surely not difficult to find) one blot. The villain had almost won the game after all. " Alec d'Urberville would be thoroughly in his element in an Adelphi Drama of the most approved type, ancient or modern. He is just the sort of stage-scoundrel who from time to time seeks to take some mean advantage of a heroine in distress, on which occasion said heroine will request him to ' unhand her ', or to ' stand aside and let her pass '; whereupon the dastardly ruffian retaliates with a diabolical sneer of fiendish malice, his eyes ablaze with passion, as, making his melodramatic exit at the O.P. wing, he growls, ' Ah ! a day will come ' or, ' she must and shall be mine ! ' or, if not making his exit, but remaining in centre of stage to assist in forming a picture, he exclaims with fiendish glee, ' Now, pretty one, you are in my power ! ' and so forth. 'Tis a great pity that such a penny-plain and twopence-coloured scoundrel should have been allowed so strong a part among Mr. Hardy's excellent and unconventional *dramatis personae.*"

While the serial publication of *Tess* was still going on, the author received a great many letters appealing for a happy ending, but as he saw the matter, to meet his correspondents' wishes was impossible on more than one account. The theory of heredity, in which he was at the period inclined to believe, necessitated the murder ; a sin was sure of its wages ; death and the law's revenge apart, there could not be happiness between two such temperaments as Angel Clare and Tess. So the risk of driving the public away from him and his book was taken ; and Hardy rejoiced, a little sadly, to witness that the public did not at all shun the bitter draught so rarely offered within his recollection. His sadness arose from the receipt of more letters, from those who had become in disgrace with fortune, expressive of the tragic side of experience,—Tesses and Clares urgently seeking the personal guidance which not even Shakespeare could have given. When the fifth edition of the novel appeared, Hardy included one of the prefaces which he liked to write, fulfilling the philosophical part of his mind, and therein he thanked the general reader and the majority of the reviewers for supporting his experiment in " laying down a story on the lines of tacit opinion, instead of making it to square with the merely vocal formulae of society ".   At the same time, he was not going to let off those professional writers who had " manipulated " his book ; and among others, he retorted to Andrew Lang (though not naming him) for this pitying sentence let fall from the firmament of rectitude : " He does but give us of his best ".

Among the unpublished valuations of *Tess* (and Edmund Gosse could report, " Wherever I go I hear its praises "), those of two great novelists should not be overlooked here.   Henry James wrote to Stevenson : " The good little Thomas Hardy has scored a great success with *Tess of the d'Urbervilles*, which is chock-full of faults and falsity and yet has a singular beauty and charm " ; but a year afterwards he did not quite maintain this verdict.   Stevenson apparently had not admired the book, and James replied, " I am meek and shamed where the public clatter is deafening—so I bowed my head and let *Tess of the D's* pass.   But oh yes, dear Louis, she is vile.   The pretence of ' sexuality ' is only equalled by the absence of it, and the abomination of the language by the author's reputation for style.   There are indeed some pretty smells and sights and sounds.   But you have better ones in Polynesia."   George Meredith, in a letter to Frederick Greenwood, called Hardy " one of the few men whose work I can read ", and regretted the way in which the heroine was treated at last : " Tess, out of the arms of Alec into (I suppose) those of the lily-necked Clare, and on to the Black Flag waving over her poor body, is a smudge in vapour—she at one time so real to me ".

Whatever faults were found in Hardy's novel and
in the sub-title, " A Pure Woman ", the impression
that it made was profound ; such observers as William
Sharp and Mrs. Humphry Ward assure us that it " did
more to bring about a true recognition of the author
than the whole range of his writings ", and its readers
returned to his former productions with a new regard.
Clergymen preached sermons suggested by *Tess*. "Spy"
(Sir Leslie Ward) included Hardy in the series of
coloured cartoons in *Vanity Fair* (June 4th, 1892.)
Topographical enthusiasts, who had been busy with
Thomas Hardy's Wessex, now took their notebooks to
the d'Urberville country.   Kindly journalists from
town, with a feeling of adventure, went into Dorsetshire and talked to Hardy at home.

They found him a little different from the common
notion of him, the old Bucolic Fallacy.   " In truth
there is nothing ' truly rural ' about Mr. Hardy's
features.   There is a town paleness about them not at
all suggestive of long rambles by field and hedgerow.
With broad, white forehead, eyes that seem slightly
weary, and dark moustache to accentuate these features,
Mr. Hardy might well pass for a Londoner in the prime
of life.   But probably he gives one this impression
because of his recent attack of influenza which was exceptionally violent in Dorchester."   Another visitor
did not think of that explanation.   " Of middle height
with a very thoughtful face and rather melancholy eyes,
he is nevertheless an interesting and amusing companion.   He is regarded by the public at large as a
hermit ever brooding in the far-off seclusion of a west
country village.   A fond delusion, which is disproved

by the fact, that he is almost more frequently to be seen in a London drawing-room or a Continental hotel than in the quiet old-world lanes of rural Dorsetshire. His wife, some few years younger than himself, is so particularly bright, so thoroughly *au courant du jour*, so evidently a citizen of the wide world, that the, at first, unmistakable reminiscence that there is in her of Anglican ecclesiasticism is curiously puzzling and inexplicable to the stranger, until the information is vouchsafed that she is intimately and closely connected with what the late Lord Shaftesbury would term ' the higher order of the clergy '."

Hardy would point out in his drawing-room the original drawings for illustrating his novels which Herkomer, du Maurier, Alfred Parsons and others had done, and there also hung some water-colours of local scenes by Mrs. Hardy which " went far to prove the verisimilitude of her husband ". A portrait of himself with a full beard, by a Dorsetshire artist, hung over an old carved sofa, opposite an engraving of Admiral Sir Thomas Hardy, the novelist's kinsman in whose arms immortal Nelson died, and whose monument on a hill-top could be seen from Max Gate. The house was indeed a post of observation appropriate to its maker. " A vast perspective is before one from almost any one of the windows, rolling downs, acres of arable land and pastures, upland ranges, and dark belts of woodland, with, valley-ward, the white gleam of the Frome meandering among the daisy lands and through and past ancient Dorchester. To the south-west are the broken ridges of that extraordinary freak of nature (and toil of man) known as Maiden Castle. In front of the house itself stretches away an immense swelling meadow, some three thousand acres in extent, the largest in England."

The topics on which Hardy was persuaded to hold forth were not the only ones on which his talk could be revealing. He had come to be regarded as a champion of simple Hodge, and was by no means tired of declaring that there was really no such person ; yet, of course, the country people did merit a general description. Hardy was proud of them : " They are full of character, which is not to be found in the strained, calculating, unromantic middle classes ; and for many reasons this is so. They are the representatives of antiquity. Many of these labourers about here bear corrupted Norman names ; many are the descendants of the squires of the last century, and their faces even now strongly resemble the portraits in the old Manor-houses. Many are, must be, the descendants of the Romans who lived here in great pomp and state for four hundred years. I have seen faces here that are the duplicates of those fine faces I saw at Fiesole, where also I picked up Roman coins the counterpart of those we find here so often. They even use Latin words here which have survived everything. . . . The labourer as a rule is, as I depict him, rather fetichistic. Susan Nunsuch, in *The Return of the Native*, still exists. In some parts, the girls go out on Midsummer's Eve as they did in *The Woodlanders* in the hope of meeting him who will be their husband. They are wonderfully good at description if you know their words, but it takes a lifetime to understand them, accent and turns of phrase mean so much with them." Hardy agreed that he was sometimes described as the novelist of the agricultural labourer, but with his usual

dryness commented, " That is not inclusive, I think."
Conversation naturally found its way to his latest book,
and gave him the cue to tell a pretty story of a village
girl who had lately retorted to his compliments on her
good looks with " Ah, but you don't think me so nice
as Tess." Hardy replied, " But she isn't real ; you
are." " What ! " said the girl. " Oh, I thought she
lived in that house over the hill there." She was much
relieved, Hardy gathered, to know that Tess was no
practical rival.

Questioned further about his book, Hardy admitted
that he was sorry not to have been able to rescue Tess
at the last, as so many had hoped, but so it had to be.
" You must have felt it a pain to bring her to so fearful
an end." " Yes. Such dreams are we made of that I
often think of the day when, having decided that she
must die, I went purposely to Stonehenge to study
the spot. It was a gloomy lowering day, and the skies
almost seemed to touch the pillars of the great heathen
temple." As for " a pure woman ", it was suggested
that Tess's first love-trouble did not deprive her of
that name, but that " her absolutely unnecessary return
to Alec d'Urberville " did ; to that Hardy replied,
" But I still maintain that her innate purity remained
intact to the very last ; though I frankly own that a
certain outward purity left her on her last fall. I
regarded her then as being in the hands of circumstances, not normally responsible, a mere corpse drifting with a current to her end." When it was forecast
that the broad result of the book would be a greater
freedom for open and serious discussion of some deep
problems of human life, Hardy went slow. (He had
of course no desire to set himself up as a protagonist

in the manner of W. T. Stead.) " That would be a very ambitious hope on my part. Remember I am only a learner in the art of novel-writing. Still I do feel very strongly that the position of man and woman in nature may be taken up and treated frankly."

The great and dramatic advancement of Hardy in the foreground of living novelists was also reflected in the rapidly increasing number of studies of his work as a whole. Such estimates had of course been written before there was any mention of *Tess*, and examples have already been touched upon. Before 1892 (to linger over another of these contemporary contemplations) John A. Steuart had included Hardy in his series of " Letters to Living Authors ", with Meredith, Hall Caine, Stevenson, Blackmore, Mark Twain, Tolstoi and others. Steuart began, " Sir,—I think it would be safe to say that you are the most distinctively modern of our living novelists of note. Mr. Besant may occasionally seem to deal more directly with the perplexing problems of the day ; Mr. Meredith may appear, to some, to be more emphatically the intellectual child of the age ; but of certain broad aspects which are as characteristically nineteenth century as they are characteristically English, you are, I think, beyond rivalry as a delineator." Steuart found in the Wessex novels a union of the ideal and the realistic which struck him as masterly ; " your work has really much of the Greek spirit in it, and is, therefore, unique in the present day ". With some reservations on the score of the improbable, even the absurd (the wife-sale in *The Mayor of Casterbridge*), Steuart delivered a panegyric, and prophesied permanence for *The Wood-landers*, *Far from the Madding Crowd* and *Under the*

Greenwood Tree. He acknowledged a thing remarked by Gosse and others, that " you are no favourite with the young lady who patronises the circulating libraries. She is in the habit of making marginal notes in your books which are sometimes more entertaining than complimentary. Precisely why the fair one quarrels with you is, of course, among the mysteries of the world, but it is vaguely understood she considers herself slandered in your female characters, so she calls you ' that horrid man Hardy '."

Nevertheless, we find in the *Westminster Review* for February 1892 " A Study of Mr. Thomas Hardy ", methodical and unbiassed, by Janetta Newton-Robinson. The critical power and eloquence of William Sharp's " Thomas Hardy and his Novels ", in the New York *Forum* for January 1892, it must be confessed, were of a higher order altogether. Sharp was attracted by the unusualness of Hardy's progress and triumph, and his deliberations on the matter are worth quoting, partly for the light they throw on the chronicles of this novelist. What had been against his reception before *Tess* (and even there, " the immense swing by which he has recently been carried to the front place was due in no slight degree to causes independent of the literary quality and value of his work ") ? Characteristics out of the common.

" His robustness of thought and speech does not appeal to most readers. They dislike him as crudely natural, even as they dislike the strong smell of the earth. . . . To speak of him as a pessimistic writer would be misleading because inadequate. He does not preach pessimism, for he has the saving grace of having no ' ism ' to support or to exemplify. . . .

Life, movement, humour, and the endless play of the forces of nature, afford him more than he reveals his intimate sense of the insoluble mystery of existence, of our unguided way across a trackless plain of whose lost frontiers there is no resemblance, and whose horizons are seen of none. It is this steadfast austerity which has stood between him and so large a portion of the reading public. . . . A noteworthy factor in the matter of Thomas Hardy's acceptance by the public, is his style, or to be more exact, certain idiosyncrasies of style. Though the most exclusively and natively English of all the great writers of the Victorian age, he is in point of diction the most Latinical writer we have had since Dryden and Milton. . . . Perhaps one must know something of Wessex in order fully to enjoy Thomas Hardy's novels."

In 1892 the earliest study of Hardy to appear as a separate volume was announced by Elkin Mathews and John Lane : *The Art of Thomas Hardy*, six essays by Lionel Johnson. This publication, by a young poet of considerable merit, whose first book it was, did not come out until 1894, and has kept its place upon the whole as a fine critical performance. Its author had intellectual strength and training enough to deal with the big problem of Hardy's latest search for a true tragedy, and style such as is after all part of the critic's own problem. Another book on Hardy was published in 1894,—the work of Annie Macdonell ; and, though she admitted that she could not pretend to any finality in her criticism, Hardy being in the full vigour of his genius and having prepared the public for further surprises, she did something which commands respect and attention if we refer to her pages now. Hardy might have specially commissioned her to say for him, " Not that he has posed as philosopher, or even as poet. . . . Story-teller, picture-maker, humorist, it is entertainment he offers us."

By way of pastime and keeping his hand in, Hardy was writing more of his short stories, and he collected several of them in *Life's Little Ironies*, 1894. Some were sinister enough, others merry and countrified. They must have been popular, for they originally appeared in many of the most astutely edited magazines of the day ; one, " The Fiddler of the Reels ", was printed in the number of *Scribner's Magazine* produced in honour of the Chicago Exhibition, May 1893. That month, Hardy was invited to stay with Lord Houghton at Vice-Regal Lodge, Dublin ; and the visit led to a collaboration with Mrs. Henniker, Lord Houghton's sister, in a tale called " The Spectre of the Real ".   On June 3rd, 1893, a short play based on " The Three Strangers ", and called *The Three Wayfarers*, was produced with one of Barrie's, who had suggested the dramatization, at Terry's Theatre.

But Hardy was not principally concerned with short-story writing or one-act plays.   He had generally some scheme in his mind for a work of full stature, to be attacked on some destined day ; in 1887 or 1888 he had noted the possibility of an imagined student's tragedy ; and by 1894 he had brought this plan through its trial stages to fulfilment.   He called this book in the end *Jude the Obscure*.   Whether or not he anticipated its effect on his name and on public opinion when he was at work on it, he obviously determined on treating it with relentless black shades, and iteration of a knell-like complaining.   But once again he had to face the first necessity of a professional novelist at the time, and contrive that his book should make its appearance as a magazine serial entitled " Hearts Insurgent ", which was done in *Harper's* from December 1894 to November 1895. Then it immediately came out with the imprint of Osgood, McIlvaine—in its original and final form, by itself, " a novel ", its writer held, " addressed by a man to men and women of full age ".

There are not wanting in the biographical history of this country cases of men of humble birth whose inclination for literature or learning in one direction or another was at once their blessing and their calamity. When the poet John Clare, " The Northamptonshire Peasant ", had become a sort of show-piece in a lunatic asylum, he was apt to be a little fierce with those who too readily asked him about his life story. For them, with whatever inward reservation, he had one answer : he wished he had never left the labours and habits of his fathers. We have seen society considerably modified and the distribution of opportunities improved ; in particular the universities have become much more accessible to merit and diligence irrespective of class ; and yet, the fate of a John Clare or a Jude Fawley is still within the bounds of possibility, under different externals. Still, Hardy's tragic narrative was not confined to the disillusion and rejection of a self-taught man. He had long been capable of more complex plots and psychological labyrinths than that.

It was Hardy's belief that the " Christminster " to which Jude was lured as a seeker after the higher knowledge was not, as " everybody " knew it must be, just Oxford. In the text of his novel, allusions occur which might easily be taken as demonstrating the conventional identification. Jude, for example, is found reading Matthew Arnold's rapt apostrophes to Oxford ; but in the book those celebrated phrases are addressed to Christminster. In the map of Wessex, as Hardy deals with it, Christminster inevitably occupies the present site of our most ancient university city ; and Dr. Rutland prints a set of " approximate " references from the novelist's autograph, wherein Fourways is not unconnected with Carfax, Cardinal College with Christ Church, and so on. But notwithstanding all such details, Hardy's Christminster was essentially a vision, a " city of youth and dream " which he surely in his boyhood had beheld in the summer clouds, like Keats's undiscoverable " little town by river or sea shore, or mountain-built with peaceful citadel " in his " Ode on a Grecian Urn ". For practical purposes Jude could not walk the clouds of heavenly academe, and Hardy's own close and emotional observation of Oxford (one of his early delights as an architect) duly supplied the tangible surroundings.

Whatever the University of Oxford thought about Hardy's apparent indications of its dons and its traditions and its ceremonies, the larger public was naturally exercised in mind by a more extensive aspect —by the painful portrayal of a man caught in the thorns of life, trapped in the pits of dangerous dreams and false marriage, and altogether sent here below to accumulate bitter disasters about him. " Everyone ", wrote the novelist who called herself John Oliver Hobbes, on November 26th, 1895, " is jumping on Hardy's last book. It is much finer in reality and as a work of literary, philosophic value than *Tess*, but the subject is, of course, very painful." A little later, *Punch* expressed an opinion by including a parody, not one of the most adroit, headed " Dude the Diffuse. By Toomuch Too Hardy." Then the *Review of Reviews* for January 1896, on " Thomas Hardy and Marriage ", brought together two notices " which differ about as widely as it is possible for two articles to differ ". In the *Free Review* Mr. Geoffrey Mortimer blessed his fate for letting him live in an age which had given forth two such novels as *Jude the Obscure* and *Esther Waters*. Hardy had crowned his achievement. But one who had herself written some novels, Mrs. Oliphant, in *Blackwood's Magazine* took up the parable " against the anti-marriage league which had Mr. Grant Allen, Mr. Thomas Hardy and Mr. Dowie as its exponents ". The character of the new novel, to her, was easily summed. " Nothing so coarsely indecent as the whole history of Jude . . . has ever been put in English print ;—that is to say, from the hands of a master. There may be books more disgusting, more impious as regards human nature, more foul in detail, in those dark corners where the amateurs of filth and garbage ", and so forth.

Let us glance at one or two more of the reviews. That January the first number of *Cosmopolis, an International Review* appeared, a work of great promise, assembling many capable writers. Here Edmund Gosse wrote so well on Hardy that his words live still. He began by naming three novelists as having become classical : as having risen above profit-and-loss accounts. " Still a great number of English novelists, and many of them with no small success, hear the voice yet speaking which said two hundred years ago :

Travaillez pour la gloire, et qu'un sordide gain
Ne soit jamais l'objet d'un illustre écrivain ;

and among these we say Meredith, Hardy, Stevenson, as one hundred and fifty years ago we might have said Richardson, Fielding, Sterne." He would therefore avoid the impertinence of " purely indulgent eulogy ". He thought that Hardy had, first of all, arranged his new plot with too rigid a mind, though not because he meant to " join the ranks of deciduous troublers of our peace " who had lately been casting forth " a sheaf of ' purpose ' stories on ' the marriage question ' (as it is called) ".

Next, Hardy was wrong to try for fresh fields, to leave South Wessex for North ; " where there are no prehistoric monuments, no ancient buildings, no mossed and immemorial woodlands, he is Samson shorn ". He had done his best with Marygreen, but it remained just a dull hamlet ; and " to pass from the landscape to the persons ", it seemed to Gosse that the neuropath had taken the pen from the poet. And yet, ghastly as the story was, it made " an irresistible book ". And yet, again, why did Hardy insist increasingly on being a rebel ? " What has Providence done to Mr. Hardy that he should rise up in the arable land of Wessex and shake his fist at his Creator ? " To conclude, as though wagging a monitory finger at his friend, Gosse produced a little Apologue : " A fact about the infancy of Mr. Hardy has escaped the interviewers and may be recorded here. On the day of his birth, during a brief absence of his nurse, there slipped into the room an ethereal creature known as the spirit of Plastic Beauty. Bending over the cradle she scattered roses on it, and as she strewed them she blessed the babe. ' He shall have an eye to see moral and material loveliness, he shall speak of richly-coloured pastoral places in the accent of Theocritus, he shall write in such a way as to cajole busy men into a sympathy with old, unhappy, far-off things.' She turned and went, but while the nurse still delayed, a withered termagant glided into the room. From her apron she dropped toads among the rose-leaves, and she whispered, ' I am the genius of False Rhetoric, and led by me he shall say things ugly and coarse, not recognizing them to be so, and shall get into a rage about matters that call for philosophic calm, and shall spoil some of his best passages with pedantry and incoherency. He shall not know what things belong to his peace, and he shall plague his most loyal admirers with the barbaric contortions of his dialogue.' So saying, she put out her snaky tongue at the unoffending babe, and ever since, his imagination, noble as it is, and attuned to the great harmonies of nature, is liable at a moment's notice to give a shriek of discord."

Another splendid piece of criticism appeared in the *Illustrated London News*. " The reader closes this book with a feeling that a huge pall has blotted out all the light of humanity. In one way that sensation is a tribute to Mr. Hardy's mastery of his art." But the writer was going on to convict Hardy of points of failure as an artist. When a doctor in the story was made to say that child murderers and suicides were becoming common, owing to " the universal wish not to live ", it was " too much. . . . We all knew perfectly well that baby Schopenhauers are not coming into the world in shoals." For this critic, such errors caused the tale to border upon the ludicrous, but the closing sentence gave no encouragement to any who presumed to ridicule Hardy. " Read the story how you will, it is manifestly a work of genius, moving amid ideas and emotions of so large a significance that most of our fiction is to *Jude the Obscure* as a hamlet to a hemisphere." A similar proposal of the comparative eminence of Hardy closed the article in the *Saturday Review* : " Had Mr. Hardy never written another book, this would still place him at the head of English novelists. To turn from him or from Mr. Meredith to our Wardour Street romancers and whimpering Scotch humorists is like walking from a library into a schoolroom." So too the *Westminster Review* insisted upon the supremacy of Hardy with all his faults or foibles ; and, after a few months, one who had been among the first to make a pilgrimage through Wessex and write an account of Hardy's product in its fullness —Havelock Ellis—asserted the same kind of veneration in the *Savoy*. He indeed refused to treat *Jude* as a surprise : he once more considered Hardy's whole course, found " no real break and no new departure ", and named the Elizabethan dramatic poets Fletcher, Heywood and Ford as the class of genius to which Hardy belonged.

Here, however, it is time to take into the reckoning the way in which *Jude the Obscure* aroused feelings other than veneration, and we return to the *Saturday Review* in which the immediate history of the popular opinion, or substitute for opinion, was registered with valuable vigour. Hardy was unlucky, he was just too late. " It is doubtful," the *Saturday Review* declared, " considering not only the greatness of the work, but also the greatness of the author's reputation, whether for many years any book has received quite so foolish a reception. . . . By an unfortunate coincidence it appears just at the culmination of a new fashion in Cant, the cant of ' Healthiness '. It is now the better part of a year ago since the collapse of the ' New Woman ' fiction began. The success of *The Woman Who Did* was perhaps the last of a series of successes attained, in spite of glaring artistic defects, and an utter want of humour or beauty, by works dealing intimately and unrestrainedly with sexual affairs. It worked a crisis." The pendulum had swung back; the respectable public had abandoned its temporary fashion; " and the reviewers, mindful of the fact that the duty of a reviewer is to provide acceptable reading for his editor's public, have changed with the greatest dexterity from a chorus praising ' outspoken purity ' to a band of public informers against indecorum. . . . So active, so malignant have these sanitary inspectors of fiction become that a period of terror analogous to that of the New England witch mania is upon us. . . . And at the very climax of this silliness, Mr. Hardy with an admirable calm has put forth a book in which a secondary, but very important interest is a frank treatment of the destructive influence of a vein of sensuality upon an ambitious working man. There probably never was a novel dealing with the closer relations of men and women that was quite so free from lasciviousness as this. But at one point a symbolical piece of offal is flung into Jude's face. Incontinently a number of popular reviewers, almost tumbling over one another in the haste to be first, have rushed into print under such headings as ' Jude the Obscene ' [*Pall Mall Gazette*] and denounced the book, with

simple libellous violence, as a mass of filth from beginning to end."

Such reviewing was not confined to English journals,
and one American example, the work of Jeannette L.
Gilder, disturbed Hardy so much that he addressed
the following letter to Messrs. Harper (December 24th,
1895) : " I am much surprised, and I may say distressed, by the nature of the attack on *Jude* in the New
York *World*, which has just come into my hands. This
is the only American notice of the novel I have yet
seen, except Mr. Howells's in the *Weekly*. I do not
know how far the *World* is representative of American
feeling and opinion. But it is so much against my
wish to offend the tastes of the American public, or to
thrust any book of mine upon readers there, that if it
should be in your own judgment advisable, please
withdraw the novel. You will probably know that it
has been received here with about equal voices for and
against—somewhat as *Tess* was received. All sensible
readers here see at least that the intention of the book
is honest and good. I myself thought it was somewhat
overburdened with the interests of morality." Jeannette Gilder later asked Hardy for an interview, being
in London, but he was not willing.

There was a run on the book at the free libraries,
however " degenerate " or " decadent " its author
might have become, which disturbed guardians of
national virtue. Among them the Bishop of Wakefield,
the Rt. Rev. William Walsham How, did most for
that abstraction, writing a letter to the *Yorkshire Post*
to announce his burning a copy of *Jude* (or some other
book by Hardy) and persuading Messrs. Smith to keep
this work out of their library and to be on their guard

against others by the same hand. Hardy's comment on the Bishop's published letter is well known—the Bishop had burned the novel in a temper because he had not nowadays the chance of burning the author. And there were, even in the grey region of this novel's history, some points of amusement. Professor Flinders Petrie and Hardy were enjoying an idle day at Framlingham when they saw across the front of a large shop, in bold gilt letters, thrice repeated, GEORGE JUDE. 'Well," said the Professor, " you wouldn't call that ' Jude the Obscure '."

The whole affair certainly depressed Hardy and did not soon die away in his mind. Nine years later he summed it up, with a vulnerable simplicity, by inscribing in a first edition of the book : " The criticisms which this story received in England and America were a monumental illustration of the crass Philistinism of the two countries, and were limited to about 20 pages out of more than 500. It was left to the French and Germans to discover the author's meaning, through the medium of indifferent translations."

During these years Hardy was not entirely submerged in his work and agitations as a writer of fiction. He was quite a familiar figure in literary society, away from Max Gate, and in 1894 made one of Edward Clodd's Whitsuntide party at Aldeburgh, a party (as Grant Allen rhymed it)

> That was none the limper
> For holding in it Edward Whymper.

Whymper told of his ascent of the Matterhorn on July 14th, 1865, when four of his companions lost their lives. Little need to add that the story from

Whymper's own lips stirred Hardy's imagination ; in 1897 he was at Zermatt, eyeing the scene of this triumph and catastrophe, and he wrote a sonnet with a vision of the seven mountaineers.   And sixteen years after the first meeting with Whymper, by Hardy's desire, Clodd arranged another of the same kind. Hardy brought and read his poem, and had with him too a copy of the *Ascent* in which he asked Whymper to write an addition ; this book went back as a special treasure to Max Gate.   Those things are worth mentioning because they illustrate a characteristic of Hardy, his admiration and affection for men of action—the same spirit which led him to friendships with General Buller and Lawrence of Arabia, to name no others. He might so easily have been one of this stamp himself.

Strangely enough, when Hardy was at Zermatt in June 1897, a fatality occurred which he was drawn to enquire into.   An Englishman, ascending, had disappeared.   Hardy " walked up to the Riffel Alp by the way Mr. Cooper must have taken, and down again, examining narrowly such slight precipices as occur on each side of the very rough bridle path which forms the route, and came to the conclusion that no human body could fall over at any point and lie invisible ". During this tour Hardy stayed at the Hotel Gibbon, Lausanne, and the experience was such as he could have hoped for : its strange power is preserved in the poem or ghost-story that he wrote in Gibbon's Garden.

The growing habit of comparing Meredith and Hardy, although the latter had still to reveal fully one essential part of such a comparison, lent a particular excitement to a meeting held by the Omar Khayyám Club in 1895 at the Burford Bridge Hotel, with its memories of Nelson and Keats and Hazlitt. For both Meredith and Hardy were there, Hardy being brought along by Edmund Gosse. In 1890 Gosse had introduced one of his appreciations of Hardy with the fact that the two writers were being " spoken of in the same breath ", but he had added that Meredith was approaching twilight, whereas Hardy was still vaguely one of our young writers—a young writer of fifty. It was singularly true.

Meredith marked the Burford Bridge occasion by making his first speech ; Hardy replied for the guests, and " wittily and happily described " the meeting with the other speaker long before in Chapman and Hall's dusty back room. When Hardy had done, there was a call for George Gissing, whose book, *The Unclassed*, had greatly impressed the Wessex novelist ; and Gissing rose to mention how he also, in connection with that book, had had an interview at the publishers' with Meredith " when I didn't know who he was ". Hardy invited Gissing to Max Gate, no doubt for a cheerful interchange of sombre selections.

One of the diners contrasted the appearance of the two representative writers while they talked with a window half enclosed with green leaves as background. " Hardy's features gave the impression of ' many thought-worn eves and morrows ' ; Meredith looked as if he had met and mastered life." Some thought that, in the friendly competition of the novelists, Hardy was losing ground by being temporarily obsessed with a limited topic. Meredith's diversity promised to win. At all events, those who wrote retrospects of the novel at the time of Queen Victoria's Diamond Jubilee naturally placed Meredith and Hardy at the head of living novelists. In his *Victorian Age in Literature*, 1913, G. K. Chesterton produced a variation of his own on the theme, of which some words are remembered by lovers of epigram : " Hardy went down to botanize in the swamps, while Meredith climbed toward the sun. Meredith became, at his best, a sort of daintily dressed Walt Whitman ; Hardy became a sort of village atheist brooding and blaspheming over the village idiot." Presumably running short of blasphemy or village idiots, in 1898 Hardy was one of the thirty authors who offered Meredith a congratulatory address on his seventieth birthday.

In his time Hardy was honoured with the dedications of a good many books, which were sometimes embarrassing. The voluminous Robert Buchanan, who surprisingly enough was a year younger than Hardy, inscribed to him his *Come Live with Me and be My Love* in 1892. The comment of one journal was, " The book is dedicated to Thomas Hardy, and it is not difficult to see that the author of *The Woodlanders* is in some sort responsible for it. It is a heavy responsibility, and we tender to Mr. Hardy our respectful sympathy. He has written of English country life as no man else has ever written of it yet. Mr. Buchanan writes of it as we hope no man will ever write again." Then, the business of sitting to artists who wished to make pictures of Hardy was becoming usual. It was felt at once that the etched portrait by William Strang (reproduced in Lionel Johnson's book) was the most successful likeness yet done. In 1897 the first part of Mr. Will, now Sir William, Rothenstein's *English Portraits : a Series of Lithographical Drawings* contained portraits of Sir Frederick Pollock and Thomas Hardy.

As for the inner world of Hardy in the years when *Tess of the d'Urbervilles* and *Jude the Obscure* were at once extending his fame and subjecting him to obloquy, it is hard to speak without anxiety ; but there are signs that he was often in a deep melancholy. A personal loss must have been contributory to this. Under " Deaths " in the *Dorset County Chronicle* for July 28th, 1892, appeared : " July 20th, at Bockhampton, in the house of his birth, Thomas Hardy, son of the late Thomas Hardy and Mary Hardy of the same place, in his 81st year ". The mason's grave was marked with a stone designed by the surviving Thomas Hardy. The novelist's father had been an invaluable friend, as well as a touchstone of local tradition and wisdom ; with his passing, the austerity of fate seemed to strike at Hardy more plainly. For Hardy himself had no child. But a broader shadow was settling upon him, in consequence of the many big and small, declared or lurking enmities aroused or mobilized by what was summed up as the pessimism of his writings. We have Hardy's insistent warning not to assume that all his poems with " I " as their apparent speaker are in any way autobiographical ; yet the small group entitled " In Tenebris ", dated 1895 and 1896, and headed with appropriate verses from the Psalms (in Latin), can scarcely represent anything but the spiritual anguish of the writer himself. They are, as nearly as anything can be, Hardy's parallel to James Thomson's *City of Dreadful Night*. Some of the lines in these soliloquies have been often quoted :

> Let him in whose ears the low-voiced Best is killed by the
>   clash of the First,
> Who holds that if way to the Better there be, it exacts a
>   full look at the Worst,
> Who feels that delight is a delicate growth cramped by
>   crookedness, custom, and fear,
> Get him up and be gone as one shaped awry ; he disturbs
>   the order here.

Outwardly in those years Hardy would scarcely have
betrayed the torment of isolation and infertility which
such private utterances perpetuate. The brief description by an unnamed writer accompanying the
Rothenstein portrait, is anything but gloomy : " Retiring and almost timid in personal demeanour, he has
yet the courage of his convictions, his art, and his
processes. As lovable as he is modest, and as genial
as he is great, he has endeared himself long since to
all who know him, and to thousands who have never
seen his face." Or, one might add, his bicycle. He
was still exploring his native regions, with that modern
advantage.

Early in 1897 Hardy put forth the last of his novels
to appear in book form, though it cannot be called the
last in order of composition. A version of *The Well-
Beloved* had come out serially (" The Pursuit of the
Well-Beloved ") five years earlier, " but ", Hardy says,
" it was sketched many years before that when I was
comparatively a young man and interested in the
Platonic Idea, which, considering its charm and its
poetry, one could well wish to be interested in always ".
Then, in answer to an editorial request for " something light ", he had developed and emphasized his
theme. When *The Well-Beloved ; a Sketch of a Tem-
perament* was finally sent on its way by the author, it

did not give the critics much to talk about. The *Athenaeum* regarded it as a sign that Problems were going out, Temperaments coming in, but more particularly felt that Hardy's reviving his story for book publication should signify " a desire to renew those pleasant relations with his readers that should never have been interrupted ". How agreeable it would be if he would go back, receding beyond his episode of tragic and ugly imaginings, to recapture the pastoral spirit which had once pleased so well ! Meanwhile, Hardy could write to Mrs. Craigie, " My *Well-Beloved* has been much better received, and *bought*, than I expected such an intangible person to be ".

During the same year, in a new edition of Black's *Guide to Dorset*, A. R. Hope Moncrieff thanked Hardy for advice and assistance and showed how a great many readers regarded all his books as a series, unbroken by any special purposes in any one or two of them, by including a topographical table of all. Indeed, from this list of fictitious and real places, it appears that most of the enthusiasts visiting Dorset because of the Hardy interest wanted to be with the phantom of Tess. They were desired to bear in mind, even when authoritatively guided to the family vault and tombs of the Turbervilles in Bere Regis church, that there was some insecurity ever " in drawing comparisons between hard fact and the vagueness of romance ". In the " first uniform and complete edition " of the novels, which was being published by Osgood, McIlvaine and Co., there was now a map of the Wessex they concerned, drawn by the author. Another approach to Hardy's novels, neither rustical and local nor sociological and world-weary, was already being

made. Technique never stands still. At the beginning of 1897 Enoch Arnold Bennett was looking into
The Trumpet-Major, and noting " what an excessively
slow method of narration " Hardy used ; it was to
him already as old-fashioned as Richardson, and the
humour " obvious and Dickens-like " ; but, with so
many other readers of Hardy, Bennett felt that " some-
how his persons have individuality ".

In whatever light it might be regarded, Hardy's
work in prose fiction was now practically at an end.
It had been begun, almost thirty years before, with
some uncertainty and it had gone on with recurrent
consciousness of the practical and spiritual limitations
which it imposed.   So far back as Good Friday, 1892,
Hardy had been confiding to his notebook, after reading and even in some measure praising the *Quarterly
Review*'s article on *Tess*, a feeling that he was on the
verge of a farewell.   " If this sort of thing continues,
no more novel-writing for me.   A man must be a fool
to deliberately stand up to be shot at."   Something
has been said of the miasma in which *Jude the Obscure*
was enveloped, in some quarters ; the matter may be
still further detailed.   The outcry against the work
was taken up in America and Australia, on the general
line " Aside from its immorality there is coarseness
which is beyond belief ".   Anonymous letters and
postcards arrived at Max Gate, and Hardy found that
the press campaign had an unhappy influence on his
country neighbours, reverencers of newspaper opinions,
though in London society he was received as before.
(We have allusions to various functions there, including
a masked ball where Henry James and he were the
only two not in dominos and were very popular.)

Even *The Well-Beloved* was attacked as smuggling in " unmentionable moral atrocities ", and Hardy, on being asked to make a public reply to such charges, refused with some animation. The attack was too silly. " There is more fleshliness in *The Loves of the Triangles* than in this story—at least to me. To be sure, there is one explanation which should not be overlooked : a reviewer *himself* afflicted with ' sex mania ' might review so—a thing terrible to think of."

So the most original and imaginative English novelist of the last part of the nineteenth century, after strenuous discussions, arrived at the decision to attempt that way of writing no more. Hardy may be called on here to state the case as he saw it at this point : " Tragedy may be created by an opposing environment either of things inherent in the universe, or of human institutions. If the former be the means exhibited and deplored, the writer is regarded as impious ; if the latter, as subversive and dangerous ; when all the while he may never have questioned the necessity or urged the non-necessity of either." He was even glad that a decision had been forced upon him, for he had wished to resume another " and more instinctive kind of expression ", the earliest he had loved.

V

AN EPIC DRAMA

THE passion for poetry which came into prominence in Hardy's life as his novels grew more troublesome to him, and which indeed had been frequently a powerful instrument in the shaping and unifying of those books themselves, urged him towards more than one ample design. He had long been within sight, though the view was changeable and misty, of a really mighty poetical work, for the construction of which a number of impressions received in childhood and youth would be necessarily combined with a completed enquiry among the historians, the old dramatists of Greece and our own country, and afoot in the scenes of the actions to be described. To that slowly matured intention we will revert later. A simpler endeavour was at hand. " Songs of Five-and-Twenty Years " had been planned in 1892, but we hear no more of that scheme. In September 1898 there appeared instead, by Thomas Hardy, *Wessex Poems and Other Verses*, being, as the author explained, a miscellaneous collection and much of it written long before. Messrs. Harper advertised the book modestly above a much louder call to the Novels, with the note, " Hundreds of Thousands of these Novels have been sold " ; they must, however, have felt that the new volume had something rich about it, for they offered a number of copies in a special binding, suitable for presentation. The volume had also this distinction : it was illustrated with what the author called " rough sketches, recently made, and inserted for personal and local reasons rather than for their intrinsic qualities ". After all his heavy labours and his buffetings in the battle of opinion or fashion, Hardy was treating himself to a sort of holiday with his old favourites, many of the drawings being reminiscent of his training as a " Gothic " architect.

One hundred years before, a volume entitled *Lyrical Ballads* had been published, without any author's name on the title-page, but discovered presently to be the work of William Wordsworth and Samuel Taylor Coleridge. At first little noticed, and reviewed rarely and coldly, that book was in the end recognized as a portent of remarkable discoveries in the region of modern English poetry. The fortunes and the significance of *Wessex Poems*, 1898, bear comparison with those of *Lyrical Ballads*. Hardy's first published venture in verse was to be followed in his own instance by numerous and substantial additions, and in the view of many critics of our poetry it opened the way for other writers and a renewal, away from the most popular Victorian tradition, of urgency and simplicity. This is not to say that *Wessex Poems* item by item was an ungainsayable achievement ; and the very first poem in it, " The Temporary the All ", although it had something to say of a curiously fresh and bitter-sweet nature, must have perplexed readers who saw it offered specifically as an example of Sapphics. The metre set forth, indeed, in that direction, but mainly got into trouble on the way.

How did Hardy's new manifestation affect the

critics ? They did not trouble themselves with it overmuch. A writer in the *Academy* was struck by the notion that celebrities were inclined to try some art other than that which had brought them fame : " A parliamentary leader writes philosophy, a queen turns poetess, a Kaiser becomes everything by turns, and nothing long. Leaders of society take to the stage, leaders of the stage to society." And likewise prose-writers popped forth among the poets. The critic did not count Meredith, but he named Blackmore, Quiller-Couch, Conan Doyle as recent, and Charlotte Brontë and George Eliot as elder instances of this. Hardy was just one more, and as one would have expected and in the same way as Conan Doyle, whose *Songs of Action* were published at the same time, Hardy had " relied for most of his success on the ballad ". Yet these ballads of his only set up a feeling of frustration : their matter should have been left to the novelist to treat in prose narrative. Hardy's versification was immature. The odd thing was, to continue further with the *Academy*, that he had managed to hit off several charming lyrics ; and among those approvingly quoted were " Neutral Tones " (the point of its date, 1867, was not seen) and the " Ditty " (1870), which is so Hardyan without any obvious aim at being " different " :

> Beneath a knap where flown
> > Nestlings play,
> Within walls of weathered stone,
> > Far away
> From the files of formal houses,
> By the bough the firstling browses,
> Lives a Sweet : no merchants meet,
> No man barters, no man sells
> > Where she dwells.

In *The Bookman* the author of one of the earliest books about Hardy, Annie Macdonell, was more decisive. The book was a surprise to most of his readers, but not to all. " He remains, as a poet, very nearly where he was before *Wessex Poems* saw the light. The strongest note of his fiction has been a poetical one. The creator of the tragedy of Jude, of the gracious comedy of Mellstock folks, of the Titanic personality of the Mayor of Casterbridge, the revealer of untamed powers that sleep and wake mysteriously in Egdon Heath, is essentially a poet." Miss Macdonell allowed that Hardy's mastery of the verse medium was uncertain, but maintained that fault-finding over his technique was of small value when the poems were so vivid, so concentrated, " flashing sudden flame on some characteristic and original mood, the dark path whereto must be sought for in his other work ". To another sympathetic reviewer, William Archer, Hardy expressed his pleasure at seeing his way with words appreciated. Archer had written, in reference to " The Peasant's Confession ", that Hardy sometimes seemed " to lose all sense of local and historical perspective in language, seeing all the words in the dictionary on one plane, so to speak, and regarding them all as equally available and appropriate for any and every literary purpose ". Hardy noted, " Concluding that the tale must be regarded as a translation of the original utterance of the peasant, I thought an impersonal wording admissible ".

Hardy sent his old hero, and now reader, Swinburne a copy of *Wessex Poems*, which was acknowledged with admiration not only for some of the poems but for several " splendid illustrations " as well. It is strange

that Hardy's drawings, which were as distinct from
other people's as his verses were, did not excite more
general interest by their symbolism and their phantasmal quality. Perhaps they were considered, like the
poetry, as honest but untutored and uncomfortable
endeavours to do that which others had standardized.
The catalogue of those poets who have practised the
art of illustration in England is not a brief one, nor is
Hardy the least striking performer included therein.
In the pages of *Literature* he was given some praise as
an artist, but it cannot have been entirely welcome :
" The whole [book], we fear, is conclusive as to the
unfitness of this medium of expression for Mr. Hardy's
genius. The illustrative sketches which are all of them
interesting, and not a few of them singularly powerful
little studies of the wide and rolling pastures that he
loves, express that genius far more adequately." One
reviewer caused Hardy some amusement, mixed with
censure : " This gentleman said that when he first
read the book he thought it rather good, but being
determined not to be taken in, and to be conscientious
at all hazards, he made a point of getting up to re-read
it on a wet morning before breakfast, and then found
that it was worth very little ".

A second edition of *Wessex Poems* had still to come
when Hardy in 1901 demonstrated that he really meant
what he was now doing by publishing another collection
of verse, *Poems of the Past and the Present*. The list
of editors of periodicals to whom he offered his thanks
in reprinting his contributions shows that he had won
a position already among the poets. Once again, it
was a copious and various collection, and some of the
pieces had been waiting for the light of day since the

Sixties and Hardy's Bayswater lodgings ; on the other hand, some were of immediate appearance, including the elegy on Queen Victoria and the group on the South African war. Another group testified that Hardy was by no means the hermit of Dorchester, but a Continental traveller (these " Poems of Pilgrimage " being the fruit of his tours in Italy and Switzerland in 1887 and 1897). In the well-known stanzas entitled " Lausanne : in Gibbon's Old Garden " probably certain readers could catch the voice of personal experience, the author's epitaph on his novels of questioning and candour : as when Gibbon's ghost is imagined asking,

> " Still rule those minds on earth
> At whom sage Milton's wormwood words were hurled :
> *' Truth like a bastard comes into the world*
> *Never without ill-fame to him who gives her birth '* ? "

At the same time, be it recollected that Hardy was profoundly aware of the history of unconventional thinkers from the remotest times known, and that he was not a specimen of the kind of complainant whose own troubles and dissonances are the only basis for an attitude.

How desirous Hardy was to be acknowledged in his new phase is shown in a reminiscence by Professor William Lyon Phelps, who came over from America for a bicycle tour in 1900 and was able to call at Max Gate. Phelps replied to a direct question directly, and said that the poetry was less great than the prose works. " Evidently pained ", Hardy disagreed by a long way, and showed that " he wished to be regarded as an English poet who had written some stories in prose ". How far the critics of new verse approved of his desire, now that he had submitted to them two quite extensive collections, will perhaps be sufficiently measured by reference to *The Times*, *Spectator* and *Saturday Review*. The first appreciated highly an intellectual kind of lyric though it had its excess of strenuous harsh touches, yet altogether Hardy's poems were " harmonies that are far removed from the placid jingle of popular rhyme ". The *Spectator* was respectful, but declared, " Poetry is not his proper medium. He is not at home, he does not move easily in it. . . . Mr. Hardy is a master of fiction, but not a master of music." And yet there was much which the reviewer could discuss in detail, mood, picture, thought : " he has a wonderful, almost too great command of vocabulary. His diction bristles with rare words, but if far-fetched and bizarre, they will always be found to be the words of a scholar, and of a good pedigree." He was apt to be coarse, to use in one piece even " a Swiftian turn " (probably the words " some sturdy strumpet "), which was not permissible in the twentieth century. The *Saturday* allowed the chief claim : " so far as it is possible to be a poet without having a singing voice, Mr. Hardy is a poet, and a profoundly interesting one ". He had been studying metre much more elaborately than people thought, and if in the end he had not a style in verse, neither had he in prose ; but he had a quality of mystery and wild nature quite unlike others, in this " grey book ".

The other and more daring of Hardy's enterprises away from fiction now calls for our consideration. Compelled by early memories which were refreshed every time he walked or bicycled or talked with old people in his native country, he inevitably worked out year by year the large shape of an artistic interpretation of what had passed once between the menacing forces of Napoleon and, in the end, the character and faith of Britain. The space of time covered by Hardy's conjecturings and trials, studies and first-hand observations in connection with his big plan is characteristic of him ; it is likely that even before 1875, under which date we have a memorandum of his on the foreshadowed " Iliad of Europe from 1789 to 1815 ", he was examining ways and means, and it was not until 1897 that he fixed more or less upon the final structure. By that time he described it in a note as " Europe in Throes. Three Parts. Five Acts each." The dramatic form had gained the day.

Upon his original idea of ballads or other verses in imagination of the Napoleonic wars, a much more difficult and exciting conception had imposed itself, apparently in the winter of 1881. It was said long ago that history is philosophy teaching by examples. Hardy had by nature tended to read philosophy, to compare such theories as he could find of the mystery of things ; and Dr. W. R. Rutland has followed him with great skill in his study of thinkers famous in his early life, with the general conclusion that Hardy was more indebted in forming his speculations to Herbert Spencer and to J. S. Mill than to Schopenhauer and von Hartmann, " whose works he nevertheless perused ". Before long, then, the vision of a tremendously movemented period of wars, exemplified in picturesque and heroic incidents, was modified into a philosophic history, wherein all outward shows however in appearance brought on by the conflict of mortal men different in character, aim and opportunity, were perceived as proceeding from a first great cause. In 1886 the author was still finding his way in this imaginative or cosmological region, and a memorandum tells us how far he had got : " The human race to be shown as one great network or tissue which quivers in every part when one point is shaken like a spider's web if touched. Abstract realisms to be in the form of Spirits, Spectral Figures, etc." Something more was required before the immense task of composition could be, indeed could not but be, carried through ; and it grew clear as the fantasy of an Immanent Will automatically working or pulsing through the " network or tissue " obtained central place in Hardy's mind. He had found It, the god unlike the others.

So, in 1897, fresh from visiting Brussels and the field of Waterloo, which, apart from a few shepherds, ploughmen, dogs and cats, he had to himself, Hardy really set down an outline for the epic drama entitled *The Dynasts*. He worked upon it for several years, but we are given hardly a glimpse of him in this connection, quietly purposeful among his books and at his writing-table. In 1900, when Professor W. L. Phelps called on him, there was no invitation into the study, although kindness and hospitality shone. These qualities were enjoyed not only by human visitors. The place was a paradise of cats. " Are all these your own cats ? " " Oh, dear, no, some of them are, and some are cats who come regularly to have tea, and some are still other cats, not invited by us, but who seem to find out about this time of day that tea will be going."

He found time for other affairs while the great composition was thriving, and travelled with his Glad-

stone bag and a set of proofs to stay with Edward
Clodd in Suffolk at the end of May 1903, when Mr.
H. W. Nevinson first met him. That observer of
many changes and chances has portrayed Hardy at
the time when he was achieving his greatest work.
There was nothing of the country cousin about him,
except in his shy talk. " Face a peculiar grey-white
like an invalid's or one soon to die ; with many scattered red marks under the skin, and much wrinkled—
sad wrinkles, thoughtful and pathetic, but none of
power or rage or active courage. Eyes bluish grey
and growing a little white with age, eyebrows and
moustache half light brown, half grey. Head nearly
bald on the top, but fringed with thin and soft light
hair. . . . Figure spare and straight ; hands very
white and soft and loose-skinned." Slow to join in
the conversation, Hardy claimed little attention for
himself when he did so, merely " stating his opinion
or telling some reminiscence or story ", and " attempting no phrase or eloquence as Meredith does ". A
year later A. C. Benson found himself at the Athenaeum
Club seated (" like Alice between the two Queens ")
between Henry James and Hardy, neither of whom
could hear what the other said. Hardy talked of J. H.
Newman (" no logician "), describing the *Apologia* as
simply " a poet's work, with a kind of lattice-work of
logic in places to screen the poetry " ; and after James
had uttered something very oracular on Flaubert,
" Hardy went away wearily and kindly ".

Another impression of Hardy at this stage of his life
(1901, to be exact) is preserved in William Archer's
Real Conversations, published at the beginning of 1904.
Warmed by a fire of elm-logs in Hardy's library, Archer

had led the talk round to the supernatural. " I am
most anxious to believe in it," said Hardy ; " I should
think I am cut out by nature for a ghost-seer. My
nerves vibrate very readily. . . . If ever ghost wanted
to manifest himself I am the very man he should
apply to. But no—the spirits don't seem to see it."
Another topic emerged. " People call me a pessimist ;
and if it is pessimism to think, with Sophocles, that
' not to have been born is best ', then I do not reject
the designation. I never could understand why the
word ' pessimism ' should be such a red rag to many
worthy people ; and I believe, indeed, that a good
deal of the robustious, swaggering optimism of recent
literature is at bottom cowardly and insincere. I do
not see that we are likely to improve the world by
asseverating, however loudly, that black is white, or
at least that black is but a necessary contrast and foil,
without which white would be white no longer. That
is mere juggling with a metaphor. But my pessimism,
if pessimism it be, does not involve the assumption
that the world is going to the dogs, and that Ahriman
is winning all along the line. On the contrary, my
practical philosophy is distinctly meliorist." And as
if in demonstration of this, Hardy added that war was
doomed ; men were becoming better able to see other
men's points of view, or the sense of humour was
growing. " Not to-day, nor to-morrow, but in the
fullness of time, war will come to an end, not for moral
reasons, but because of its absurdity."

The first part of Hardy's extraordinary epic drama
of war was published at the end of the year 1903,
with a second and larger issue a month later. It met
with few critics capable of comprehending it all in the

short space of time allowed for the purposes of reviewing. There was an ominous touch of evasion even
in Swinburne's letter of thanks for a copy : " I never
read any dialogue of yours that gave me more delight
than the fifth scene of the second act, nor any verse of
yours that I more admired than the noble song which
closes the fifth act. But if I may say it without offence
—I trust you do not mean to give over your great work
in creative romance even for the field of epic or historic
drama." Swinburne could read the answer to that
in the next number of the *Saturday Review*, where
Mr. Max Beerbohm pointed out that Hardy's ceasing
to be a novelist was not a matter of being hurt by the
attacks on *Jude the Obscure*, but something deeper.
" Mr. Hardy writes no more novels because he has
no more novels to write." Still, for him, in the new
form Hardy had attempted the impossible, and failed
in " a really great book " with a reading of will and
life that would not do. For Mr. Beerbohm, it was an
autumnal work of a great writer ; " in England, during
recent years, great writers in their autumn have had a
rather curious tendency : they have tended to write
either about Napoleon or about Mrs. Meynell. The
late Mr. Coventry Patmore wrote about Mrs. Meynell.
Mr. Meredith has written both about Mrs. Meynell
and Napoleon. Mr. Hardy now readjusts the balance,
confining himself to Napoleon. So far, his procedure
is quite normal ; a new theme, through a new form.
But I mislead you when I speak of Mr. Hardy as
' confining himself to Napoleon '. ' Excluding Mrs.
Meynell ' would be more accurate. He is so very
comprehensive." The crowded scenes of the panoramatist did not entirely fill Mr. Beerbohm with a sense

of historic magnitude, but even the opposite; the
scene of Nelson's death, for instance, " irresistibly
reminded " him " of the same scene as erst beheld by
me, at Brighton, through the eyelet of a peep-show,
whose proprietor strove to make it more realistic for
me by saying in a confidential tone, 'Ardy, 'Ardy, I
am wounded, 'Ardy.—Not mortally,[1] I 'ope, my
lord ?—Mortally I fear, 'Ardy." All told, the Immanent Will was an artistic nuisance. " Mr. Hardy's
puppets are infinitesimal—mere ' electrons ', shifted
hither and thither, for no reason, by some impalpable
agency. Yet they are exciting."

Upon this question of his Immanent Will and his
philosophical sketch-book Hardy was not disposed to
give way, though it would not have been against Mr.
Beerbohm that he intended to move in writing a letter
to *The Times Literary Supplement* soon afterwards.
He might perhaps have done best to let his reviewers
go their ways, but he had a habit (it may express his
simple attitude towards the world) of commenting
on them in this manner ; and after all, he naturally
felt a disappointment when what was to him the harvest
of a lifelong profundity of meditation and of a strenu
ously perfected literary armoury was treated casually,
even flippantly, above all with a tone of moral reproba-
tion. He had suffered before at the hands of *Spectator*
reviewers, but he could still be pained by what they
said ; and the charge this time was that he was an
incompetent dabbler in philosophic terms. Elsewhere,
the line of his philosophy was disapproved : but, he
protested, it was surely " as old as civilisation. Its fundamental principle, under the name of Predestination,

---

[1] There is a variant reading, " mortually ".

was preached by St. Paul. . . . It has run through the history of the Christian Church ever since." Latterly it had been transferred to the scientists as determinism ; but from its Pauline form he himself had only made the modification from an assumption of externality to immanence.

Hardy's attention was drawn to an article by Mr. H. G. Wells in the *Fortnightly* during 1903. He seemed just a little hurt, though glad to read the item. " It is, indeed, an interesting and suggestive look ahead. To be sure, what he says as to the desirability of establishing an ' adult ' literature has been anticipated : many years ago some of us wrote about that. But his essay has much more in it than this ; and it reads like that of a writer of long experience of life, a quality I am surprised to find in one who is, I believe, yet a young man." Later on Mr. Wells was to write in one of his works presented to Hardy, " The Master, and long may he reign ! "

On Easter Day, 1904, Hardy's mother died, aged nearly ninety-one, having been active almost to the end. One of her latest acts was to make a wreath from the old-fashioned flowers in her garden at Higher Bockhampton, for the funeral of Henry Moule, the curator of the Dorchester County Museum. Her son wrote a poem upon her death, which turns away from the fact of bereavement to " a numb relief "—a dark joy that " she had escaped the Wrongers all ". Such a poem betrays that Hardy was still liable to sink into a dire enmity with life, for his mother's experience of the world through her long sojourn was surely not a succession of wrongs, an unblessed valley of the shadow. To quote from the *Dorset County Chronicle*, " the calm beauty of Stinsford in the lovely weather of Wednesday afternoon, when the body of Mrs. Hardy was laid at rest in the churchyard, befitted the funeral of one who had completed her patriarchal life by such long beautiful stages of old age ". Moreover, Hardy himself wrote to the press in order to correct some erroneous statements about her : " The late Mrs. Hardy was a woman of character in many ways. The first book that she gave her son, after those merely for the nursery, was Dryden's *Virgil*, for which she had a great liking. By the time that he was twelve she had him regularly instructed in Latin, and at fifteen in French by a governess. The house in which she died was built by the Hardys more than a century ago, but it passed out of their hands, some years back. Yet though she was the owner of several comfortable freehold houses not far off, she preferred to remain in the original inconvenient one, which she was enabled to do, as long as she chose, by the courtesy of the present possessor." She was noted for her " extraordinary store of local memories ", which spanned the era of modern progress and change. It has been suggested to me that Hardy's mother was one of the strongest influences on him even when he himself was becoming a veteran, and through her he was greatly enabled to keep in view a past order of men and things—in a word, Mellstock— which could always arouse his imaginative powers.

Signs that Hardy's repute was in very good order, no matter how much this or that work of his called forth hostile journalism, increased through the early years of this century. The Wessex worshippers did not worry about his philosophical battles. In 1901 Sir B. C. A. Windle published, and dedicated to Hardy,

The Wessex of Thomas Hardy. It was illustrated by
Edmund H. New, and author and artist were obliged
to Hardy for personal kindness and authoritative direction. The dedication copy bore the graceful inscription " Sic redit ad dominum quod fuit ante suum ".
C. G. Harper, whose topographical books were so many
and deservedly popular, followed in 1904 with *The
Hardy Country* ; and about the same time Hermann
Lea put forth a shilling *Handbook to the Wessex Country
of Thomas Hardy's Novels and Poems* (enlarged in later
years). You could buy also, at Wareham or elsewhere,
" Pictorial Post Cards of a Unique Distinctive Character " in sets, each illustrating one of the novels.
Mr. Lea mentions another effect of Hardy's creations :
" the vast number of artists who have been drawn
hither in quest of fresh subjects. Of these, Mr. Fred
Whitehead probably enjoys the greatest popularity,
judging by the number of his works that have appeared
on view at the Royal Academy, New Gallery, and other
exhibitions. The fact that by far the larger proportion
of his pictures represent either actual places and scenes
described in the Wessex Novels, or are taken from the
immediate vicinity of the towns and villages mentioned,
points a deduction that is obvious." In the early
years of the century the Dorset novels of " Agnus
Orme " obtained passing comparisons with Hardy's
books : the *Athenaeum* protested, though it found a
word of praise for one more writer on " so characteristic
a country ". In 1906 A. H. Hyatt's *The Pocket Thomas
Hardy* was published, a collection of " beauties " from
the writings in prose or rhyme, which some will remember gratefully although Hardy expressed a certain
dissatisfaction with it, probably with all the class of

snack-bar anthologies. The 1908 edition of Mr. Wilkinson Sherren's *The Wessex of Romance* contained a picture of Hardy the cyclist, standing in a lane with his machine, check knickerbockers and panama hat : great days !

In January 1905 Hardy served as Grand Juror at the Winter Assizes, and then, in April, the first of his academic distinctions arrived. The case cannot be concealed. It came not from England but from Scotland. He was bidden to Aberdeen to receive from the University the honorary degree of LL.D. The Principal and Mrs. Marshall Lang entertained him at the Chanonry Lodge, Old Aberdeen. This occasion gave Hardy a sense of the triumph of Wisdom's " radiant form ", evidenced in a short poem of high beauty. He passed some days with Meredith at Box Hill, and Meredith afterwards commented, " I am always glad to see him, and have regrets at his going, for the double reason that I like him, and am afflicted by his *twilight view of life* ". When Hardy visited Swinburne in June, he found the old poet pleased with a sentence gleaned from a Scottish newspaper : " Swinburne planteth, Hardy watereth and Satan giveth the increase." Like Satan, Hardy could now claim to be an international figure : indeed, he had for many years attracted some notice overseas. Ten years earlier he could say of his novels that many had been " published simultaneously in England, America, Australia and India, and translated into Continental languages ". It was natural, and it illustrates his standing, that at the end of 1903 the editor of *L'Européen* should ask for Hardy's views on the condition of France ; and Hardy's answer is curiously readable at the present hour : " I am not of opinion that France is in a decadent state. . . . A true judgment of the general tendency cannot be based on a momentary observation, but must extend over whole periods of variation. What will sustain France as a nation is, I think, her unique accessibility to new ideas, and her ready power of emancipation from those which reveal themselves to be *effete*."

From time to time Hardy gave his support to movements at home intended to clear away the effete. He was much concerned with the weakness of the acted drama, and was among the signatories of an appeal in 1904 (" What can be done to help the British Stage ? ") and of a protest in 1907, after the theatrical censorship had vetoed Granville Barker's play, *Waste*. In joining others on this ground, Hardy brought a sense of his own frustration as a dramatist who might have been : for he had long felt that for one reason and another, from the timidity of managers to the asperity of censors, all that he could offer as a sincere artist was beyond practical consideration.

Still, he was producing, in printed form, one prodigious dramatic piece. The hazy way in which the first part of *The Dynasts* had been received by the critical world had not dulled his interest. On February 2nd, 1906, his friend Gosse was writing to him after a perusal of the second volume, every word of it, " I have but to pray you to go on. Slacken not in winding this glorious poem up to a noble and thrilling conclusion." Two years later the same correspondent, who liked his poets to be very meticulous with their metrical patterns, had had a preliminary view of the third volume, and he was well satisfied : " Surely

you must have been giving a good deal of attention to
the technique of prosody ? The ingenious turns of
versification in this latest volume were not lost on me.
Even a rondeau, as correct as one of Benserade." In
connection with Gosse's compliment, there is the story
of Hardy's being seen at the reading-room of the
British Museum with Saintsbury's formidable *History
of Prosody* before him—but that was *after* the publication of *The Dynasts*.

The second and third parts of *The Dynasts*—the
draft of the third was completed on the eve of Good
Friday, 1907—appeared in 1906 and 1908 respectively.
Criticism steadily advanced from the stage of regretting
that Hardy had dropped novel-writing to admitting
that he was a great writer knowing his own way best;
and to a competent view of the work which he had
designed and done with a Victorian amplitude. Meanwhile he remained unaffected—the watchful craftsman
who would have been no more or less important to
himself had he chanced to be constructing a drinking-
fountain or laying out an allotment. Once again it
is to Mr. H. W. Nevinson that we turn for an impression of the author during the progress of the
long-meditated and assured edifice. At Max Gate
there would be the walk to William Barnes's rectory
and grave, with stories of Louis Napoleon ; or the
road to Dorchester would be preferred, and a pause
before " the shop that had been kept by the father of
Treves, the great surgeon, and the house where Judge
Jeffreys lived during the Bloody Assize ". Going
further on his bicycle, Hardy would lead to a point
commanding a view of the Channel " over Weymouth
and Portland " as well as " far inland to nearly all the

places mentioned in his books ". And of course there
was a visit to the Roman amphitheatre. In London,
going to a play by Gorky at Terry's Theatre, Mr.
Nevinson was lucky enough to find Hardy also arriving ; " he was in his usual mood, gentle, sensible,
unpretentious. He thought the books appearing on
Wessex might help to advertise his own books a little.
. . . For himself he enjoyed concerts better than
theatres, and thought Tchaikovsky's music had exactly
the modern note of unrest. Best of all he liked to go
to St. Paul's to hear the chanting, always choosing out
his favourite chant according to the day's programme.
Afterwards we went to a Lyons tea-shop, at which he
was a little alarmed, being used only to an A.B.C.,
and unfortunately, as we came out, he caught sight
of a broadsheet announcing ' Family Murdered with
a Penknife '. He couldn't get over that. The vision
of the penknife seemed to fascinate him. But we
parted most amiably, the Strand quite unconscious of
his greatness—unconscious as was Dido how powerful
a god lay nestling in her lap."

As for the Roman amphitheatre, and incidentally
the intensity with which Hardy's thoughts could be
seized by pictures of inhuman outrage of modern or
of ancient date, his article on " Maumbury Ring " in
The Times of October 9th, 1908, is uncommonly illustrative. Hardy had been following the excavations
undertaken through the Dorset Field and Antiquarian
Club (of which he had been elected an honorary
member) with eager interest, notwithstanding his age
and the weather ; his account of the proceedings is
naturally an unconscious fragment of autobiography,
and must not be too sparingly used. " As usual,"

he wrote, " revelations have been made of an unexpected kind. There was a moment when the blood of us onlookers ran cold, and we shivered a shiver that was not occasioned by our wet feet and dripping clothes. For centuries the town, the county, and England generally, novelists, poets, historians, guidebook writers, and what not, had been freely indulging their imaginations in picturing scenes that, they assumed, must have been enacted within these oval slopes ; the feats, the contests, animal exhibitions, even gladiatorial combats before throngs of people

> Who loved the games men played with death,
> Where death must win

—briefly, the Colosseum programme on a smaller scale. But up were thrown from one corner prehistoric implements, chipped flints, horns and other remains, and a voice announced that the earthworks were of the paleolithic or neolithic age, and not Roman at all. This, however, was but a temporary and, it is believed, unnecessary alarm."

Hardy was a little inclined to regard the amphitheatre as defying the specialists who came and went. " While the antiquarians are musing on the puzzling problems that arise from the confusion of dates in the remains, the mere observer who possesses a smattering of local history, and remembers local traditions that have been recounted by people now dead and gone, may walk round the familiar arena, and consider. And he is not, like the archaists, compelled to restrict his thoughts to the early centuries of our era. The sun has gone down behind the avenue on the Roman Via and modern road that adjoins and the October moon is rising on the south-east behind the parapet, the two terminations of which by the north entrance jut against the sky like knuckles. The place is now in its normal state of repose and silence, save for the occasional bray of a motorist passing along outside in sublime ignorance of amphitheatrical lore, or the clang of shunting at the nearest railway station. The breeze is not strong enough to stir even the grass-bents with which the slopes are covered, and over which the loiterer's footsteps are quite noiseless." Under such circumstances of lonely night, Hardy reflected upon the history of Maumbury since before the Romans adapted it, with thoughts too of Sir Christopher Wren [1] passing by and discerning the Roman genius ; and then he dwelt on an episode of 1705–1706, which it is clear was as freshly hideous to him as the family murder mentioned by Mr. Nevinson. The story, which Hardy had partly from ancestral tradition and partly from an enquiry into the records, was that of the trial and execution at Maumbury of young Mrs. Channing on a charge of murdering her husband, a grocer in Dorchester, by poison. To Hardy this business, with its frightful details, was as moving as the tragedy which made his old friend Browning write *The Ring and the Book.* His narrative closed with the question, " Was man ever ' slaughtered by his fellow man ' during the Roman or barbarian use of this place of games or of sacrifice in circumstances of greater atrocity ? "

[1] Even in this, Hardy was following in the footsteps of William Barnes, who had contributed to the *Gentleman's Magazine* for May 1839 a letter headed "The Roman Amphitheatre at Dorchester," and a plan. Barnes mentions the association of Wren with the locality, and the strangling and burning of Mary Channing.

But Maumbury Ring meant something more to Hardy than its appeals to his imagination of vanished civilizations and of a civilized savagery in the days of Swift and Newton. It was one of those local land-marks with which all his actual experience, his life from earliest to latest, was deeply connected, and which held him as if timelessly watching what it had been his destiny to see and feel. He could thus sum up almost sixty years of his life, as though his literary ardours and productions had been a parergon, and as though the real world which he possessed was unaffected by any of the apparent actions and sometimes the dis-quiets of Thomas Hardy the celebrated writer. " A melodramatic, though less gruesome, exhibition within the arena was that which occurred at the time of the ' No Popery ' riots, and was witnessed by this writer when a small child. Highly realistic effigies of the Pope and Cardinal Wiseman were borne in procession from Fordington Hill round the town, followed by a long train of mock priests, monks and nuns, and pre-ceded by a young man discharging Roman candles, till the same wicked old place was reached, in the centre of which there stood a huge rick of furze, with a gallows above. The figures were slung up, and the fire blazed till they were blown to pieces by fireworks contained within them.

" Like its more famous prototype, the Colosseum, this spot of sombre records has also been the scene of Christian worship, but only on one occasion, so far as the writer of these columns is aware, that being the Thanksgiving Service for Peace a few years ago. The surplices of the clergy and choristers, as seen against the green grass, the shining brass musical instruments, the enormous chorus of singing voices, formed not the least impressive of the congregated masses that Maumbury Ring has drawn into its midst during its existence of a probable eighteen hundred years in its present shape, and of some possible thousands of years in an earlier form."

The progressive attitude of many readers towards *The Dynasts* is probably mirrored in the *Spectator*'s reviews of the three parts as they appeared. Of the first, it was apprehended that the author's reach exceeded his grasp, for " he has no turn for transcendental poetry ". In Wessex scenes he could do very well. Part II, 1906, drew a brief iteration of the old protests : " The blank verse tends to be spasmodic and unrhythmical, and the lyrics suffer from a deplorable lack of music. The diction is strained, and when metaphysics begin we flounder among quasi-technical platitudes. But in spite of a hundred faults, there is a curious sublimity. . . . We can at least acknowledge the magnitude of the conception." The last Part, in 1908, was the occasion for a considerable recantation. " We wrote in 1904 that Mr. Hardy's reach seemed to exceed his grasp. After laying down the last volume we admit that we were wrong. Taking the complete poem, we feel that the poet has attained unity, and that the dramatic quality of the whole is his great achievement." Among other notices, one by a poet yields one particularly striking observation : " Many a stone has been thrown at the blank verse ; yet does not this very verse seem by some diabolical ingenuity to reveal all the sawdust that went to stuff that monstrous zany of the fates, Napoleon ? " The writer of this was Walter de la Mare.

Apart from *The Dynasts*, Hardy in the early years of the reign of King Edward VII was not inactive nor unconcerned with public matters. A few instances may stand for all. On June 20th, 1906, at the general meeting of the Society for the Protection of Ancient Buildings, a magnificent paper by Thomas Hardy called " Memories of Church Restoration "—it has been already mentioned in these chapters—was read ; but it was read by Colonel E. Balfour. In September 1906 it was reported that Hardy had started a movement for adding a tower to the south-west side of Holy Trinity Church, Dorchester ; for, said he, " the church is sadly deficient in external dignity at present, and no stranger passing by it can realize that such a large church stands there ". The old zest for new Gothic architecture was still stirring. In November 1907 it was announced that, in succession to Sir Frederick Treves, Hardy became president of the Society of Dorset Men in London. He held the office for two years, and if some of the members complained that they saw very little of him, he was very willing to plead guilty ; for, as he wrote at the time of his retiring, " I feel that I have filled the office very unworthily. Authors do not, as a rule, make good official members of anything ". Still, he was incomparably valuable to the Society, as its year-books demonstrate. His presidential address in 1908 on the subject of " Dorset in London " was a first-rate contribution, and for years he was the source of curious and entertaining matters proper to such a company of friends. In the year-book for 1910–1911, for example, there were published in facsimile of Hardy's invariably clear and proportioned manuscript " Some Old-fashioned Psalm-Tunes Associated with the County of Dorset ". How lovingly he had assembled them, " Wareham ", " Blandford ", " New Poole " and the rest, as part of the inheritance which had sustained him secretly all the years of his pilgrimage !

Meanwhile another of his interests was enthusiastically supported by the Society. In 1908 he welcomed the request of Mr. A. H. Evans to be allowed to dramatize one of the Wessex novels. *The Trumpet-Major* was chosen, and played by the Dorchester Debating and Dramatic Society ; in 1909 *Far from the Madding Crowd* was taken, and performed not only in the county town but also in London. The adapter disclaimed any high ambitions, merely desiring to give the characters of the novels another sort of realization ; and the experiment pleased. The following year *The Mellstock Quire*, based on *Under the Greenwood Tree*, took its place in the series, and Hardy chose some carols to be sung in it, out of his local collections. In 1911 a variation (not an altogether new composition) was offered. " This year the Society were able to present a novelty in the shape of a play and not merely adapted from the novels, but actually prepared for the stage by Mr. Hardy himself. This was a close version of his short story from *Wessex Tales* entitled ' The Three Strangers ', and styled ' The Three Wayfarers '." Once again Hardy brought out an ancient traditional tune for the Hangman's song in this piece. Here for the moment we may leave what was becoming an annual institution at the Corn Exchange, Dorchester, and in London. But as for more arduous attempts to conquer the British stage, Hardy was still holding back. A letter of his to John Galsworthy, printed in *The Times* on August 13th, 1909, shows that his sense of the difficulty there had not changed. " All I can say is that something or other—which probably is consciousness of the Censor—appears to deter men of letters who have other channels for communicating with the public, from writing for the stage. As an ounce of experience is worth a ton of theory, I may add that the ballad which I published in the *English Review* for last December entitled ' A Sunday Morning Tragedy ', I wished to produce as a tragic play before I printed the ballad form of it, and I went so far as to shape the scenes, action, etc. But it then occurred to me that the subject—one in which the fear of transgressing convention overrules natural feeling to the extent of bringing dire disaster—an eminently proper and moral subject—would prevent my ever getting it on the boards, so I abandoned it."

Hardy's poems were by this time frequent in the contents of various magazines, and he also contributed them freely to those handsome miscellanies which were fashionable, at that period, in favour of charitable objects. One may name as reminders of the tribe Mrs. Aria's *May Book*, 1901, *Wayfarer's Love*, edited by the Duchess of Sutherland, 1904, and *The Queen's Carol*, 1905—the latter for the benefit of the unemployed. In the matter of occasional prose, Hardy was now and then to be found among the correspondents of *The Times* (we have noticed his letter on J. S. Mill of May 1906 and his article on Maumbury excavations). He contributed his valuable share to F. W. Maitland's *Life and Letters of Leslie Stephen*, 1906, and in 1908 he appeared as an editor, and performed the best known of his services to the name

and work of William Barnes. " I have been moved ",
he wrote, " to undertake the selection [of Barnes's
poems] by a thought that has overridden some immediate objections to such an attempt,—that I chance
to be (I believe) one of the few living persons having
a practical acquaintance with letters who knew famili-
arly the Dorset dialect when it was spoken as Barnes
writes it, or perhaps, who know it as it is spoken now."
On that subject Hardy liked to dream sometimes.
Winchester should have remained, in the interests of
our language and other things, the royal, political and
social capital of England, leaving London as the com-
mercial capital. He conceived that this would yield
a relation like that of Paris with Marseilles or Le
Havre ; the overgrowth, the fog and grime of London
would incidentally have been precluded.

Chronological commemorations were beginning to
be incomplete without some words from the seer at
Max Gate, or the Athenaeum Club, of which he had
been made a member as a person of distinction in
literature in 1891 ; here are one or two. For the
eightieth birthday of George Meredith (February 12th,
1908) he answered the request of the *Daily News* : " I
have known Mr. Meredith for so long a time—forty
years within a few months—and his personality is such
a living one to me, that I cannot reach a sufficiently
detached point of view to write a critical estimate of
his great place in the world of letters ". In the Jubilee
number of the *Cornhill Magazine* (January 1910) his
" Impromptu to the Editor " showed how even a date
in the history of periodicals could be employed as
an opportunity for a criticism of life. Hardy also
marked the twentieth anniversary of the Humanitarian

League (May 1910) with a published letter, part of which, as the rights of animals kept him busy thinking and doing all his life, may be given now : " Few people seem to perceive fully as yet that the most far-reaching consequence of the establishment of the common origin of all species is ethical ; that it logically involved a readjustment of altruistic morals, by enlarging, as a necessity of rightness, the application of what has been called ' The Golden Rule ' from the area of mere mankind to that of the whole animal kingdom. Possibly Darwin himself did not quite perceive it. While man was deemed to be a creation apart from all other creations, a secondary or tertiary morality was considered good enough to practise towards the ' inferior ' races ; but no person who reasons nowadays can escape the trying conclusion that this is not maintainable." If it came to the point, Hardy would act with determination when humane principles were violated ; as he did in 1911, when (we may imagine how unwillingly on one side of the question) he was the principal witness in a prosecution at Dorchester for cruelty to a cow. He received the thanks of the magistrate and of the Royal Society for Prevention of Cruelty to Animals.

The first item in the *Fortnightly Review* for August 1904 had been a lengthy lyrical ballad of a doleful character by Hardy called " Time's Laughingstocks : a Summer Romance ". The title was transferred to the new volume of poems which he published in 1909, including once again a number dated forty or more years before. The group of sketches and episodes to which the title especially applied was certainly worked in a gloomy manner. Even the consolation of the old man who, reduced to the workhouse at last, had counted on the rule that men would be in one wing and wives in another, was snatched from him by the untimely philanthropy of a perspiring curate, who just then succeeded in getting the Guardians to put married couples together. But for power Hardy had never revealed himself so greatly : " Reminiscences of a Dancing Man " and " The Homecoming " are tremendous though brief. His visions of a universal tragedy of nescience and conscience too had increased in intensity.

Upon the death of George Meredith, which Hardy saw announced on a poster in Piccadilly, he paid his poetical tribute in *The Times* (it is one of the optimistic pieces in " Time's Laughingstocks ") ; and the presidency of the Authors' Club passed to the rather hesitating Wessex novelist. In July 1909 Queen Alexandra was present at a production of *Tess* as an opera at Covent Garden, by Baron d'Erlanger. The author of *Tess* attended the dress rehearsal, and a word on the subject has been written by Mr. S. L. Bensusan : " He could be infinitely patient. . . . Baron d'Erlanger wrote delightful music, and I remember Sammarco as Alec and Destinn in the name part. The effect was strange. Wessex had passed into Italy and lost everything truly characteristic in the passing. But Hardy gave no sign, and when afterwards I asked him what he thought, he answered smiling, ' I thought they all worked so hard.' "

And not long afterwards, a month after Hardy's seventieth birthday, another notable election marked the succession in English literature. It was announced in July 1910 that His Majesty the King conferred the

Order of Merit on Sir William Crookes and Mr. Thomas Hardy,—Hardy thus taking the place which Meredith's death left vacant. Hardy was invested on July 19th, but, he said, " afterwards felt that I had failed in the accustomed formalities ". This high honour was probably not dearer to Hardy than the local one which followed at the end of the year. Wearing his Order, Hardy was present in the Town Hall of Dorchester to receive, like his friends Dr. Handley Moule and Sir Frederick Treves, the freedom of the borough—which was symbolized by a scroll within a silver-gilt casket designed by T. Braybrooke, a Dorchester silversmith, " in the Renaissance style, adorned with Mr. Hardy's monogram and the borough arms enamelled, and also with a list of his principal books engraved on the ends ". The Mayor, Mr. Symes, gave this casket into Hardy's hands and quoted to him those words from Marty South in the last page of *The Woodlanders* : " If ever I forget your name, let me forget home and heaven. But no, I never can forget 'ee, for you was a good man and did good things."

To this Mr. Hardy replied in a speech which survives the particular occasion, and ranks among the numerous autobiographical moments of his which make one wish he had found time for a comprehensive story of his own life. " I may be allowed to confess that the freedom of the Borough of Dorchester did seem to me at first something that I had possessed a long while, had helped myself to (to speak plainly), for when I consider the liberties I have taken with its ancient walls, streets and precincts through the medium of the printing press, I feel that I have treated its external features with the hand of freedom indeed. True, it might be urged that my Casterbridge (if I may mention seriously a name coined off-hand in a moment, with no thought of its being localized) is not Dorchester—not even the Dorchester as it existed sixty years ago, but a dream place that never was, outside an irresponsible book. Nevertheless, when somebody said to me that ' Casterbridge ' is a sort of essence of the town as it used to be, ' a place more Dorchester than Dorchester itself ', I could not absolutely contradict him, though I could not quite perceive it. At any rate, it is not a photograph, that inartistic species of literary produce, particularly in respect of personages. But let me say no more about my own doings. The chronicle of the town has vivid marks on it. Not to go back to events of national importance, lurid scenes have been enacted here within living memory, or not so many years beyond it, whippings in front of the town pump, hangings on the gaol roof. I myself saw a woman hanged not one hundred yards from where we now stand, and I saw, too, a man in the stocks in the back part of this very building. Then, if one were to recount the election excitements, Free Trade riots, scenes of soldiers marching down the town to war, the proclamation of Sovereigns now crumbled to dust, it would be an interesting local story."

E. T. Raymond has told, in illustration of Hardy's powers of self-protection, how one young London journalist visited him on his seventieth birthday, and retired with small result. He had been treated with courtesy, but " mechanical courtesy, veiling inflexible disapproval ". Hardy appeared to know nothing about interviews as one of the possibilities in his existence. He certainly pointed to the landscape outside and agreed that it had given one man a great deal,—might be as generous to another. He was Hardy the country gentleman.

VI

CHANGE AND CONSTANCY

AFTER Hardy's seventieth birthday and the honours
which came to him at the time, his life went on for a
year or two much as before. In 1911 he was almost
offered a peerage when the Government had a plan of
strengthening its ranks in the House of Lords with
some well-known Liberals. His literary eminence was
clearly acknowledged when his publishers proposed to
him a definitive edition of his prose and verse, which
he agreed to arrange. There could be little question
of the appropriate name for this handsome publication
—the Wessex Edition ; and it was now that Hardy
grouped his ' fictitious chronicles " under the three
heads, " Novels of Character and Environment ",
" Romances and Fantasies " and " Novels of Ingenuity ". He advised his readers not to assume
" that these differences are distinctly perceptible in
every page of every volume ". The General Preface
which Hardy composed for this edition was both stately
and redoubtable, and remains as one of the strongholds
of his critical eloquence and his self-revelation. Here,
for example, he compares himself to Boswell in the
care he had taken " to authenticate some detail " of his
Wessex, but goes on, " Unlike his achievement, however, on which an error would as he says have brought

discredit, if these country customs and vocations, obsolete and obsolescent, had been detailed wrongly, nobody would have discovered such errors to the end of Time. Yet I have instituted enquiries to correct tricks of memory, and striven against temptations to exaggerate, in order to preserve for my own satisfaction a fairly true record of a vanishing life."

On his attitude to all life, Hardy naturally included " one word ", disclaiming any attempt in " imaginative writings extending over more than forty years " at a " coherent scientific theory of the universe ", and urging that though some natures " become vocal at tragedy, some are made vocal by comedy ", their silences do not mean limitations of perception. And now that he was collecting his poems, he felt a regret : he had " wished that those in dramatic, ballad and narrative form should include most of the cardinal situations which occur in social and public life, and those in lyric form a round of emotional experiences of some completeness. But

The little done, the undone vast ! "

The Preface is dated October 1911. Hardy continued to be the most unorthodox and perceiving poet of the time on public events,—the death of King Edward VII, the coronation of George V, the disaster of the *Titanic*. His poem on that ocean tragedy, which so struck the world, was one of extraordinary visual imagination. It was given by Hardy for the programme of a Dramatic and Operatic Matinée in aid of the *Titanic* Fund, in May 1912.

To his poems we go for the most obvious traces of the great change that came over Mr. Hardy's life at the

end of that year.   His wife, who had alarmed him by
a " first strange fainting-fit " in the summer of 1906,
and latterly had been rather an invalid, gave her last
garden party on July 16th, 1912.   Her health grew
worse, and yet there seemed no serious urgency.   Before
a doctor arrived, she died on the morning of November
27th, 1912.   It was the day when *The Trumpet-Major*
was produced in Dorchester.   As soon as he could,
Hardy travelled into Cornwall and caused a tablet
of his own design to be placed in St. Juliot Church
in memory of her who had once been so vivid a
figure there.   A curious solitariness had settled upon
both her and him in later years, which held to the
last:

> Why did you give no hint that night
> That quickly after the morrow's dawn,
> And calmly, as if indifferent quite,
> You would close your term here, up and be gone
> Where I could not follow
> With wing of swallow
> To gain one glimpse of you ever anon !
>
> Never to bid good-bye,
> Or lip me the softest call,
> Or utter a wish for a word, while I
> Saw morning harden upon the wall,
> Unmoved, unknowing
> That your great going
> Had place that moment, and altered all.

For months Hardy was talking to himself in verse of
the heavy change, of the romantic joy of forty years
before, of the way in which time had eluded him and
had made some things that should have been so easy
and usual now for ever impossible, of the way in which
even this human grief and chasm would soon be
overgrown.

> Soon will be growing
>   Green blades from her mound,
> And daisies be showing
>   Like stars on the ground,
> Till she form part of them—
> Ay—the sweet heart of them,
> Loved beyond measure
> With a child's pleasure
>   All her life's round.

Within these poems, which have not gone unrecognized as making in their entire sequence one of the most unconventional and impressive elegies in English, there may be discerned a voice of self-punishment, of realization that the writer had failed in some questions of approach and contact ; but there was the larger feeling that conditions of our existence had been more powerful in the history of that married life than the personal attitude or quality on either side. And now, what remained for Thomas Hardy alone again, at the considerable age of seventy-three ?

It might have appeared that his work was essentially all done, that he had said his say in the forms that were proper to his genius ; the Wessex Novels, his epic-drama on a period of crisis symbolizing national histories, his lyrical annotations on man and Nature, his occasional and laconic declarations upon questions which divide thinking people—these might have seemed to constitute a life-work accomplished.

> I seem but a dead man held on end
> To sink down soon. . . .

That thought, in the early hours of his isolation, certainly attacked him ; but it did not overwhelm. After all, Hardy came of a race that did not mostly acknowledge seventy years or so to be an oppressive old age.

He possessed a fascinating quickness, which waited to prove itself even though (as has been already seen in the notices by contemporaries) the impression of the burden of years was superficially strongest.

People in general were certainly not inclined to regard Hardy as past his real day, though there may have been something to stir his love of ironies when Mr. (now Sir) Sydney Cockerell, during the year 1911, brought to his notice the desirability of his allotting some of his manuscripts to public libraries. Hardy was willing, and called it a convenience to do this, " for I have no descendants, and short shrift may be allowed any leavings of mine ". The process thus initiated by the provision of one who has excelled in securing valuable memorials of literature and art for the general benefit was continued until on both sides of the Atlantic a great deal of Hardy's manuscript is permanently accessible. For the Fitzwilliam Museum at Cambridge, Mr. Cockerell obtained the first draft, with the markings for magazine issue, of *Jude the Obscure*. In May 1912 Hardy's friend sent him a memorial which had been submitted at Cambridge in favour of Hardy's receiving an honorary degree there. It did not succeed immediately, but in 1913 the University conferred the proposed distinction, and once more Hardy " walked gowned ", but not, according to A. C. Benson, correctly gowned. Benson records on the occasion of the ceremony, under June 10th, 1913 : " Hardy (in a LL.D. gown by mistake) looked very frail and nervous, but undeniably pleased. . . . Then we all adjourned to hall. I read grace sonorously, and found myself at the end of the high table between Sargent and Hardy."

Later in the year Hardy was in Cambridge again, having been elected an Honorary Fellow of Magdalene College, and now seeking formal admission. Dr. Donaldson, " the Master " (to call on Benson's *Diary* again), " was afraid that Hardy might dislike a religious service. But Hardy said that he often went to St. Paul's and other London churches, like Kilburn, and knew a lot about ecclesiastical music and double chants. He had ordered a complete set of robes, too—bonnet, gown and hood. This restored the Master's confidence. We sate and talked and smoked ; and the old man wasn't a bit shy—he prattled away very pleasantly about books and people. He looks a very tired man at times, with his hook nose, his weary eyes, his wisps of hair ; then he changes and looks lively again. He rather spoiled the effect of his ecclesiastical knowledge by saying blithely, ' Of course it's only a sentiment to me now.' "

Next day, November 2nd, the Master pronounced the admission of Hardy in the Latin tongue, before the altar of the College chapel ; and a sermon was preached by the Archdeacon of Zanzibar, who may not have had any special purpose of reforming the new Honorary Fellow by reasoning that God was " a God of *desire*, who both hated and loved—not a mild or impersonal force ". During the visit Hardy talked to Benson about his writings : " he was ashamed of his little book of republished stories, and surprised at its good reception ". He could only nowadays put up against Benson's output a scanty production of verses, he had enough of these by him for a book : " but he didn't know whether he ought to include in it some verses he wrote when his wife died—' very intimate, of course—but the verses came ; it was quite natural ; one looked back through the years, and saw some pictures ; a loss like that just makes one's old brain vocal ! ' "

The published collection of prose also mentioned in their conversation was entitled *A Changed Man, The Waiting Supper and Other Tales*. As to its reception, that was partly a matter of sentiment. The golden days were not quite gone, the Wessex novelist was still on the scene. We may catch the note from one or two of the reviewers. In the *Saturday Review*, panegyric began thus : " A new book by Thomas Hardy—what a chance it is for every critic ! How we wish every critic seized it ! It is his chance to remind the public that Thomas Hardy is now the one living figure of fulfilled genius in English literature. What is the use of hiding or denying it ?—There is no other. . . . Critics often have a chance to praise the work in fiction of Mr. Bennett, Mr. Galsworthy, Mr. Wells, Mr. Maxwell, they have it at any rate two or three times a year as regularly as clockwork ; and they take it. . . . But this should not be forgotten. When (or if) one says a book by Mr. Wells or Mr. Mackenzie is a masterpiece, is a very powerful effort, is great, one means a masterpiece, or very powerful, or great compared with the novels being produced by the other writers of today. . . . It is extremely important that people should be brought to understand that Thomas Hardy's stories—stories of how supreme a sincerity ! —are in a class by themselves."

Similarly, John Bailey in *The Bookman*, cautious as he was in his inspection of the actual contents of this eighteenth volume of the collected Hardy, summoned readers to an act of homage. " Why is Mr. Hardy

incomparably the greatest of living English novelists ? "
His own answer was, " What he gives us in his novels
is always, or almost always, truth seen in the light of
poetry, not realism seen in the light of the fashion, or
scandal, the social or political propaganda of the hour.
He is never a High Churchman or a Low Churchman,
never a Christian apologist nor, with occasional unfortunate exceptions, an anti-Christian controversialist.
So in political matters. A Conservative may feel that
Mr. Hardy is a Radical. But his Radicalism is just
one of the two eternal halves of the eternal whole of
the human being in the sphere of politics ; it is a thing,
one may almost say, of all time and existence ; not a
thing that cannot open its mouth without declaiming
about the wages question, or the woman's question,
or the problem of birth-rate ; in fact, not journalism,
but poetry. He has always been a man of much more
than his own generation, caring about things that no
single generation can claim for its exclusive property."
Seeking a name among the living novelists by which
to test his answer, Bailey could only come upon one.
" The only possible contemporary rivals to the peasants
of Wessex are perhaps Mr. Kipling's private soldiers.
However little we know of the barrack-room, we are
for the moment as sure of them as we are of Gabriel
Oak. But does not the actuality in them overweight
the poetry ? Are they not a little too much of their
own generations ? Will they be as alive a hundred
years hence as they are now ? But Gabriel Oak will ;
he belongs to all generations, and is above all accident
of time and place."

Hardy himself set no great store by the tales which
he now recovered from periodicals of a distant date

(the *Bolton Weekly Journal* of the eighties, for example), but he felt that as some of them had been pirated in America he had better attend to the matter.

In December 1913 Hardy was one of the committee who arranged a banquet in honour of Anatole France in London, but he could not attend there, sending instead a message ; he described his contemporary as one " who never forgets the value of organic form and symmetry, the force of reserve, and the emphasis of understatement, even in his lighter works ". Lionel Johnson, perhaps, had been the first to define some qualities in Hardy himself which might be considered as more often shown in French than English authors.

The mystery of the perpetual menace of war had travelled with Hardy all his life, and it was not yet departing from him. His greatest work had been inspired by this haunting. His poems had not infrequently been almost an automatic statement of its rumours and oracles. He had gone out of his way to appeal plainly to his fellow-men on the subject. Thus, reading in his *Times* of June 27th, 1904, a translation of " Count Tolstoi's philosophic sermon on war ", he had taken his pen : " This sermon may show many of the extravagances of detail to which the world has grown accustomed in Count Tolstoi's later writings. It may exhibit, here and there, incoherence as a moral system. Many people may object to the second half of the dissertation—its special application to Russia in the present war (on which I can say nothing). Others may be unable to see advantage in the writer's use of theological terms for describing and illustrating the moral evolutions of past ages. But surely all these objectors should be hushed by his great argument, and every defect in his particular reasonings hidden by the blaze of glory that shines from his masterly general indictment of war on a modern principle, with all its senseless and illogical crimes." Presently, roused by an anti-war activity of W. T. Stead, he had urged that the nations should at least agree not to make use of horses in the battlefield. In 1911 he had signed a protest against what was as yet principally a theme or scare of the future—the use of aerial vessels in war, and an appeal to all governments to save the world from that. But Hardy well knew how far such ideas as his were able to affect the contending forces of the powers in those years; how modest their hope was to help in removing quickly the " incubus of armaments, territorial ambitions smugly disguised as patriotism, superstitions, conventions of every sort ".

And so it was not surprising that in the ill-fated year 1914 he should be among those most prescient of the storm. That May his poem " Channel Firing " stood first among the contents of the *Fortnightly Review*, and its strange and terrible note travelled out to some who had hitherto known little of Hardy's poetry and conjectured little of the dangers of Europe. In this poem the guns at night aroused the dead and alarmed the creatures,

> Till God called, " No ;
> It's gunnery practice out at sea
> Just as before you went below ;
> The world is as it used to be :
>
> " All nations trying how to make
> Red war yet redder.   Mad as hatters,
> They do no more for Christ his sake
> Than you who are helpless in such matters. . . "

> Again the guns disturbed the hour,
> Roaring their readiness to avenge,
> As far inland as Stourton Tower,
> And Camelot, and starlit Stonehenge.

Only a few weeks more and these and many more guns were roaring in a world war. Hardy had been striving to believe that the horror might not materialize : but, on August 4th, while he was at lunch at Athelhampton Hall, a telegram announced the fact. Publishing his new book of verse that autumn, called *Satires of Circumstance*, with some distaste for releasing satire at such a moment, Hardy had just time to include in it as Postscript his vigorous and still famous stanzas " Men Who March Away ".

The immensity of the turn of events at first caused Hardy to " sit still in an apathy ", or perhaps to make an ironical comment or two on the failures of civilization in logic and in humanity. But the lyric just mentioned is dated September 5th, 1914. As he read accounts of the German invasion of Belgium, and of North-East France, he began to express himself in verse and prose, yet ever with the faith that the blame for the violence released did not lie on the ordinary man in the ranks of our enemy. That faith was most characteristically exemplified in the sonnet published in the *Fortnightly* for April 1915, " The Pity of It ", which opens :

> I walked in loamy Wessex lanes, afar
> From rail-track and from highway, and I heard
> In field and farmstead many an ancient word
> Of local lineage like " Thu bist ", " Er war ",
> " Ich woll ", " Er sholl ", and by-talk similar,
> Nigh as they speak who in this month's moon gird
> At England's very loins, thereunto spurred
> By gangs whose glory threats and slaughters are.

The accounts of the mutilation of Rheims Cathedral
drew from him, in October 1914, a letter communi-
cated to *The Times*, and quoted there ; arising partly
from general feelings, partly from his educated love
for noble architecture, and again in a desire to find
that the destruction was not predetermined. " Is there
any remote chance of the devastation being accidental,
or partly accidental, or contrary to the orders of a
superior officer ? " He was inclined to suppose that
Germany might have been demented by the " bom-
bastic poetry—for it is a sort of prose-poetry ", of
Nietzsche, eclipsing the humane philosophers such as
Kant and Schopenhauer. His epitome of Nietzsche is
well worth recapturing from another letter of that time :
" He used to seem to me (I have not looked into his
works for years) to be an incoherent rhapsodist who
jumps from Machiavelli to Isaiah as the mood seizes
him, and whom it is impossible to take seriously as a
mentor. I may have been wrong, but he impressed
me in the long run, owing to the preternatural absence
of any overt sign of levity in him, with a curious suspicion (no doubt groundless) of his being a first-class
Swiftian humorist in disguise."

The volume *Satires of Circumstance* took its title,
not very happily, from a group of fifteen short poems,
in a bald style and of an acid content. He had been
collecting, if not devising, pictures of the meaner
situations into which human beings may come. He
had given these short stories a verbal and metrical
form which, for hardness and concentrated stroke, reminds one of village church gargoyles. But all the
book was not of this make. There were in it poems
which seemingly had nothing to do but be beautiful,

like " When I set out for Lyonnesse ": poems of
bright colour, like " Self-Unconscious ", and of pride
in man, like " The Abbey Mason ". Among the elegies
for E. L. Hardy, too, there were some of a tender and
lingering luxuriance.

Some readers perhaps noted the gracious melody
and the spiritual gaiety — the close excepted — in the
poem called " After the Visit : to F. E. D."

> Come again to the place
> Where your presence was as a leaf that skims
> Down a drouthy way whose ascent bedims
> The bloom on the farer's face.

The poem as he published it bore no date, but was
related to one of the occasions on which a young
writer of stories for children, Florence Emily Dugdale,
had come to Max Gate ; on one of these, in June 1907,
Hardy had presented her with a copy of *Wessex Poems*,
and their friendship had continued and deepened.
When *Satires of Circumstance* appeared, " F. E. D."
had for some months been Mrs. Thomas Hardy. The
marriage took place quietly at St. Andrew's, Enfield,
on February 10th, 1914. " We thought it the wisest
thing to do," Hardy observed, alluding particularly to
the fact that F. E. D. had been his admirably skilful
secretary for years past. Probably no one who saw
his life at home after 1914 ever formed any other impression than that it was the wisest thing to do ; the
fame of Hardy had brought with it a daily round of
various problems and engagements and requests which
he could not have tackled alone. The second Mrs.
Hardy, of " the large luminous living eyes ", sacrificed
much in order that she might shield the man of genius
in his age from the most tedious and worrying of these

affairs. But to say that is infinitely far from expressing the community of tastes and aspirations and affections which made the disparity in the ages of Thomas and Florence Hardy often as though it was not. One wonders what would have been Thomas Hardy's fate had the World War found him in 1914, him the saddened spectator of man's desperate remedies and apparently unescapable battlefields, " alone, withouten any companye ".

It has been noted that Hardy's salutary lyric, " What of the faith and fire within us ? " was dated September 5th, 1914, and it may be that this call to patriots was connected with a conference at Wellington House, Buckingham Gate, two days earlier. Eminent authors had come together, under the chairmanship of C. F. G. Masterman and with Government representatives attending, to discuss how our writers might state Britain's case to neutrals. Arnold Bennett was there, and set down his notes : " Zangwill talked a great deal too much. The sense was talked by Wells and Chesterton. . . . Thomas Hardy was all right." To Hardy it was a memorable afternoon, " the yellow sun shining in upon our confused deliberations in a melancholy manner that I shall never forget ".

By the end of 1914 Hardy had given a good many signs of his presence among the authors who were up and doing. A glance through *The Times* newspaper between August and the close of the year soon finds some of these signs. In the campaign of poets organized by *The Times* editor (one sees many of the old hands there, Newbolt, Bridges, Watson, Hewlett, A. E. among them), his friend Kipling and he struck with the greatest effect : Kipling's " For All We Have, and

Are " appeared on September 2nd, Hardy's " Song of the Soldiers ", spoken of already under another title, came a week later. It bore a footnote, on behalf of author and journal, to say that the copyright was *not* reserved. These two energetic and straightforward lyrics, in the ancient line of Tyrtaeus, remain vocal while the majority of the verse of late 1914 slumbers. On September 18th Hardy was found among the authors who published a declaration that, with all their feelings against war, they believed that Britain could not have refused to take part in that war without dishonour ; and on December 23rd Hardy again figured as a signatory of an authors' address " To Our Russian Colleagues ". It was pointed out, in a long article in *The Times Literary Supplement* (August 27th) on " The Soldiers of Thomas Hardy ", that he was one of only two modern masters of fiction who had given us genuine characterizations of the English soldier, beginning forty years earlier with Sergeant Troy. Hardy was naturally among the contributors to *King Albert's Book*, edited by Sir Hall Caine ; but a far more conspicuous manifestation of what his writings meant to the national spirit at that emergency came in November, when Mr. Granville Barker's excerpts from *The Dynasts* were acted at the Kingsway Theatre. Hardy supplied a new prologue, unassuming and temperate :

        . . . We gather that it may not be amiss . . .
      To raise up visions of historic wars
        Which taxed the endurance of our ancestors ;
    That such reminders of the feats they did
    May stouten hearts now strained by issues hid. . . .
    —What matters that Napoleon was our foe ?
    Fair France herself had no ambitious ends ;
    And we are happy in a change that tends
    To make of nearest neighbours closest friends.

The abridgement, of course, emphasized the English elements of *The Dynasts* and the scenes of Trafalgar, the Peninsula and Waterloo. John Freeman the poet commented, " This enormous and continental work has been boldly cabined within the two hours' traffic of the stage, brightening many a winter afternoon and evening at the Kingsway Theatre—a success no less delightful than unlikely ". The production was for the imagination : the lights were dim, the scenery very simple ; and the problem of explaining the action was given to a reader (Mr. Henry Ainley) at a desk below the stage and to two ladies in grey robes seated in impressive immobility on either side.

It was not only the vast shape and the pervading sympathy of *The Dynasts* which the outbreak of a new war of Napoleonic range brought more strikingly into the reflective moments of English people. That access of recognition, that search for the wisdom and healing power of a master of humane understandings, was to be expected. Thackeray's daughter might be expected to write to her old friend, though this was a little later in the war, " I have just finished *The Dynasts* with *awe* and with absolute admiration. It is a relief for my excitement to write to you and I feel as if I were one of your spirits speaking. I have almost forgotten the war for a day or two, in wonder at your inspired history of *now*, written in 1907." But the anxious time also sent readers to Hardy's other works. " Your old novels ", Gosse wrote, " take on a fresh bloom in the light of this new war, which reproduces so many of the psychological features of the Napoleonic time." Amidst all the tempest and upheaval, the appearances of doom and things past prophecy, Hardy's works had set up a steady rule or inviolable standard of English qualities, not unworthy of the comparison with Shakespearean embodyings of those which had been made often enough in spite of all the attacks on *Tess* or *Jude*.

VII

THE GREAT WAR AND AFTER

The year 1915 came in, and the visionary glory which had been expressed in life and literature during the first months grew less sparkling ; the matter-of-fact aspects of so tremendous a war, such variety of demands on the nation, so strong a probability of years of fierce fighting began to tell. Thomas Hardy, like so many others whose age deprived them of the comparative relief of participation, could only wait and watch the appearances of the conflict, doing now and then such services as any civilian can, or as only this eminent author could, in war-time. For example, he was able to send to the great Red Cross Sale of April 1915 two manuscripts which were distinctly useful for the purpose, namely, " The Night of Trafalgar " and the more recent " Men Who March Away ". And that July he made an unusual appearance in the rôle of a translator, among those called on by Miss Winifred Stephens for *The Book of France*. Hardy translated the contributions of J. H. Rosny and Rémy de Gourmont. Another occasion which Hardy gladly supported was the Shakespeare Tercentenary of April 1916. His poem, founded on an acceptance of the ordinary " biography " of Shakespeare of Stratford, was probably the best thing in *A Book of Homage to Shakespeare* collected by Israel Gollancz.

A childless man, Hardy was nevertheless bereaved when the war had been a year in progress by the death in action of his young relative, " the most promising young relative I had in the world, F. W. George." This boy, who held a commission in the Dorset Regiment, was killed in the Dardanelles, and is commemorated in the verses " Before Marching and After ", which catch with keen reality the feeling of the young officer at that period, visiting his home before going overseas to " that Game with Death ". By this time Hardy had begun to think over the whole war with a degree of anxiety ; yet he had an advantage over most who did not like the way things were going in 1915, the fact that he could rest his thought on stability long seen and known in contemplation. It was in 1915 that he wrote the fulfilment of a long-concealed outline, and achieved one of his most widely appreciated lyrics— " In Time of ' the Breaking of Nations ' ".

Hardy also had the strong keep or tower to retreat into, when he would, that all the original artists have : he might well join Wordsworth in echoing the assertion of William Cowper,

> There is a pleasure in poetic pains
> Which only poets know.

Throughout 1915 and 1916 he was so fortunate as to feel many impulses for new poems on many and diverse topics homely or supernatural, from his father's violin to " the clock of the years " going backward with horrid cancellations. The moon looking in on his nightly task might seem to be just

Curious to look
Into the blinkered mind
Of one who wants to write a book
In a world of such a kind.

But the writing did not cease.   It yielded, at Christmas
1915, one more of Hardy's exceedingly simple " ballad
successes " (and perhaps, closely examined, one of the
most surprising)—the poem called " The Oxen ".
Here was the celebrated pagan of Wessex appealing
very beautifully to the world as a Christian in desire.
Like so many of his poems, this one sprang from lonely
musing on scenes of the past and their application to
the present.   In this sense, Hardy's poetry may often
be called racial ;   nameless men and women, quietly
repeating matters of common knowledge and tradition,
had passed on to this man with the gift of expression
the substance of their feeling and fancy.—The picture
is one to delight us still in troubled times.   A quiet
Christmas Eve almost a hundred years ago, in a Dorset
cottage, by firelight, and an old man, unaware of anything remarkable in his talk, says that the cattle in the
shed are on their knees now.   Everyone agrees silently.
A boy looks especially attentive.   The years run by,
and there is the attentive boy Hardy himself grown
an old man, realizing the universal appeal in that
local [1] superstition, the reviving life in it : wording it
thus :

---

[1] Widespread.   " ' James, tell me the truth, did you ever see
the oxen kneel on old Christmas Eve at the Weston ? '   And he
said, ' No, I never saw them kneel at the Weston, but when I was
at Hinton at Staunton-on-Wye I saw them.   I was watching them
on old Christmas Eve and at 12 o'clock the oxen that were standing
knelt down upon their knees and those that were lying down rose up
on their knees, and there they stayed kneeling and moaning, the
tears running down their faces ' " (*Kilvert's Diary*, vol. iii., edited
by William Plomer).

So fair a fancy few would weave
  In these years ! Yet, I feel,
If someone said on Christmas Eve,
  " Come ; see the oxen kneel

In the lonely barton by yonder coomb
  Our childhood used to know,"
I should go with him in the gloom,
  Hoping it might be so.

Another bereavement befell Hardy during these early months of war. The place of his sister Mary in his affections and in the growth of his imaginative sympathies is to be inferred from the many poems with which her initials are connected. She was a school teacher and a village organist ; her activities had prevented her from doing as much as she and her brother wished in the art of portrait painting. Her portrait of her mother was said to be the best ever done. Hardy was fascinated by her character, which he thought of in the Psalmist's sentence, " I held my tongue and spake nothing : I kept silence, yea, even from good words ". She was buried in the cold and wet on November 29th, 1915, " under the yew tree where the rest of us lie ".

Towards the end of 1916 Hardy was enabled to visit the camp of German prisoners of war near Dorchester. " He came home ", says Mrs. Hardy, " very moved by the experience, and glad that he had gone, although he went most unwillingly." Quickly making contacts with the captives, treating them as individuals, he continued to show them practical kindness which, the same authority tells us, resulted in some similar kindness being shown to British prisoners in a similar camp in Germany. At the same time, Hardy was unfailing in his desire to join in any national service that

could influence the prospects of England's victory.
His sonnet of March 1917, " A Call ", reflects the side
of his nature which could be perceived in his personal
appearance and manner—a marching, adventuring,
military liveliness ; but the years had seen to it that
this Thomas Hardy never fixed a bayonet, or flew a
Handley Page.

> Would years but let me stir as once I stirred
> At many a dawn to take the forward track,
> And with a stride plunged on to enterprize,
>
> I now would speed like yester wind that whirred
> Through yielding pines ; and serve with never a slack,
> So loud for promptness all around outcries !

But all that Time had left for him, apart from writing,
was the unromantic job of adjudicating locally on cases
(such as there were) of food profiteering.

From the pen of Arnold Bennett we have another
rapid sketch of Hardy in London, in July 1917. It
was at Sir J. M. Barrie's, and Bennett was meeting
Mrs. Hardy for the first time : he liked her greatly,
and saw how well he and she harmonized. There was
a discussion, begun by Hardy, of the elements of good
tales : " he kept his head and showed elasticity and
common sense, and came out on the whole well. He
has all his faculties, unimpaired. Quite modest and
without the slightest pose. They both had very good
and accurate appraisements of such different people as
Shorter and Phillpotts." When darkness had fallen,
they stood outside one of the windows, watching the
searchlights : then more famous authors arrived, not
without arousing some irony in Bennett. " The
spectacle of Wells and G. B. S. talking firmly and
strongly about war, in their comparative youth, in front

of this aged. fatigued and silent man—incomparably their superior as a creative artist—was very striking."

In the winter of 1917 Hardy's new volume of poems was published, with the appropriate title *Moments of Vision*. His friend Gosse, who particularly welcomed all tokens of increased confidence and hope in Hardy, wrote in high spirits, " Your command of stubborn material was never more remarkable ", and soon afterwards undertook a short but richly expressive account of all Hardy's lyrical poetry up to that point. A number of especially striking and much-welcomed poems were found in the new work : " Heredity ", " To the Moon " (with its fierce but quiet close), " The Blinded Bird ", " The Robin ", " The Coming of the End " and " Afterwards ", besides the items already touched on, soon became part of the general stock of familiar verse. But many other things in *Moments of Vision*, possibly of less immediate attractiveness, were of a deep beauty and meaning, and once again Hardy had produced a volume which would stand the test of being searched and studied many times over ; even where the style faltered into something eccentric or trite, there was the sense of beloved life and courageous thought. In the margin, one would note that he was still able to gather in from almost half a century earlier sometimes a finished poem, sometimes a piece that could be revised, and often the idea for a new writing. As for the war poems, they were duly included ; yet from one that did not stand officially under that classification it may be seen that Hardy, after all, was not able to remove his philosophic position far from what he had shaped imaginatively in past years. In " The Blow ", he still inclined towards a view of the war as a catastrophe due to the blindness or clumsiness of the First Cause :

> That no man schemed it is my hope—
> Yea, that it fell by will and scope
>   Of That Which some enthrone,
> And for whose meaning myriads grope.
>
> For I would not that of my kind
> There should, of his unbiassed mind,
>   Have been one known
> Who such a stroke could have designed ;
>
> Since it would augur works and ways
> Below the lowest that man assays
>   To have hurled that stone
> Into the sunshine of our days ! . . .

When he was asked what he thought the effect of the war on literature would be, Hardy more than once replied in a way which proves his willingness to see good come even out of the seeming worst. He reminded his questioners of Hebrews xii. 27 : " the removing of those things that are shaken, as of things that are made, that those things which cannot be shaken may remain ".

In the early days of 1918 an unexpected relic of Hardy in the seventies was reported : it was the manuscript of *Far from the Madding Crowd*, and it had reposed in the offices of Smith, Elder since that book came out. Hardy agreed to make a present of it to the Red Cross Sale then being arranged, and it figured there as the gift of Mrs. Reginald J. Smith and himself; the price reached was £250, besides which some other autographs of his benefited the Red Cross, especially the last chorus of *The Dynasts*. The latest price paid for the *Far from the Madding Crowd* manuscript is $8,200.

One of the poems in *Moments of Vision* was a memory of William Barnes, or rather of his funeral, signalled to Hardy on Winterborne-Came Path by the October sunshine flashing from the coffin. Possibly someone will one day put together a pamphlet covering all the writings and sayings of Hardy about his honoured predecessor in Wessex poetry and story. In the fifth volume of T. H. Ward's " British Poets ", 1918, Hardy edited the section given to Barnes, and he then discoursed on Barnes's too little known poems in common English and the cocksureness of the critics who received them with displeasure. He has been known to accuse these censors of quenching, in that as in other instances, a poetic light that should have shone abroad ; but, as Mr. Siegfried Sassoon once remarked, seeing that Barnes was sixty-seven years of age when his volume of poems in common English appeared and was rejected, the damage may not have been so serious. Still, to Hardy, what was a sexagenarian but a youth of possibilities ? Mr. Sassoon's name having been introduced, it should be explained that he came into Hardy's circle in 1917 or 1918, being known as an officer of outstanding gallantry in the Western Front battles, and as a poet who had published a series of daring poems in several kinds condemning the appalling sacrifice of youth in a war of which the battlefields grew worse and worse. He was one of the younger authors who, from the later years of the war, formed a new companionship for Hardy while they honoured his genius. Mr. Sassoon assembled, and bore to Max Gate, an offering for Hardy's seventy-ninth birthday in the shape of a volume of autograph poems by several hands.

The signing of the armistice on November 11th, 1918, ultimately drew from Hardy one of his finest and most observant poems, wherein he had a word for all, men and women, of the battlefield or home, horses, birds even, whom the war had so long bound down. About this time signs of his slowing-down were appearing, but they did not appear in his writing, nor in his reception of friends. Mr. Llewellyn Powys, who as a child had seen Hardy and stored away some imaginative things he said, found him in 1919 " as full of interesting conversation as ever ". The picture drawn by Mr. Powys is memorable. " Presently I found myself seated near a good log fire. A little white dog lay stretched on the hearthrug. Near the chimney-piece I noticed the portrait of Shelley, and on the top of the bookshelf a small bust of Sir Walter Scott. He came in at last, a little old man (dressed in tweeds after the manner of a country squire) with the same round skull and the same goblin eyebrows and the same eyes keen and alert. What was it that he reminded me of ? A night hawk ? a falcon owl ? for I tell you the eyes that looked out of that century-old skull were of the kind that see in the dark." And when Mr. Powys went his way, he left Hardy gazing into the October night.

The " Mellstock Edition " of Hardy's Works, occupying thirty-seven volumes, came out in 1919 and 1920—a prominent example of many productions of his writings, at that period, for the bibliophile.

Early in 1920 two attractive arrangements lured Hardy from his retirement to Oxford, where the University was making a cheerful recovery from the ravages of the war ; and one token of this revival was the decision of the Dramatic Society, of which Mr. Charles Morgan was the manager, to perform Mr. Granville Barker's selection from *The Dynasts*. This was felt to be " perhaps the biggest venture in all the long annals of the Society ", and remains in memory as not only a high endeavour but a captivating achievement. Some of those in the audience who had recently experienced years of war were spellbound by Hardy's imaginative realization of what they had come to know, and more than that. The acting and reading were admirable, though someone was found to censure the make-up of two principal characters : " Nelson was forty-seven when he died, and he had led a hard life in more senses than one ; but he was represented as a young man of apparently about twenty-three. Wellington, on the other hand, was forty-six when he fought Waterloo, and was in full vigour of manhood, as the Spanish portraits of him show ; but his representative had chosen to make up as a doddering old gentleman of sixty-five at least, decrepit in figure, and strong only in the strength of his language." Some press critics wanted much more noise during the battle scenes. But these discrepancies did not much disturb Hardy's audience, enthralled with his supernatural questionings and conjectures working in such forms as had lately haunted Europe. A Church newspaper was found to attack Hardy, the play and the production ; it was supposed that the use of a vicar as an object of fun was responsible.

The other cause of Hardy's journey to Oxford was the conferment of the honorary degree of D.Litt., on which the Public Orator, A. D. Godley, made a speech (in Latin) comparing Hardy's rural muse with Virgil's, forecasting the long survival of his writings on country scenes and manners, declaring that Hardy, even had he not written his novels, would have merited immortality in his verses. No allusion to *Jude the Obscure* is discernible in this oration. But Hardy must have had a perplexing moment of vision there at Oxford as he listened to his praises and thought of his farewell to fiction. Another honour awaited him at Oxford : it was an honorary fellowship of Queen's College, to which he rejoiced to be admitted, in November 1922. Nor should it be forgotten that Hardy the architect was given his reward—an honorary fellowship of the R.I.B.A. (1920).

Upon his eightieth birthday Hardy received a message from the King, and a deputation of authors at Max Gate. He had humorously deprecated the suggestion, " a deputation ". He said he was still one who " goes about bicycling (though in mitigation let me state that I don't bicycle *far* nowadays). I ought to be a dignified figure sitting in a large armchair (gilded for choice) with a footstool." But he hailed the authors who celebrated June 2nd, 1920, at Max Gate : they were " Anthony Hope ", Augustine Birrell and John Galsworthy. His cheerfulness and serenity seemed to have increased with his years. That July he wrote a poem, in a script as decisive as ever he wrote, describing his feelings at Wentworth Place, Hampstead, some time the home of John Keats. His attitude towards Keats was not only that of love of the poet ; it was a keen curiosity about the man, ever springing from the persuasion that Keats's people also came from Dorset. I do not think that anyone has yet quite accepted this theory in spite of the number

and the pugnacity of the Keatses in the district of the
Hardys, and we must also wait for confirmation of
another notion beloved by Thomas Hardy. " He told
me ", says Mr. Powys, " that he considered it possible
that John Keats on the occasion of the landing at
Lulworth, at the time he composed his last sonnet "
(Hardy was following the then usual dating) " may
have gone to visit relatives at a village called Broad-
mayne which lies between Dorchester and Winfrith,
quite some distance inland. He himself, he said, remembered people of the same name who lived in this
village and were stablemen like Keats's own father ;
one of them, so he asserted, born about 1800, being
remarkably like John Keats in appearance." Having
found graves of two " John Keates ", who both died
about the same year as the poet, in Berkshire and in
Suffolk, I may wonder if Dorset has any better claim
to the poet's family ; but the hope strongly pleased
Hardy, and in September 1920 he was inspired by his
reflections to write still more verses in memory of
Keats, entitled " At Lulworth Cove a Century Back " :

> Had I but lived a hundred years ago
> I might have gone, as I have gone this year,
> By Warmwell Cross on to a Cove I know,
> And Time have placed his finger on me there :
>
> " *You see that man ?* "

It was appropriate, then, that when 106 younger writers,
led by Mr. St. John Ervine, marked Hardy's eighty-
first birthday with a loyal address, they should accom-
pany it with a copy of the 1820 edition of *Lamia,
Isabella, etc.*, by John Keats.

While the nation at home was doing its utmost to

establish a happier age, and while the literary world
in special had the appearances of a fuller life and
opportunity, the after-pains of the war were not concealed from such a practised panoramatist (to use Sir
Max Beerbohm's word) as Thomas Hardy ; and in
spite of his vivacity in the daily encounter and his
eager collaboration in every promising plan among his
country's authors, he could not always keep back the
judgment that he was forming from a kind of evidence
long familiar on the condition of humanity.   Professor
Albert Cock, who visited him for a discussion of " a
University for Wessex " (which has indeed proved a
fruitful idea), was speaking of the optimism found in
the closing chorus of *The Dynasts*, and he was naturally
praising that finale.   But Hardy " shook his head as
he replied : ' I shouldn't write that now.'   ' Not write
those lines of hope again, why not ? '   I eagerly
questioned.   Came the brief, the pregnant, the un-
answerable reply : ' The Treaty of Versailles.' "

But should we ever take a detached saying of
Hardy's as comprehending all that he had in his mind ?
It was never his instinct to abandon all hope, and,
whatever the broad aspect of history past and future
might seem to him, he was not going to say that he or
anybody else could calculate the chances of good or
evil with certainty.   He was not unlike Marshal Foch,
whose remark on his being told he was obviously de-
feated right, left and centre is familiar ; why then,
strike !   The individual should get on with his job.
The rest ?—these shapes of dynasty might not work
out according to formula however positive and total it
looked.   While Hardy was impressed with the gathering phenomena of grim things to come, he remained

sedulous in the minor affairs of life ; and he balanced
his dismay at certain immense historical generalities
with a loving respect for man as a modest, enduring,
trusting wayfarer.

In some such light we may set beside the glimpse
of him given by Professor Cock another of the same
period, picturing his delightful good sense as a friend
of the unambitious many : " Mr. Thomas Hardy said
that in his view the best design for a war memorial is a
flat tablet in a public place with the names clear.   Such
a tablet devised in detail by Mr. Hardy himself was
unveiled within the Post Office at Dorchester.   Returning to his old career of architect, he drew out the
design in detailed form, even to the lettering, and
though he is eighty-one the writing is firm and good
as ever.   He has added a motto from his own verse :

> None dubious of the cause, none murmuring."

Again, although Hardy's works have impressed upon
our minds the non-Christian interpretation of the universe which was most elaborately bodied forth in *The
Dynasts*, and which (through the Sinister Spirit and
the Spirit of Pity) is the fable of his poem on the end
of the war in 1918, still the evidence of his readiness in
real life to honour the Church of his fathers is abundant.
He could not but hold in veneration, as a light long
obscured yet still helping the simple in a conflict of
darknesses, the common creed.   A reminiscence published by Brig.-Gen. J. H. Morgan, from an experience
in October 1922, is much to the purpose.   He walked
with Hardy to Stinsford Churchyard, talking " by the
way through the meadows of the eternal riddles of
human destiny, chance, free will, immortality, whence

we arrived at the subject of religion, and the Church of England. Thereupon he said, ' I believe in going to church. It is a moral drill, and people must have something. If there is no church in a country village, there is nothing. . . . I believe in reformation coming from *within* the church. The clergy are growing more rationalist and that is the best way of changing.' " Pressed to charge the clergy, in that case, with casuistry in subscribing to articles in which they did not believe, Hardy would have nothing of it. He looked on it as a necessity in practical reform. And as he laid his flowers on the grave of his first wife, he began a long talk on the theme, " The liturgy of the Church of England is a noble thing. So are Tate and Brady's Psalms. These are the things that people need and should have."

So too he understood the trouble that many excellent people felt when they came upon the tragic protests in some of his novels. He included such men and women and their uneasiness within his own personality; they had his respect. He had written to Sir Sydney Cockerell, " When *Jude* comes out at the end of this month in the new series and you read the Preface and Postscript you will say to yourself (as I did to myself when I passed the proof for press), ' How very natural, and even commendable, it is for old-fashioned cautious people to shy at a man who could write that ! ' " He was no exotic, no outlaw, though his intellectual imagination could set him apart.

LAST WORKS AND DAYS

ADDRESSING a new audience, most of whom had no complaints to make that he wrote no more novels and were thoroughly satisfied that he had for so many years expressed his wisdom in verse forms,—seizing the opportunity, moreover, of the temporary renewal of peace and culture and meditation,—Hardy prefixed to his new collection of poems an " Apology " of some length. It is dated February 1922. The book, *Late Lyrics and Earlier*, may be considered as inaugurating the last phase of his literary life, a time of extraordinary alertness and energy when we reflect that it was his ninth decade. But he could be in no doubt over the honour in which he was held by the generation that had endured the actual war, and the intellectual position which was acknowledged by some of them and some of their elders as his, and his only, in a country which did not lack thinkers of a high order. The old habit of noticing and countering indolent reviewers and their misrepresentations had not quite left him, and so long as it set him upon publishing such powerful replies and reasonings as the " Apology " it was a good thing that it persisted. In reading the " Apology ", with its considerations not only on his personal outlook but also on the characteristics of the age and the hope of a cure for the disease of modern life in a reanimated

theology, many will again feel the regret that Hardy
was not more various an author even than we see :
that in all his long course he did not set apart one season
for a volume such as Sir Thomas Browne once perfected, a Religio in ordered prose. Granted that his
delight was to shape his perceptions as they chanced
in symbolic verses, and that the tax for writing poetry
on the writer's energies is a very severe one, yet there
is one great work by Hardy missing for ever from the
potential catalogue of his compositions. Perhaps, had
his early friend Horace Moule survived, the impetus to
accomplish such a Religio would not have been wanting.

   Late Lyrics and Earlier contained its share of poems
which at once took the fancy ; the opening song,

This is the weather the cuckoo likes
And so do I;

the " Voices from Things Growing in a Churchyard ",
" Surview " and especially " An Ancient to Ancients "
with its air of perfected Victorian culture, were some
of these noted poems. Another, " The Wood Fire ",
outwardly referring to the crucifixion but in reality
inspired by the news of the clearance of the wooden
crosses on the old Western Front, brought down on
Hardy the allegation of blasphemy, which he very
keenly resented It is remarkable that even at this
date he could bring out poems dated 1866, and that
he had also reserved some of the poems written upon
the death of his first wife for this new volume ; some,
too, which the death of his sister Mary in 1915 had
called forth, were now appearing.

   Emma Hardy's presence in the spirit was manifest
in the next of Hardy's productions, *The Famous Tragedy*

of the Queen of Cornwall at Tintagel in Lyonnesse, begun
in 1916, completed in 1923, and performed in Dorchester and then London by the Hardy Players early
in 1924. It is not one of the grand versions of the
legend of Tristram and Iseult, and on the stage its
weaknesses were all too obvious, but it served to keep
up the revived tradition of Wessex acting and Hardy.
The players had performed some of his scenes in 1921
at Sturminster Newton, a place of intense memories
for him. They appeared last at the Corn Exchange,
Dorchester, in November 1924, and then the Pavilion
Theatre, Weymouth, with the stage version of *Tess*,
which was afterwards acted in London at Barnes
Theatre. Hardy took a natural pleasure in their local
productions, never missing the first night, and con-
triving mostly to find some new item for the enrich-
ment of the programme.

Writing an introductory note for Mr. J. J. Foster's
Wessex Worthies in 1920, Hardy observed that the
province had not been commonly considered remarkable " for the energy and resourcefulness of its
natives ", but " ventured to say that in the arts and
sciences which soften manners and tend to make life
tolerable the people of South-Western England had
certainly not been behind those of other countries ".
One of these worthies, long known to Hardy, and in
his own way to a grateful part of the reading public,
died at the end of 1923,—the surgeon Sir Frederick
Treves. The loss affected Hardy deeply, but he wrote
a philosophic elegy on his friend for *The Times*, helped
in the funeral arrangements and chose the hymns.

There was a last visit to Oxford, and Queen's College, in June 1923, which is picturesquely recorded by

Lord Elton : " The Provost [Dr. Magrath] was only one year Mr. Hardy's senior, but with his patriarchal white beard appeared a great deal older, and as we left the party—Hardy sitting bright-eyed and upright on the edge of his chair—it seemed almost like leaving a new boy in charge of his headmaster ". The impression goes deeper than the outward look.

The Prince of Wales, after opening a new Territorial Drill Hall in Dorchester and meeting many of his Wessex tenants, visited Hardy on July 26th, 1923. He drove with the novelist in an open car to Max Gate, amid the bright faces of numerous onlookers. It was a simple and informal occasion, no other guests were present at the house, and Hardy's principal feeling was one of thankfulness that Max Gate had pleased and refreshed the overworked Prince, even for a little while. The same day, Dr. Marie Stopes informs me, " Hardy drove twenty miles with his wife to have tea with me and my husband in my lighthouse, which is the one he knew as a boy, and is mentioned in his *Well-Beloved*".

Such outings and briefer perambulations, with the constant arrival of visitors familiar or new, did not keep Hardy from literary work. He managed to retreat into his study almost as much as he wished, and when something was required from his pen he would generally and liberally produce it. Thus in 1924, in the same week, we find newspaper notices of his contributions to *The Book of the Queen's Dolls' House* and to *A Centenary of Work for Animals* (edited by E. G. Fairholme and W. Pain). He did not himself pen the miniature book which was made for the library of the Queen's Dolls' House, but he signed it, with the wish (as he wrote to Princess Marie Louise) " to have a whole library of such books " himself.   He was once again amassing the contents of a volume of poems, which he entitled *Human Shows, Far Phantasies, Songs and Trifles* (1925).   When it came out, it was seen that he had once more unearthed from his Bayswater period of sixty years before at least two poems, but he had also been on the spot with poems on happenings of 1923 and 1924—a terrible murder trial, the centenary refusal of a memorial to Byron in Westminster Abbey. In *Human Shows* his London memories evidence themselves more than in his previous collections, but not to the exclusion of his usual topics and theories.

His own dramatization of *Tess*, transferred to London in 1925, was the subject of great interest and much journalism.   With Miss Gwen Ffrangcon-Davies as heroine, it was performed for above a hundred nights, at the Barnes and then the Garrick Theatre.   I am fortunate in being able to quote a letter from Mr. A. E. Filmer, who produced it, which is a valuable record in more than one way : " The script as I received it was a theatrical impossibility.   I use the words quite deliberately.   There was not a curtain in the whole piece, and the writing throughout was of the story, not of the theatre—thus the psychological *speaking cue* would often occur in the middle of a sentence and be followed by several lines of monologue—' look at all the pretty things I've given you ' and at least six lines before the reply (of Tess) ' I hate my pretty things ! ' That is not *speech*.

" I had some interviews with Mr. Hardy and my shyness and trepidation at the contemplation of the first, were grotesque.   (Unfortunately I am a born respecter of persons.)   But T. H. was sweetness incarnate, his whole personality emanated gentleness. I do not remember any other so unlike the portraits of him—drawings, photographs, and so on. Well, when I had screwed up my courage to the point of making, with sincere humility, certain suggestions, he literally gave me *carte blanche*. He said, ' Do exactly as you think fit,' and when I left him, ' I am very happy, sir, that the play is in your hands.'

" I took scissors, cut up the script and rebuilt the play. So far as my memory serves me I made no cuts, and I need hardly say that I made no alterations in the text ; it was a matter of rebuilding (mainly to give each scene an effective curtain) and readjustment of speaking cues . . . all that sounds—and I hope is— very theatrical. For if a play is not to be made effective and attractive, why produce it ? "

The many who were privileged to see and converse with Hardy at this stage must have been always a little puzzled by him, or rather by the natural problem of finding some terms in which to define his personality. The " obvious explanation " was sometimes accepted, the " characteristic anecdote " gladly passed round, but even the obvious was not always the real point. For example, Hardy's apparent passion, outdoing Words-worth's, for graves and burial-grounds, which probably is treated here and there in any account of him, in-cluding this, as a profound and essential element in him, need not have been what it seemed. Commenting on it himself, in a letter to Sir Sydney Cockerell, Hardy does not find it difficult or basic, but explains it as merely an effect of association : " I think the reason why the scenes of many of the poems are churches and churchyards is that I used to spend much time in such places sketching, with another pupil, and we had many pleasant times at the work. Probably this explains why churchyards and churches never seem gloomy to me." On his eighty-sixth birthday he reflected, in a charming little melody, upon his own way through the world ; he had from boyhood been aware that life " did not promise overmuch ", and so he had come through, despite all his great endeavours of thought and imagination, as a child,

> And hence could stem such strain and ache
> As each year might assign.

He had the Lucretian stability—or was it the countryman's creed ?—and that was even disappointing to some who half expected that his presence would disclose a phantom of the tempest and mystery of his principal writings. He lived in the still centre.

A very able observer, Mr. Leonard Woolf, was among those who called on Hardy in 1927 at Max Gate, " which, with its sombre growth of trees, seemed to have been created by him as if it were one of his poems translated into brick, furniture and vegetation. He talked about his poems, and London as he had known it in his youth, and about his dog ' Wessex ', all with great charm and extraordinary simplicity. He was a human being, not ' the great man '. And then he told a story. . . ." The resulting impression, to which this story led, was one " of simplicity and of something which is almost the opposite of simplicity ". In the same manner, one could not call Hardy ethereal, in spite of his sympathy with the ethereal Shelley ; he stood firmly and realistically on this solid ball, as an oak or ancient stone in a meadow ; yet coexistent with this, through his talk of plain local and diurnal business, there came the feeling that he was also attending to some quite different, distant, unspoken, incommunicable world of consciousness. The clock, the calendar, the small circumstances of the room or the pathway or the wood-gate were there ; he had them all registered ; but they did not contain him after all, and his time and place were suspiciously distant. However,—here he was, at your service, and tea would be at four. Sir Edmund Gosse, making several visits to his friend that summer, was more struck than ever : " He is a wonder if you like. At 87½ without a deficiency of sight, hearing, mind or conversation. Very tiny and fragile, but full of spirit and a gaiety not quite consistent in the most pessimistic of poets."

The round of literary and Dorset life found the old man always willing, though birthdays with their telegrams worried him a little. In November 1926 we catch him at Higher Bockhampton, studying his old home with a view to " tidying and secluding " it; or again, as Mr. Bensusan describes, he is in one of his old villages, examining the taproom of an inn, to see if it had changed since he sat there over forty years earlier finishing a chapter of a serial story. In July 1927 he fulfilled a duty which must have been to him almost a religious rite. He appeared in public to lay the commemoration stone of the new Dorchester Grammar School, of which he had been appointed a governor some years before by the court of the Dorset Quarter Sessions. Hundreds of spectators cheered him, marked that " his handling of the solid silver trowel to spread the cement before the actual stone-laying was workmanlike in the extreme ", and enjoyed his speech, which he " delivered in clear and resonant tones audible to everyone ".   His words are recorded, and once again they yield some light upon his un-shakable trust in the tribe of which he came : " What I have to say is mainly concerning the Elizabethan philanthropist Thomas Hardy, who with some en-couragement from the burgesses, endowed and probably built this ancient school in its first shape—him whose namesake I have the honour to be and whose epitaph inscribed upon his tablet, unlike many epitaphs, does not, I am inclined to think, exaggerate his virtues, since it was written not by his relatives or dependents, but by the free burgesses of Dorchester in gratitude for his good action towards the town.   This good deed was accomplished in the latter part of the sixteenth century, and the substantial stone building in which it merged eventually stands to dignify South Street and I hope it may remain there.

" But what we know very little about is the person-ality of this first recorded Thomas Hardy of the Frome Valley here at our back, though his work abides.   He was without doubt one of the Hardys who landed in this country from Jersey in the fifteenth century, acquired small estates along the river up-wards towards the source, and have remained here-abouts ever since, the Christian name of Thomas having been especially affected by them.   He died in 1599, and it is curious to think that though he must have had a modern love of learning not common in a remote county in those days, Shakespeare's name could hardly have been known to him, or at the most but vaguely as that of a certain ingenious Mr. Shakespeare who amused the London play-goers, and that he died before

Milton was born. . . . But we may shrewdly conceive that he was a far-sighted man and would not be much surprised, if he were to revisit the daylight, to find that his original building had been outgrown, and no longer supplied the needs of the present inhabitants for the due education of their sons. His next feeling might be that he rejoiced in the development of what was possibly an original idea of his own, and wish the reconstruction every success." And on that note of congratulation, honouring this example of vital and valuable change in a manner strange for an alleged pessimist, Hardy proceeded to end his address. At home afterwards, he said that he had made his last public appearance.

One of his lifelong enthusiasms found a new occasion soon after when a beautiful Roman pavement was uncovered at the Dorchester Foundry. With Mrs. Hardy he paid more than one visit to the site. In old days this would have meant a fine page or two in a new Wessex tale.

In October 1927 he acceded to a request from the editor of the *Nineteenth Century and After*, that he should write about George Meredith. It was again a centenary matter, and centenaries had their place in Hardy's likings. " Unfortunately I am not physically able to write anything that can be dignified by the title of an article ! But I will get it ready when wanted." He did, once again gathering his reminiscences of the ancient days when he first saw Meredith, and dealing out a knock to the *Spectator* and other Victorian reviews for some failure in acclaiming his old friend's genius and presumably " putting a damper on the circulation of *Modern Love* till years after ". The short essay, which was to appear in print only when its writer had passed away, ended with a consideration on Meredith's permanent effect in our literature : " The likelihood is that, after some years have passed, what was best in his achievement—at present partly submerged by its other characteristics—will rise still more distinctly to the surface than it has done already. Then he will not only be regarded as a writer who said finest and profoundest things often in a tantalizing way, but as one whose work remains as an essential portion of the vast universal volume which enshrines as contributors all those that have adequately recorded their reading of life."

Another literary occupation of the autumn was the revision of his selected poems for a new edition of the volume included in the Golden Treasury Series in 1916. He remarked one day, in some talk about ambition, that he had done all he meant to do, but did not know whether it had been worth doing. " His only ambition, so far as he could remember, was to have some poem or poems in a good anthology " such as that with which Palgrave opened the Golden Treasury Series in 1861. How well he had justified the anthologist ! But, " if he had his life over again, he would prefer to be a small architect in a country town, like Mr. Hicks at Dorchester, to whom he was articled ".

During the same year, 1927, a stately edition of *The Dynasts* was published, the author signing the copies in accordance with the fashion then prevailing. A poem of melancholy grace, " Christmas in the Elgin Room, British Museum : Early Last Century ", published in *The Times* in December 1927, might have assured the reader that the author was still as full of

health and power as ever; his friends were quite
prepared to see him excel even the other Hardys in
spirited longevity; but when the poem appeared he
was already yielding to his last illness. Moreover, a
thing had already happened which distressed both him
and his wife infinitely. Wessex, " a dog known rather
well ", had been with them all their married years;
but he died at last. Hardy, like Edward Lear with his
ancient cat Foss, did not disdain to have a headstone
carved in his own design for his constant companion.
The loss certainly troubled Hardy, affected his hold.
" His brain is tired," Mrs. Hardy sadly recognized;
and yet, it was not beyond reasonable hope that a quiet
period would set him up again, to go daily to his desk
and stroll to his wonted posts of observation. Sir
Henry Head was called in. But, as Hardy had pointed
out, making the old and worn and neglected truth his
own, things come to an end; and on January 11th,
1928, with a wild night out of doors, Hardy's life ended.
He had been conscious until very near the moment.
He wrote out his cheque for the Society of Authors the
day before in his usual handwriting. He listened to
poems read by Mrs. Hardy, including " Rabbi Ben
Ezra ", Mr. De La Mare's " The Listeners ", and a
passage from FitzGerald's *Omar Khayyam* which he
knew rather well:

> O Thou, who Man of baser earth didst make
> And didst with Paradise devise the snake,
>   For all the sins wherewith the face of Man
> Is blackened. Man's forgiveness give—and take.

At that point he signalled his wife to read no further.
An hour after his death, she saw that his face was
wearing a look of radiant triumph.

There was inevitably an Irony awaiting Hardy's decease, but he does not appear to have foreknown it. He had desired that his body would be laid among his people in Stinsford Churchyard. It was his home, and he had been loyal to it in a great many thoughts and actions. It was part of Wessex, which was the kingdom he had well won. After attending Tennyson's funeral in 1892, he had reflected that " the scene was less penetrating than a plain country interment would have been ". But of course there was the other view : this great English man of letters ought to be entombed (after cremation) among others of similar eminence in Westminster Abbey. Representing this view, Sir James Barrie lost not a moment in putting it into action ; Mrs. Hardy's assent, however reluctant, was obtained, and the Abbey authorities very cordially accepted Barrie's plan and gave leave. However, it was ingeniously provided that Stinsford should not be entirely deprived of the remains of the last of the Thomas Hardys, and his heart was assigned to the old place for burial. The Abbey funeral, though a quarrel ensued over the distribution of tickets (as if, Sir John Squire wrote, it had been a matinée), was profusely attended, and the service was unconnected with any of Hardy's strivings for or against the Church. Those who acted as pall-bearers were Lord Baldwin, Mr. Ramsay MacDonald, Sir James Barrie, Sir Edmund Gosse, Mr. Galsworthy, Mr. G. B. Shaw, Mr. Kipling, Professor Housman, Dr. A. B. Ramsay as Master of Magdalene College, Cambridge, and the Rev. E. M. Walker, Provost of Queen's College, Oxford. If one may guess what Hardy would have said to all this, it appears that he would have sympathized with the

principle of honouring the literary man, privately enjoyed the queer dilemma and fuss caused by his death,
and regretted the rule by which only name and date
are allowed on stones in the Abbey nowadays : he
would have liked some interesting inscription, pre-
ferably in Latin, for the benefit of those to come who
like himself cared for such things, and pondered over
all biography.

Sir Edmund Gosse did not long survive his old
friend. The dispersal of Gosse's library revealed how
long the two lovers of poetry had been associated ; as
also, the status of Hardy at the time in the estimate
of the world's great book-collectors. The MS. of a
single poem, " God's Funeral ", was bought for £340.

Hardy left behind another volume of poems which
he had prepared for the press, except to give it his
final revision, entitled *Winter Words*. It was published
in 1928 with his preface, wherein he repeated his
obstinate rejection of the allegation that he was an
unvaried pessimist, his complaint that reviewers do
not invariably read the books they review, and his dis-
claimer of any attempt in any of his pages to supply a
" harmonious philosophy ". Once more Hardy had
amused himself by discovering verses written sixty years
earlier to include in the collection ; his vein of learned
wit had not failed, as witness his doggerel on Liddell
and Scott (1898) and the Drinking Song on the arrival
and the overthrow of the famous theories of the universe, which breaks off with a pretty epigram on
Einstein's contribution, and a rallying call to men to
do good things no matter what happens to theories.
For the rest, there were his usual and diverse meditations, mimes, ditties, epigrams, anecdotes, pictures ;

and perhaps at the finish he forgot that he was no pessimist, for the series ends with " We Are Getting to the End " and " He Resolves to Say No More "— poems quite terrible, if regarded as indeed the last words of this far-sighted man to a world that he loved in so many of its showings. But, at the moment when these words are penned, even those premonitory poems can hardly be said to justify the branding of Hardy as a pessimist ; they appear simply as the impartial observations of one who could see what was on the way, at so short an interval from what could have been supposed a tremendous opportunity to frustrate such monstrous recurrences.

In 1931 a column of Cornish granite embellished with laurel wreaths of bronze was erected opposite Hardy's birthplace. It was the gift of American admirers, and an American speaker of deserved literary fame unveiled it,—Professor Livingston Lowes. " In this heath," he said, " as in no other spot, Hardy's sense of an enduring past, and of the indissoluble oneness of humanity with the earth from which it sprang, found its supreme impression. And as it has dealt with man's memorials for centuries, that aged, watchful heath will in time incorporate this trespasser upon its solitude with itself."   Among those who were present, a Dorchester journalist named C. Lacy could recall Hardy as a schoolboy, coming to the town from Bockhampton " wearing a brown holland pinafore—a pinafore, mind you, not a smock—and a canvas dinner-bag hanging over his shoulders ".

Florence Hardy, to whose memory nothing but admiration is due, and who completely subordinated her own independent abilities to her loving care of

Thomas Hardy, survived until 1937. It is observable that the series of pleasant little books for children which she wrote ended with her marriage. In the first period of her widowhood she collected her energies, which had naturally been already taxed by the task of dealing with the complex practical side of a celebrated writer's life, for the two volumes which preserve so many details about her husband's works and days. She published a number of additional poems, and facilitated such studies of Hardy's writings as promised to be valuable. After her death, Max Gate came on the market, and many were relieved to read that it was bought by Hardy's sister, Miss Kate Hardy. Some could not repress a sigh a little later when the library was dispersed by public auction. It was not much, perhaps, that the big things in it were scattered among new owners, but there was something pathetic in the appearance of items like these (in Messrs. Hodgson's exemplary catalogue) :

Hardy (T)—Selections from Browning, 1906, and other Pocket Editions, etc., *given by Hardy to Miss Florence Dugdale, from the latter to Hardy,* or *bearing Hardy's autograph.* 24 vols.

        „   —The Tutor's Assistant, *inscribed " Thomas Hardy's Book,* 1849 " [aetat. 9], fcp., 1849, and other school books, *mostly bearing* his autograph or with MS. notes. 25 vols.

        „   —Baedeker's Traveller's Manual, *with additional words and phrases scribbled in by Hardy,* 1873 ; Garbett (E. L.) Elementary Treatise on Architecture, 1850, and others of personal interest, *mostly with Hardy's autograph.* 25 vols.

        „   —Baedeker's Continental Guides, 11 vols. 1875–95, and others, *some with Hardy's autograph, a few with pencil notes.* 3 parcels.

Here, at length, was the real and unmistakable flitting. Hardy had written his poem " The Strange House (Max Gate, A.D. 2000) " in acceptance of the future, when, to vary Cowper's lines a little,

> It had become a history little known
> That once he called the curious house his own ;

but the process of hiding away and effacing the associations had begun a little earlier than he could have apprehended.

Some of my readers may perhaps be curious to see what were the books with which Thomas Hardy lived, for he was one whose books were truly his intimate friends. It was not hard to discover that he possessed the *Dictionary of National Biography* among many masterly works of reference, the *Oxford English Dictionary*, *Chambers's Encyclopaedia* (1895), the *Encyclopaedia Biblica* edited by the Rev. T. K. Cheyne and J. Sutherland Black (1914), *Webster's English Dictionary* (1864), Liddell and Scott's *Greek-English Lexicon* (1851) and others. His considerations of philosophies were shown in several acquisitions such as the *Histories of Philosophy*, by F. Ueberweg and by G. H. Lewes, both dated 1880, editions of Hume's *Treatise on Human Nature* and *Essays* by Green and Grose (1874–1875), Herbert Spencer's 3-volume *Essays* (1868) and other writings, Schopenhauer's *The World as Will and Idea* in Haldane's translation (1896), von Hartmann's *Philosophy of the Unconscious* (1893), and the People's Edition of all Carlyle in 37 volumes dated 1872 and onwards. A first edition of Godwin's *Enquiry concerning Political Justice* in its quarto form was one of his boasts as an old book-hunter, and he was willing to believe that its numerous marginalia were in the handwriting of Shelley. For his *Dynasts* he assembled, as it is clear he would, many noted works about Napoleon and his era, of all which an account is furnished by Dr. Rutland in his larger volume on Hardy; who was also a reader in other periods of history exemplified in his Clarendon's *History of the Rebellion*, G. W. Forrest's *Indian Mutiny*, Motley's *Rise of the Dutch Republic*, and Thucydides. (The mention of the Duke of Monmouth was likely to set T. H. talking.) The Max Gate library naturally contained a selection of books splendid or modest on Dorset antiquities, genealogies and topography, including the eighteenth-century historian Hutchins, who played a part in giving Hardy's imagination some points of departure.

Hardy had the works of Swift, Fielding and Scott in extensive modern reprints, as well as those of Balzac; his Shakespeare was apt to be any ordinary sort of edition, and he was generally content with unpretentious pocketable forms of favourite poets like Byron, Shelley, Coleridge and Keats, though he was rumoured to have been slow in consenting to a pocket edition of his own writings. He housed old sets of *The Spectator* and *Tatler* by Addison and Steele. And he bought or he received as gifts a great many books by the writers of his day, a diversity of persons including "Lucas Malet" and Sarah Grand, Alfred Austin and Hubert Crackanthorpe, H. G. Wells, T. E. Lawrence, Charles Whibley, John Galsworthy, Mrs. Humphry Ward, Rider Haggard, John Masefield and the younger generations of literary men and women on both sides of the Atlantic.

Hardy the reader, with his quiet good judgment

and yet his freedom from prescription and convention, probably did not change much as years went on ; he may be found in his study as usual through the following brief communication. In the *Fortnightly Review* for August 1887, edited by Frank Harris, a series of " Fine Passages in Verse and Prose ; selected by Living Men of Letters " began to appear. Matthew Arnold had the first place ; a few pages further on Thomas Hardy wrote :

" I should have replied sooner, but the words ' The one passage in all poetry which seems to me the finest ' quite bewildered my mind by their immensity. I should say that there is no one passage finest ; that the various kinds of best poetry are not reducible to a common standard. ' There is one glory of the sun, and another glory of the moon, and another of the stars.' I know that you ask ' what *seems* the finest ' ; but that seeming varies with the time and mood, and according to the class of poetry that is for the nonce nearest to the tone of our situation.

" I have very often felt (but not always) that one of the most beautiful of English lyrics is Shelley's *Lament,* ' O world, O life, O time ' ; and of descriptive poetry I do not know that anything has as yet been fairly able to oust our old friends in *Childe Harold*— *e.g.* C. III. stanzas 85 to 87.

" I know this is an old-fashioned taste ; but it is a well-considered relapse on my part, for though in past years I have been very modern, in this matter I begin to feel that more intellectual subtlety will not hold its own in time to come against the straightforward expression of good feeling.

" With regard to prose, the task is somewhat more

practicable, and yet how hopeless ! But I will go thus far : I think that the passages in Carlyle's *French Revolution* on the silent growth of the oak have never been surpassed by anything I have read, except perhaps by his sentences on night in a city, as specimens of contemplative prose (if they may be so called) ; and that in narrative prose the chapter of the Bible (2 Sam. xviii) containing the death of Absalom is the finest example of its kind that I know, showing beyond its power and pathos the highest artistic cunning."

The Centenary of Thomas Hardy was observed during the war of 1940 at Stinsford, just after the astonishing manœuvre at Dunkirk, and it is agreeable to record that the Vicar of Stinsford bears one more of Hardy's favourite names, that of Moule. " Stationed near the Porch ", Sir Hugh Walpole wrote, " were the Mellstock Choir—the violin, the bassoon, the drum. We sang the old hymn melodies so familiar to us from *Under the Greenwood Tree* and *The Trumpet-Major*. Through the open door came the scent of the roses and carnations and the songs of the birds."   At even-song Canon A. C. Deane gave an address on the word " consider " (Matthew vi. 28) as a key to Thomas Hardy's particular gift and example, and concluded with a wise appeal exactly suited to the memory of the man : " If well-to-do churches would sometimes assign collections to the National Trust, or some similar body, for the preservation of the English countryside, their action, on the highest grounds, would be amply justi-fied.   To help to preserve our rural England for people to consider would be, in the strictest sense, religious work, while it would be also the best possible way of commemorating Thomas Hardy."

IX

HARDY'S NOVELS : THE FADED PAGES

So many able expositions of Hardy's writings, studied altogether or in part, have already appeared that an anthology from those might be the best way of depicting his genius and commending it to the enquirer. There are some who, having lived while he was still producing the majority of the works in which his greatness is felt to be most decisive, do not find him at all congenial ; whether it is something in his style or alleged want of a style, or something in his metaphysical suggestions, or a feeling that his elements are not well mixed, or an insufficient degree of charm, certain it is that, Falstaff-like, they will not march with him. But the question must be, at this date, what Hardy's works are likely to mean to coming time and fresh generations. So tremendous and so swift appear the changes of this century, so prolific is the multitude of skilled authors who treat of the immediate (and almost remain contemporary for months together), so thoroughly allied to his period was Hardy in many aspects and details of his literary undertakings, that any answer must be at the mercy of time in its latest fantastic intensification. What manner of man and woman, of social order and mental and emotional need may emerge from these years, and what literature will

be effectual, typical, comprehensible even under the
inevitable reconstitution of human lives, is far beyond
my powers of guessing.   As Mr. de la Mare remarked
many years ago, when he considered the effect of Time
on one of Hardy's works, " What good that may mean,
and whose, let the Phantom Intelligences decide ".
The countenance of Hardy himself seems to dictate
caution, or even silence, since with all his faith in the
persisting past he more than any man was appre-
hensive of the strangest, widest possibilities in a world
urged hither and thither so mysteriously.   What was
it that he could have said when he determined upon
those latest lines, " He Resolves to Say No More " ?

There is a kind of friendly contention for the owner-
ship of Hardy's true greatness as a writer, and hitherto
it has swayed one way and another with the hours and
the incidents of opinion.   Fiction, with the advantage
of a long series of celebrated works making Hardy a
great name before he came out with any conspicuous
intentions in other ways, has proclaimed Hardy for
her own ; there was a day when it would have seemed
impossible to challenge this, and there is still plenty
of thought and feeling in favour of the old late-
Victorian view of Hardy's place in literature.   But
when a man, no matter what else he has written of
human life and personality, attempts a vaster scheme
altogether and a more complex harmony, fashioning
a startling interpretation of the whole history of man
through a period of extraordinary outward shows and
individualities—when a man struck with a possible
clue to the web of human history can work for years
with command of his general vast idea, and of all the
operative detail in an epic drama like *The Dynasts*,—

it is understandable that many spectators should think the novels only fragments by comparison, and even at that bearing the marks of forced industry, and should assert that the true Hardy was fulfilled in this incomparable adventure. And still a third Muse (if one may fancy a new party of Muses) may be heard declaring that Hardy's origin belonged to lyrical poetry, that beyond all other appearances whether those of the literary career or of some transient passion for an unusual form of composition, there he stayed to the end. A very numerous collection of poems, many of them already impressed on the mind of the time, exists to illustrate this definition. Under three headings, then, the expression of Hardy awaits final judgment.

What are the chances that his contribution to fiction will continue to be part of the library of his countrymen in the future, on the supposition that the huge entempesting of the present yields to something like order and serenity and (in the widest sense) religion, and that those affections and desires and questionings still characterize men and women beneath any revolution which time may have wrought ? The tentative answer must be limited to the simplest considerations. Only the few, with the gift of transferring themselves from their world into a quite different imaginary state, in order that they may give a work of art a chance to make its intended impression, will revisit successfully a considerable part of Hardy's novels and tales. The social dilemmas which were so agitating to his first public, for the most part, have already ceased to be such as are commonly understood. Even in the most ordinary terms of the novelist writing seventy years ago, there is not now the significance that once resounded : for example, the Poor Man and the Lady, to an age which thinks of poverty as a condition to be rapidly altered and of ranks and dignities as agreeable or disagreeable nonsense, do not at all suggest a sort of perpetual hopeless dawn.   They propose not a novel, not another inspection of the gulfs of convention's pain and peril, but a fairy tale or a continental express comedy.   And yet, concentrated in those plain words, there was found the deep springhead of much that Hardy the novelist had to pour forth into the willing hearts of his contemporaries.

To take an example of Hardy's writings which have probably lapsed into the registers of literary history, there to stay undisturbed except by the curious or the eccentric, let us reconsider *A Pair of Blue Eyes*.   It was one of Hardy's lucky hits, and is still of course mentioned with something of affection.   The title recalls the sentimental appetites which novelists believed, no doubt rightly, that the public wanted fed in the Seventies and Eighties : by itself, it only suggests one more of the faded and yet fragrant offerings woven then by plenty of graceful minds—as, *Red as the Rose Is She*, *Cometh Up like a Flower*, *The Vicar's Daughter*, *In Silk Attire*, *Daisies and Buttercups*, *All in a Garden Fair*.   No one will blame any generation of mortals for keeping up a dream of a modern Arcadia, just beyond the railroad, nor is it necessary to condemn the idyllic tradition, the legend of Daphnis and Chloe in its innumerable renovations and rediscoverings, because of its nature : if even Puvis de Chavannes did well what he meant to do and what others liked to see him do, then there is no apology required.   Only, the dreams of the wide world change like everything else.

We do not get far in *A Pair of Blue Eyes* before we are entertained, not as the author can have intended us to be, by his remarkable spasms of contorted and straggling English. Style at the present day—style, in the sense that the mention of Addison or Sir Thomas Browne or Landor or Arnold suggests—is not reverenced as it once was, and probably Hardy was intent on achieving a prose such as should be dignified, cultured, complete. But he often missed that without chancing upon some unusual, strenuous, rhythmic writing such as should later on attract the worshippers of that mode : I speak here of his failures. There is a sentence of Gilbert White the naturalist on passages in Milton's poetry which comes to mind in this connection—Milton, says White, sometimes " ransacks the whole circle of sciences for a set of hard words and rumbling terms that make his readers stare ". Boswell, discoursing on Johnson, smiles at his " sesquipedalian " terms. With Hardy in his early manner, rumbling or sesquipedalian terms are apt to be his labour's reward ; even when the words severally evade such description, one has the feeling that his thought itself is at any rate sesquipedalian. And in a novel which we approach unsuspectingly as an idyll (" clear, fresh and dulcet "), this must be regarded as a disadvantage not only after an interval of mortal change, but from the very first.

Here are some instances of this inartistic knottiness. An interval is announced : " It has now to be not only supposed but clearly realized that nearly three-quarters of a year have passed away. In place of the autumnal scenery which formed a setting to the previous enactments, we have the culminating blooms of summer in the year following." Speed : the Paddington porters

as a train is due out " accelerate their velocities till they
fly up and down like shuttles in a loom ", and a few
pages on, in Bombay, " Speculation moved with an
accelerated velocity every successive day, the only disagreeable contingency connected with it being the
possibility of a collapse ".   A psychological nicety :
" Meantime Elfride's countenance wore a look indi-
cating utter despair of being able to explain matters
so that they would seem no more than they really
were, a despair which not only relinquishes the hope
of direct explanation, but wearily gives up all collateral
chances of extenuation."   Another, when two rival
lovers meet : " Simultaneous operations might now
have been observed to be going on in both. They
collected their thoughts, the result being that an expression less frank and impulsive than the first took
possession of their features. It was manifest that the
next words uttered were a superficial covering to con-
straint on both sides."   Hundreds of examples of this
odd vocabulary and unhandy construction could be
singled out from the novel, but in fact the spirit of
the writing is often of this kind even where it does not
yield such precipitates.

If we feel here that the author strews some obstacles
in the reader's way while he is himself the direct
narrator, the trouble may be more rather than less
when the persons of the drama are caused to make
conversation in a similar manner. Henry Knight, we
are made aware, is an essayist and reviewer with some
fame, and doubtless our ancestors, at least those who
lived in the age of Gladstone and George Eliot, and
wrote essays and reviews, used a more elaborate dialogue than we do ; still, it is hard to stand by while

this whiskery lover is being austere with his blue-eyed lady, and not much easier when he is being amiable : as thus. Elfride begs him not to praise her for some little confession not so simple as it sounded—

" But Knight, being in an exceptionally genial mood, merely saw this distressful exclamation as modesty. ' Well,' he added, after a minute, ' I like you all the better, you know, for such moral precision, although I called it absurd.' He went on with tender earnestness : ' For, Elfride, there is one thing I do love to see in a woman—that is, a soul truthful and clear as heaven's light. I could put up with anything if I had that—forgive nothing if I had it not. Elfride, you have such a soul, if ever woman had ; and having it, retain it, and don't ever listen to the fashionable theories of the day about a woman's privileges and natural right to practise wiles. Depend upon it, my dear girl, that a noble woman must be as honest as a noble man. I specially mean by honesty, fairness not only in matters of business and social detail, but in all the delicate dealings of love, to which the licence given to your sex particularly refers.' "

Small wonder that Elfride should " look troublously at the trees ", had it been because of the essayist and reviewer's geniality : Queen Victoria herself did not like being treated as a public meeting ; but the habit of oratory was not confined to Knight among Elfride's admirers. The youthful, the spontaneous Stephen Smith has it too ; and, to be just, Elfride herself can keep up an end in the game. Thus, in a moment of urgency and bewilderment, when Stephen has been trying her with " wine and biscuit ", " tea or coffee ", " a glass of water ", this girl of nineteen or twenty produces her aphorism : " No. I want something that makes people strong and energetic for the present, that borrows the strength of to-morrow for use to-day —leaving to-morrow without any at all for that matter ; or even that would take all life away to-morrow, so long as it enabled me to get home again now. Brandy, that's what I want. That woman's eyes have eaten my heart away ! "

Be it admitted that novelists always have a convention or device for giving characters long and ingenious passages to speak in their conversations : that Hardy found this convention in especially strong command, and worked to it : yet he was not always working well. He went too far from probability ; and yet, had he presented much of his people's oratory in the form of a reading of their unspoken thoughts, he would have kept his readers at such points even now. Still glancing at the characteristics of his minor performances in fiction, as *A Pair of Blue Eyes* represents them, we are sure to notice how often he adorns his page with a brief allusion to classical learning. Does it help ? No. The reader cannot be expected to hunt up these references in order to do what his author should have done if he set out to enrich and illustrate a plain tale at all. " Stephen's manners, like the feats of Euryalus, owed their attractiveness . . .", " Mrs. Smith threw in her sentiments between the acts, as Coryphaeus of the tragedy ", " Fingers literally stiff with rings, *signis auroque rigentes*, like Helen's robe ", " Pansy went, like the steed of Adonais ",—these things remind us of poor Mr. Knight who in his love-trouble must quote his book infallibly, " Diogenes Laertius says that. . . ." To those who know their Hardy throughout and cannot but mingle their reading of his quaintest pages with a sense of his personal evolution towards supremacy, even these touches are indispensable ; but, seen without that sense or whim, they are part of an imperfect, and an outmoded, method.

Rightly, and for popular purposes, counterchanging his tale of love and correct society with sketches of simple souls, Hardy did not in this novel make a great success of them. Here, too, he was trusting to a method which was favoured by men of genius. He could point to Dickens, to Shakespeare as " labelling " their comic characters ; in real life he had found, and everyone finds individuals who grow to a great age in their haunts and are known for one or two invariable sayings or doings. But their humorous effect in life is limited, and even in books. It was in vain that Charles Lamb's friend Bob Allen endeavoured to maintain a place in journalism by popping in his patent revelation on the origin of the three balls hung outside pawnbroker's shops : and similarly these figures of fun, compelled to say their piece through the ages, become avoidable. William Worm, on whom the task of yielding amusement falls so much in *A Pair of Blue Eyes*, is to make it clear, " I be a poor wambling man." We form that opinion of him all too soon. But he might have got over this, had Dickens or even Theodore Hook been his creator, for then his stock-in-trade would have been much more extensive. Hardy, in this part of his work, had not a great deal of invention.

We must all sympathize with the novelist whose contracts require him to work piecemeal, to give readers of a magazine in each instalment a sufficient and varied nourishment for the day and the bait for

a return to the subject with an appetite, next number.
The circumstances having passed away, there stands
the whole book, and very cleverly has Hardy juggled
his way along ; but what was so desirable, and so
watchfully and promptly supplied for the original need,
of course looks different in the later reader's view.   The
tale tends to be a sort of hurried display of lantern-
slides, some gorgeous, some terrific, some weird, some
too sweet for words, but all rushing upon the attention
with too great abruptness.   Not that a show of lantern-
slides is not as good as most of our human entertain-
ments.   But it has its respects of time and place.

Coincidences are not only found in fiction, but in
the kind of fiction which young Thomas Hardy found
himself pledged to supply they certainly abound in
remarkable richness, and in the end the reader who is
not the old serial reader suspects that they are being
forced.   In the end—that suits *A Pair of Blue Eyes*
fairly enough.   The two rivals for the hand of Elfride
have been widely separated, Knight on a tour of the
Continent, then in town ; Smith on a business errand
in India : they meet by chance in Hyde Park.   They
are both, they discover, staying at the Grosvenor
Hotel, Pimlico.   They both, unknown to each other,
dash for the same train to the West of England.   And
to that very train is attached " a dark and richly-
finished van " which seizes the attention of both of
them, and in which—as they perceive at their destina-
tion—the coffin containing the dead body of Elfride
also travels to the West.   Truly a strange meeting ;
but imposed upon that is one of the novelist's feats of
surprise, which it is just possible that an extremely
experienced or suspicious reader might have seen

coming from a hint some way back in the story.   Elfride
had become the second wife of Lord Luxellian ! How
Knight, with his connection with the press and his life
in London, had failed to get word of this aristocratic
wedding, one moreover which was peculiarly interesting
to him, is not easy to see otherwise than in the arbitrary
or necessitous doings of a bold tale-teller.

Within this novel the traces of more than one theme
more commanding than the capricious love-story
which it amounts to may be recognized.   The time
was not ripe for such themes, the occasion did not
serve.   What passed when a beautiful, dutiful clergyman's daughter was loved by more than one man at
once would probably yield a great book if her character
were made fascinating enough and the gentlemen were
vigorously different and variously powerful ; but
Elfride, Smith and Knight are not tremendously exciting in their words, their thoughts, their abilities or
attempts to master life at large.   Their activities are
a little too much like those of the small stuffed personages in miniature Victorian drawing-rooms which (till
lately) could be seen in their glass shrines on seaside
piers ; a penny sets the arm and hand raising the
letter, shoes tapping the ground, the door opening
and a stern matriarchal face glaring in, all undoubtedly
signifying " Give him Up ! "   Then all dimly concludes.   Hardy in *A Pair of Blue Eyes* begins to work
in a cause which moved him strongly—the boy Smith
is not of the social rank of Elfride, and there lies the
foundation for the real tragedy, thence could have
proceeded the drama, towards a triumphal or a lament-
able end, which would have employed these lovers as
symbols of a far wider world than themselves.   Or

again, in the sketchy character of Knight, I believe that
there is the sufficient source for a complete story with
a combination of love's winding ways and of a special
dilemma in it—the effect of a great intellectual passion
and pursuit upon the man's capacities and experiences
in emotional relations. That Hardy in an improvised
novel should bring these possibilities unfulfilled into
our minds shows that he was, what subsequent writings
proved so thoroughly, out of the common as a student
of life ; but his accumulating too much for his occasion,
his inability to avoid distinctly what he could not treat
adequately, was a mistake which makes his book into
a sort of warehouse.

Among the fine things which are stacked up in that
warehouse, several landscape paintings and sketches of
detail will reward the enquiring eye. Hardy's familiarity with art galleries, and professional draughtsmanship, had not failed to tint and model his prose
descriptions, nor are those only of Nature and solitude.
The scene in the alley from Knight's London window
may serve in illustration : " Crowds—mostly of women
—were surging, bustling and pacing up and down.
Gaslights glared from butchers' stalls, illuminating the
lumps of flesh to splotches of orange and vermilion,
like the wild colouring of Turner's later pictures,
whilst the purl and babble of tongues of every pitch
and mood was to this human wild-wood what the
ripple of a brook is to the natural forest." The true
picturesque is used by Hardy here and there with a
venturesome and effective skill. Wright of Derby
might have painted the scene which, in fact, is one of
the emotional incandescences of the novel : when
Knight and Smith have to be made aware that their

lady was not theirs after all, it happens by the light of a smithy fire. A man with a parcel wants to show what is in it to the smith, who blows up the fire to help him: the parcel discloses a coffin-plate and coronet.

" Knight and Stephen came forward. The undertaker's man, on seeing them look for the inscription, civilly turned it round towards them, and each read, almost at one moment, by the ruddy light of the coals :

𝔈𝔏𝔉𝔍𝔇𝔈,

𝔚𝔦𝔣𝔢 of 𝔖𝔭𝔢𝔫𝔰𝔢𝔯 𝔥𝔲𝔤𝔬 𝔏𝔲𝔵𝔢𝔩𝔩𝔦𝔞𝔫,

𝔉𝔦𝔣𝔱𝔢𝔢𝔫𝔱𝔥 𝔅𝔞𝔯𝔬𝔫 𝔏𝔲𝔵𝔢𝔩𝔩𝔦𝔞𝔫:

𝔇𝔦𝔢𝔡 𝔉𝔢𝔟𝔯𝔲𝔞𝔯𝔶 10, 1867.

They read it, and read it, and read it again—Stephen and Knight—as if animated by one soul. Then Stephen put his hand upon Knight's arm, and they retired from the yellow glow, farther, farther, till the chill darkness enclosed them round, and the quiet sky asserted its presence overhead as a dim gray sheet of blank monotony."

Another moment of crisis in the story, and one of a fuller philosophic import, is summed up in a wonderfully keen piece of word-painting, from which one detail perhaps stands out. The scene is that in which Knight hangs over the Cliff without a Name, in frightful danger of immediate death. " From the fact that the cliff formed the inner face of the segment of a huge cylinder, having the sky for a top and the sea for a bottom, which enclosed the cove to the extent of more than a semicircle, he could see the vertical face curving round on each side of him. He looked far down the

façade, and realized more thoroughly how it threatened
him. Grimness was in every feature, and to its very
bowels the inimical shape was desolation.

"By one of those familiar conjunctions of things
with which the inanimate world baits the mind of man
when he pauses in moments of suspense, opposite
Knight's eyes was an imbedded fossil, standing forth
in low relief from the rock. It was a creature with
eyes. The eyes, dead and turned to stone, were even
now regarding him. It was one of the early crus-
taceans called Trilobites. Separated by millions of
years in their lives, Knight and this underling seemed
to have met in their death. It was the single instance
within reach of his vision of anything that had ever
been alive and had had a body, to save, as he himself
had now."

From this truly imaginative piece of sculpturing,
these meeting eyes, Hardy leads on, for " Knight was
a geologist ", into a vision of the ancient inhabitants of
the earth, primitive man and his strange and enormous
and puny predecessors ; it is a splendid fantasia, but
not of the order of the incident that started it off. For
here Hardy is really catering for the tastes of the hour—
tastes which made him install " a marine aquarium "
in the study of the Vicar of Endelstow and another in
the window of Knight's room in (apparently) Gray's
Inn. He and other novelists thought that they might,
indeed that they should diversify their romances with
useful information, disguised a little or very little.
Still considering this thrilling episode of the rescue on
the cliff, we find him creating the feeling of intolerable
suspense in various ways, but partly by assuring us of
several matters of fact. How was it that Knight got

into trouble on the edge of the precipice when he managed to catch his hat thence ? " The rain had wetted the shaly surface of the incline. A slight superficial wetting of soil of any kind makes it far more slippery to stand on than the same soil thoroughly drenched. The inner substance is still hard, and is lubricated by the moistened film." Well, there is the poor gentleman trying not to crash into the Atlantic far below : how far ? " It has been proved "—the height of the cliff—" by actual measurement to be not a foot less than six hundred and fifty. That is to say, it is nearly three times the height of Flamborough, half as high again as the South Foreland, a hundred feet higher than Beachy Head—the loftiest promontory on the east or south side of this island, twice the height of St. Alban's, thrice as high as the Lizard, and just double the height of St. Bee's." More particulars follow.

So, to those who have the fancy and the leisure, *A Pair of Blue Eyes* may be one of the most pleasing of books. Why should it be other than it is ? Hardy can afford to have produced many more of these byway books, which perhaps are more insidious than at first sight they appear ; for these comments have run to greater length, on the single example, than was intended. The appeal of the Victorians, alike in their grandeur and their nonsensicality, is waiting for us there, singularized by the striving personality and evolving interests of a youthful artist. Let it be admitted that quite lately *A Pair of Blue Eyes* has been read and appreciated by good judges of the novel in a spirit of timelessness, without any marked pause over the specimens of superannuation which beset the

scenes. Arthur McDowall, for instance, has written
a handsome eulogy of it as " a fascinating and provoca-
tive foretaste of the bigger novels ", an achievement in
pattern, a drama " strung on a symmetry of ironic
conjunctions and relations ", and, because of Elfride,
a story with the charm of youth. I cannot quarrel
with the sympathy which yields such an estimate, but
accepting the onrush (some call it the march) of time
and the natural desertion by the majority of readers of
that which is contrived for a limited and temporary
demand I must lay by *A Pair of Blue Eyes* as one of
the works of Hardy which have at best aquarium value.

With it, with them, I suspect, have gone in the long
run the larger part of his short stories. I cannot see
the world, which has been trained by other masters in
that field and in a form developing in another tone
and pace from Hardy's, going back to them with great
joy and thanksgiving. Inevitably some of them will
find at all periods the sort of reader whose mind and
function are exactly attuned to them, and then what
does the world's opinion matter ? Then, the seemingly
stilled instrument will once more make music : or, if
we consider the case in the region of Victorian aquaria,
we shall remember what a certain moment could do
with Knight's glass tank. " It was a dull parallelo-
pipedon enough for living creatures at most hours of
the day ; but for a few minutes in the evening, as now,
an errant, kindly ray lighted up and warmed the little
world therein, when the many-coloured zoophytes
opened and put forth their arms, the weeds acquired a
rich transparency, the shells gleamed of a more golden
yellow, and the timid community expressed gladness
more plainly than in words."

The short story is one of the forms of literature about which there is not an excess of critical writing. The chief rule for it seems to be that it should not be entangled with " another story ". In C. E. Montague's perfect presentation of the two young staff officers who had a malicious rivalry for embellishing their bosoms with colour-schemes of decorations, the sense of limited range and prospect is exquisite. There is no attempt to relate these figures to other questions than the one which keeps them fantastically busy ; they are made for it, and it for them, and we should not welcome any meditations on their other possibilities or circumstances for that time. The story of the Lamia which Keats found in *The Anatomy of Melancholy* is one equally well bounded ; the young man, aged twenty-five, encounters the fair gentlewoman on the road to Corinth, is enchanted, marries her, and gives a wedding feast : there one Apollonius perceives her to be a serpent, and she so detected vanishes on the instant. What else ? Nothing about the sorrows of Menippus Lycius without his lovely Phoenician : only, " many thousands took notice of this fact, for it was done in the midst of Greece ". Where the story-writer is inclined to think of the form as a strain of music, a melody of spiritual apprehension, the same instinct for beginning and ending without " explanation " is the first condition of a triumph over the hearer.—The wild geese in the dusk, at first a clangour of horn-like cryings in the distance, fly over with a half-amusing, half-frightening effect of an aerial army, and then the formation of beating wings fades into the first-heard ringing and belling and is nowhere at all. Observers of birds will have been recording this migration and will want to know, and will in the end know, the entire business that it belonged to ; the naturalist's extended story will be excellent reading, and may even be presented as a romance ; but the non-scientific man who is " used to notice such things " has no need of any additions to the brief and wonderful thing he has seen and heard within his silent horizons. It was a short story, isolated but full.

In his verse Hardy has the faculty for comprising his short story, whether it be one of those of which the queerness of circumstances in contrast or union makes the offer, or of the others expressing rather a something in the air. He found his art in this kind when he was still young, witness " Neutral Tones " (1867), a history of modern love seen in a series of grey and white maskings. In verse, he had no trouble whatever to chronicle within the compass of a few lines such a bevy of ghosts as speak in " Friends Beyond " —each comes forth with brilliant distinctness, all are gone with deepest unity of indifference, and the outside world may take its way once more. The murmuring vision has had its own dimensions. But turning to the short stories in the usual prose medium, we find the touch more erratic and, in the main, the results uneven and only good in parts.

" The Three Strangers " has always been a celebrated example of these tales by Hardy, and in its making he has employed the marvellous observation and knowledge of country humours which no writer of English fiction has possessed in the same degree. The pictures are richly realistic, the painting is that of the Dutch school sure enough—but it would have been better had the method been less stately and leisurely. The writer is not sufficiently trusting to the imagination, and appears inclined to give us rather an evening address on eweleazes and shepherds' cottages than to ensnare our sense with significances of secrets and dangers. The information of its kind is good and abundant, but it belongs to other occasions and purposes—a note of extreme remoteness might be struck more clearly without most of the second introductory paragraph, for instance : " Fifty years ago such a lonely cottage stood on such a down, and may possibly be standing there now. In spite of its loneliness, however, the spot, by actual measurement, was not more than five miles from a county-town. Yet that affected it little. Five miles of irregular upland, during the long inimical seasons, with their sleets, snows, rains and mists, afford withdrawing space enough to isolate a Timon or a Nebuchadnezzar ; much less, in fair weather, to please that less repellent tribe, the poets, philosophers, artists and others who conceive and meditate of pleasant things." No passage could be more pleasing to the lover of Hardy's character ; all great authors are beloved for their faults as well as for their perfections ; but in cold judgment this slow local minuteness is an obstacle to the creation of imaginative intensity.

It is so with other short stories by Hardy ; the scale proposed by the writer to our attention is suited rather to a novel, and to psychologies which should be given at full length if not in the briefest and acutest way. Wessex has here been a mixed blessing to her favourite son, inducing him to describe rather than to suggest, and to miss the art of a brilliant light on the

single interest for the sake of a completed history—yet
not to be truly completed without something like the
room of a novel. " A Tragedy of Two Ambitions "
is an exceedingly interesting study in circumstance and
character, and reasonably free from the strange involved style which embarrasses the novels and clogs
many of the minor tales ; the detail is brisk and for
the most part not imposed upon the action but seen
as part of it. Yet here Hardy, in my judgment, is
still out of his real road, and losing a great opportunity.
The thing looks like the ghost of a Wessex Novel that
suffered some untimely fate. There is a grim tune
here, which needed to be the recurrent and formidable
element in an extensive composition with all its dia-
logues and reveries and crises and evocations of nature
set forth in the author's longer rhythm. As it is,
transitions are found of a mechanical kind, just showing
how the business worked, and the two brothers who
should have been among the Bosolas of the English
novel are left as dreary little men ; the touch which
shuts the scene and leaves them to a certain sinister
" contingency to consider " is masterly indeed, but
only reminds us that Hardy had not let belief take
hold on him in respect of the potentialities of his idea.
The improvisation which he was content with, not
only in this but in many of his short stories, leaves the
impression that his writings in this kind were produced
because editors were calling for them and because he
had to make ends meet.

Opinions vary as greatly over Hardy's secondary
novels as over the merits of wines ; possibly a large
number of readers have set, or would set, *Two on a
Tower* very close to that group of half a dozen at the

top of the Wessex Novels which have pointed a comparison with the Waverley Novels. Yet I doubt whether anybody has escaped a final sense of disappointment concerning that book. A more magnificent announcement to the imaginative or epic sense could hardly be made than that title *Two on a Tower*. When he supplied a preface thirteen years after the first publication, Hardy certainly defined his book without hesitation as " this slightly-built romance ", but went on to speak of it more abstractedly as " the outcome of a wish to set the emotional history of two infinitesimal lives against the stupendous background of the stellar universe, and to impart to readers the sentiment that of these contrasting magnitudes the smaller might be the greater to them as men ". That was a first conception of glorious appeal, and he was not deprived of time and room enough to make the best of it ; but on this occasion also, as in the remarkable short story mentioned just now, the conception was never quite realized. It hovered about the novelist rather than burned within him ; it was as if he only half, or less than half, understood what he was on the verge of achieving, or at least could illustrate in a sentence thirteen years later. I do not protest so much that he failed in an attempt of sublime paradox as that he did not really get near it. The astronomer is there, and the love story is there, but they are not a marriage. So long as Swithin and Viviette met at all, with the proper allowance of difficulties and exaltations and misfortunes, even with an ivied tower as part of their romance, the book would be of much the same status ; as it is, the astronomy makes an attractive side-show, even if the hero has to be kept to it. " At eight o'clock

she insisted upon his ascending the tower for observations, in strict pursuance of the idea on which their
marriage had been based, namely, that of restoring
regularity to his studies." Unless we take it that an
uncertain groping for a comedy gives a twist of meaning
to *Two on a Tower*, and even if we do, this is not good
enough ; well might the equatorial be unscrewed and
the stand taken down, for the starry heavens remain
aloof, the author has kept them aloof from the characters and their social arrangements. And yet, when
he was not involved in the trade of novel-making,
Hardy was the very man to bring together in imaginative realisings the lives of mortal men and the science
or the legend of the stars.

" ' We are forgetting the comet,' said St. Cleeve."
And that is in the long run what Hardy does in this
troublesome novel, which was doomed to be blamed
less on that account than because of alleged unfair-
ness to the dignity of bishops ; even though that was
the ground of complaint, it should never have been
given could Hardy have lived up to his genius and his
admirable if amateur devotion to astronomy. " Caeli
enarrant "—he might not have been willing to proceed
from these familiar words to the assumption that the
stars declare the glory of God, but he should not have
disclosed that he knew the wonder of the work and
proposed it in relation to two imagined people of some
note only to let it all drift by. " Then by means of
the instrument at hand, they travelled together from
the earth to Uranus and the mysterious outskirts of the
solar system ; from the solar system to a star in the
Swan, the nearest fixed star in the northern sky ;
from the star in the Swan to remoter stars ; thence to

the remotest visible ; till the ghastly chasm which they had bridged by a fragile line of sight was realized by Lady Constantine." But nothing came of it all in the end. However, Hardy was for a moment within sight of a high romance or symbolical fresco such as, to the best of my knowledge, no English novelist has produced ; something at once more truly tragic and apposite to the mystery of man than the various well-contrived thrillers, which he could not have written at all, on the moon, Mars and modern politics.

No man who wrote so much fiction for the satisfying of the large public as Hardy did in his period as a novelist can be expected to have produced all of it for permanence. That public was to be attracted and held, very often, by the allusion of the moment, and by the enacting and analysing of those fashions outward or inward which were in bloom just then. It is discernible, besides, that Hardy who had come from a country life of an ancient or tardy manner into the centre of things, and was writing with the awareness that his readers were generally there before he arrived, was studious to appear as a master of the way of the world, a member of modern society. That necessary piece of literary acting went down well enough for the moment, but it was bound in the long run to look like what it was. The strained effort for modernity is left by time as an incongruity, which may be seized upon with joy by the friendly idler. " Artificial Teeth, on the united Principles of Capillary Attraction and Atmospheric Pressure.—Mr. Gray, Member of the Royal College of Surgeons, in London, has been requested, by his humane friends . . ." " Consolation to the Tremulous Writer.—The Public may look to this most unique Invention as an inestimable source of comfort to those who experience any difficulties in the command of the pen ; occasioned by tremour in nervous affection, heat or climate, agitation of spirits. . . . Made in elastic gold, 25s. each." These were modernisms once, calculated to blaze with novelty. And there is a touch of their style in a good deal that Hardy, not at his best but keeping his machinery going, offered the reader of fifty, or sixty or more years ago. It is sometimes in the phrase or the form of statement ; sometimes in the details caught into the picture, as in bad human-document paintings ; sometimes in the erudition also pressed into service ; and even in the proverbial philosophy which found its way into the psychological declarations of this observer of men and women. The complaint of Coventry Patmore and others against their admired and beloved romancer, that he *would* deform his pages with neologisms trans-ferred thither from the region of " science ", might have been deepened into an arraignment of his addic-tion to the temporary behind such terms. To sum up, it is no wonder that a quantity of Hardy's fiction is out of date and unlikely to recover, that even his great novels are a little speckled with the mortality of the deliberately modern ; but when we reflect on the tre-mendous host of later Victorian novels which, once famous or not, have now ceased to speak the language that once excited the hour, and indeed have simply vanished, this is no such matter. Hardy with his half-dozen masterpieces still eloquent and distinct can afford to have shed away what he did with less passion or liberty of mind.

X

THE NOVELS : ELEMENTS OF ACHIEVEMENT

By the number and variety of essays on Hardy's achievement in the principal Wessex Novels, some of them extending into substantial volumes, it is easily seen that he has been considered for over half a century as one of the moving forces of his age. The comparison of his tales in their technical parts with those of other novelists does not greatly affect this position, and it would not diminish his lure for studious critics if it were proved that some of his rivals could work with more of brilliance or ease in dialogue, or unfold their series of incidents with less of jerky surprise, or draw more dangerous and ambiguous villains or less whaleboned society charmers. The signs are that in the unlikely event of Hardy's books ceasing to have any general readers, they would still be pursued and correlated and interpreted by an inner circle independent of period. Perhaps the parallel would be discoverable among the dramatists who were contemporary with Shakespeare : the multitude of playgoers has long since moved away from the tragedies of Webster and of Ford, whose genius nevertheless is magnetic to those who have natural and trained sympathies for its comprehension.

In the simplest aspect, it is scarcely possible to

imagine a time when no one will be wanting to meet
Tess, there where she stands not so much for her
personal tragedy as for the English country girl, a
figure as beautiful as those in Keats's " Ode to
Autumn " and more distinctly related to these our
tilled fields, our needs and our processes. " The
women — or rather girls, for they were mostly young
— wore drawn cotton bonnets with great flapping cur-
tains to keep off the sun, and gloves to prevent their
hands being wounded by the stubble. There was
one wearing a pale pink jacket, another in a cream-
coloured tight-sleeved gown, another in a petticoat as
red as the arms of the reaping-machine ; and others,
older, in the brown-rough ' wropper ' or over-all. . . .
Her binding proceeds with clock-like monotony. From
the sheaf last finished she draws a handful of ears,
parting their tips with her left palm to bring them
even. Then stooping low she moves forward, gathering the corn with both hands against her knees, and
pushing her left gloved hand under the bundle to
meet the right on the other side, holding the corn in
an embrace like that of a lover. She brings the ends
of the bond together, and kneels on the sheaf while
she ties it, beating back her skirts now and then when
lifted by the breeze. A bit of her naked arm is visible
between the buff leather of the gauntlet and the sleeve
of her gown ; and as the day wears on its feminine
smoothness becomes scarified by the stubble, and
bleeds. At intervals she stands up to rest, and to retie
her disarranged apron, or to pull her bonnet straight.
Then one can see the oval face of a handsome young
woman with deep dark eyes and long heavy clinging
tresses, which seem to clasp in a beseeching way any-

thing they fall against. The cheeks are paler, the teeth more regular, the red lips thinner than is usual in a country-bred girl."

Or again, so long as human beings are moved by the quality of the life of tree and wood, and find it a waking dream to step aside from their own affairs into the other world of forest branches, they will not be forgetful of Hardy, not because he is the word-painter of some famous elm or some exquisite runnelled glade, but because he has seen the woodland and de-fined others' seeing in the bewildering lines and hues of its complexity. His witness is true, but such truth is difficult and unusual. " In front lay the brown leaves of last year, and upon them some yellowish green ones of this season that had been prematurely blown down by the gale. Above stretched an old beech, with vast arm-pits, and great pocket-holes in its sides where branches had been removed in past times ; a black slug was trying to climb it. Dead boughs were scattered about like ichthyosauri in a museum, and beyond them were perishing woodbines resembling old ropes.

" From the other window all she could see were more trees, in jackets of lichen and stockings of moss. At their roots were stemless yellow fungi like lemons and apricots, and tall fungi with more stem than stool. Next were more trees close together, wrestling for existence, their branches disfigured with wounds re-sulting form their mutual rubbings and blows. It was the struggle between these neighbours that she had heard in the night. Beneath them were the rotting stumps of those of the group that had been vanquished long ago, rising from their mossy setting like black

teeth from green gums. Further on were other tufts
of moss in islands divided by the shed leaves—variety
upon variety, dark green and pale green : moss like
little fir-trees, like plush, like malachite stars ; like
nothing on earth except moss."

And then besides these intensely patient and
strongly living studies in the open (the novels abound
in them and in a thousand and one glimpses resembling
them) Hardy in his right road brings us those portraits
of human worth and integrity which cannot soon fail
to inspire the thoughtful. The verse of Bunyan expresses such people of his, " Who would true valour
see, Let him come hither " ; and Tess, and Farmer
Oak, and Diggory Venn the reddleman and Giles
Winterborne are not likely to be changed with the
variations of taste or interest for some time to come.
They are the children of light. Their ways are involved with much of inglorious and unprofitable incident, but their honest and fearless natures, which
are not thrust upon us as examples, take no infection
and claim no reward. If it is a novelist's privilege to
strengthen the hearts of his readers, then Hardy, so
often waved aside as one who only thickens the en-
circling gloom, has made good use of it ; for he has
honoured the kind of characters who may best meet
the shocks of circumstance apparently more liable to
occur to mankind as the race grows more mechanically
minded. They stand for an unostentatious creed of
simplicity and endurance, and, " when the world is
burning", they assert in all they are and all they intend
the noble nature which man has offered to the fates.

I cannot but believe that these Hardyan figures,
ever beckoning to new watchers, will lead them on

through the windings and crossings of his narrations, no matter how artificial these may be or seem to be at one point or another ; he may sometimes shape their course through improbabilities, he may slow it down with something of tediousness in the disclosure of a situation, but it would be strange if one did not desire to go with them and follow out to the end what happened to them. Moreover, they are seen from time to time as the participants in scenes of crisis as sharply complete and urgent as the imagination of any of our novelists has fashioned. Some of these scenes are extraordinary in their wild force, which arises through the deliberate, authoritative way of the mind that puts them before us, and gives us the feeling of looking in through some chink at a happening quite beyond our experiences and terribly real and determined. The contrivances of Hardy for the wonder of the audience, and still for the continuation of suspense, may often be summed up as melodrama, but his best invention in this part of his craft is of a deeper perception. When Eustacia Vye is standing in the night storm on lonely Blackbarrow, herself in commotion and profound shadows, longing for the benediction of Heaven, one light is seen in the blackness. It is the light from the cottage of a poor woman, who at least should be (one would think) no agent of more blackness ; but when we are allowed to see the interior which that light commands in all its detail, the ray is identified as that of a haunting and in a way inescapable malignity. Susan Nunsuch, bewitched herself with the persuasion that Eustacia means mischief to her boy and can set it working from her dark paths, is found ceremonially melting a curiously elaborate wax image

of the person, in order to bring upon her " powerless-
ness, atrophy and annihilation ". The novelist of
course precedes this with his allusion to superstition,
but as the work goes on with minute exactness and
singleness the night side of Nature involves the
imagination ; and, just as the binder of the spell is
described as accompanying her inspired activity with
" a murmur of words ", so the prose of the master
acquires an incantatory and hypnotic insistency. It is
like some burring and whirring of a thing in a hateful
dream of ghosts. " From her work-basket in the
window-seat the woman took a paper of pins, of the
old long and yellow sort, whose heads were disposed
to come off at their first usage. These she began to
thrust into the image in all directions, with apparently
excruciating energy. Probably as many as fifty were
thus inserted, some into the head of the wax model,
some into the shoulders, some into the trunk, some
upwards through the soles of the feet, till the figure was
completely permeated with pins. . . . As the wax
dropped into the fire a long flame arose from the spot,
and curling its tongue round the figure eat still further
into its substance. A pin occasionally dropped with
the wax, and the embers heated it red as it lay."
Nothing in the old ballads with their familiar ghosts
is more decisive than that, which is as it were a gar-
goyle noticed in its stupid solidity in the edifice of the
tragedy, causing nothing, yet of a piece with what is
being caused. It is a stroke of power released from
a lifelong acquaintance with the primitive and its
peculiar intelligence, it is a profoundly understood
means of art, a resort to imaginative truth in order to
mass and enforce the smaller details of the apparently

literal and variable story. If they are to be seen all in one red and pitiless glare, they might be imaged in such an inhuman form as this.

The greatness of Hardy's novels as a whole, including but transcending all the passages of the kinds noted, has been sometimes stated in the fact that he was originally an architect, and the impression that they bear a relation to architectural edifices. That may be among the most practical ways of briefly distinguishing what it is that raises them and maintains their stature and even majesty above the general level and scope of English novels. Together with his concatenations of rival and friend, of promise and disillusion, of humour and misery and beauty and ruin, Hardy has some other work to do in the novel as he comes to envisage it ; it is the work of a spirit in love with form—but form is a dangerous and inadequate word, so far as this subtly and richly endowed nature is concerned. Besides, though the conditions under which he was obliged to serve the fiction-loving public excuse some obscurity or discontinuity of design, the fact remains that Hardy's novels do not always yield a conspicuous view of form, in the meaning of definite trace, outline and balance. Had he written them with a firm resolve to give them such order as he was trained to value in his original profession, the draughtsmanship would have been visibly different. There was no predilection on his part for irregularity or disproportion or mere violence in the production of a work of fiction : on the contrary. Mrs. Frederic Harrison mentions what he said on being shown a short story : " He wrote that as he read it he did so with fear lest the catastrophe should be overweighted, should be too strong for the

opening of the story which had been made in half-
tones ". Long after he had ceased to write novels,
he was heard to complain of novelists who broke the
" rules " of novel-writing—a code which he accepted
much as mariners accept the rules of their tradition ;
perhaps he had become more inclined to esteem such
rules as he extended his actual practice in fiction. The
day had been when he trusted in only one, according
to an anecdote of his early life by Mr. B. F. Lock. One
day in the Seventies Mr. Lock was walking with Horace
Moule at Weymouth. " Just as they entered the
Esplanade, there rose from one of the public seats a
shy young man . . . who had recently published a
novel called *Under the Greenwood Tree.* They walked
along the Esplanade, and the young novelist and the
brilliant Saturday Reviewer discussed across him the
question whether there were any, and what, canons of
constructive art which ought to be binding on the
creative artist of fiction on the practice of his art. The
young novelist maintained there was one and only one."

Whatever that giant canon was, and whatever points
of good husbandry in the elaboration of a story became
" correct " to Hardy as he advanced, it is impossible
to make his novels square with the lay-out of any minor
literary system. He heard too much as he went. He
was something of a Coleridge, and if the design of his
book were in a broad way to have been a cathedral or
a theatre of our world, with curious relationships and
correspondences effigied, pillared, vaulted, towered, yet
it might at any moment open out into an immensity of
infinite day or night,—

> So he would build his altar in the fields,
> And the blue sky his fretted dome would be.

It is Hardy's way to accept his visionary moments without anxiety for his effect. He does not expunge for safety's sake. His known habit of preparing brief schedules for his works is not a hindrance as well as a help to him ; and the form which they plot out in a few names, dates and distances is not the only one in his mind. He is aware of a powerful impulse recurrent in himself which causes, in its freedom and its exaltation, another and in the end a conformable effect through his narrative. Here he will be moved to a strenuous rendering of something in great Nature apart from the encampments of man, there he will declare and describe a tempest of the human heart or a working of apprehended universalities in similar access of mastery ; and when these passages have formed a series, they have equally composed a shape of considerable organic certainty, like the coming and going of a splendid sunset or a high tide.

The great artist, it has been asserted, is often seemingly dominated by his subject, or so lost in contemplation of it that he has no interest in the possible bewilderment of onlookers. Blake, who could laugh at life, did not draw the terrifying " Ghost of a Flea " with laughter or with any care that he might be laughed at ; he was rapt as Macbeth was when the deeps opened and he could see. Hardy, a humorist in daily life, was similarly intent on his prophetic discernings, and the question whether anyone else should perhaps find them amusing in reference to their surroundings did not trouble him. The episode of the dairymaids and Angel Clare provides an instance of his strange afflatus, when the rivers of natural force suddenly sound in tumult through his detail-work.

" The air of the sleeping-chamber seemed to palpitate with the hopeless passion of the girls. They writhed feverishly under the oppressiveness of an emotion thrust on them by cruel Nature's law—an emotion which they had neither expected nor desired. The incident of the day had fanned the flame that was burning the inside of their hearts out, and the torture was almost more than they could endure. The differences which distinguished them as individuals were abstracted by this passion, and each was but portion of one organism called sex." He continues, not departing from the figures of his story into a detached essay, but rather making them their own psychologists and equal to all that can be suffered and spoken of fatal love. They are dairymaids, and they are also tragic wraiths, seen as more representative than even that Duchess of Malfi whom Hardy had understood. But, when the wave is spent, the writer is not concerned to explain it away. He would have heard a critic specifying the Bathos in the next of his circumstances—" They tossed and turned on their little beds, and the cheese-wring dripped monotonously downstairs "—without agreeing or disagreeing. In actual life, the arrival of some more unsettling crisis than common, of some startling light on what we are and what defies all our aim and provision, is apt to be succeeded by such Bathos as that. " It is a practical joke at which even its author cannot brighten up enough to laugh "—Chesterton was referring to the black flag on the ugly tower which Angel and 'Liza-Lu saw at the close of the story of *Tess*. But the words cover many less conspicuous touches of the colourless in the wake of the flame of passion and act as Hardy's imagination presents it.

In even a story calculated to do nothing more than amuse a leisure hour—in *The Hand of Ethelberta*, for instance, that comedy in chapters—the consciousness of Hardy is wont to be drawn by the magnetism of this extraordinary globe on which we pass until he has gone beyond the bounds of normally safe construction. This is not an advantage, it may be, to the novel in question, but it is a help towards the understanding of Hardy's work altogether ; we are assured of a freedom of mind which cannot reject the sudden invitation of some glorious sight or spiritual music because of a neat scheme in progress. It is possible to regard these mighty interpolations as a sort of inverse Bathos, if we look at them from the standpoint of an everyday literary utility. We may smile at the passage which follows a careful paragraph about Ethelberta's bargaining for a ride up to Coomb Castle—" without the needless sacrifice either of dignity or cash ". We know her outlay—three shillings for the hire of a donkey. The passage into which the donkey carries the lady is certainly incongruous, in its immediate surroundings ; but what a passage of representation it is ! The hand of Thomas Hardy alone has shaped out and coloured and supplied with the right resonances such scenes as these : " Far below on the right hand it was a fine day, and the silver sunbeams lighted up a many-armed inland sea which stretched round an island with fir-trees and gorse, amid brilliant crimson heaths wherein white paths and roads occasionally met the eye in dashes and zigzags like flashes of lightning. Outside, where the broad Channel appeared, a berylline and opalized variegation of ripples, currents, deeps and shallows, lay as fair under the sun as a New Jerusalem, the shore being of gleaming sand. Upon the radiant heather bees and butterflies were busy, she knew, and the birds on that side were just beginning their autumn songs.

" On the left, quite up to her position, was dark and cloudy weather, shading a valley of heavy greens and browns, which at its further side rose to meet the sea in tall cliffs, suggesting even here at their back how terrible were their aspects seaward in a growling south-west gale. Here grassed hills rose like knuckles gloved in dark olive, and little plantations between them formed a still deeper and sadder monochrome. A zinc sky met a leaden sea on this hand, the low wind groaned and whined, and not a bird sang."

Among the many painters whose pictures he had converted into part of his being, perhaps Turner struck him as deep as any, and it is with Turner that his audacity in finding means of denoting his conceptions places him. His instinct, working through a seldom rivalled machinery of imaginative resource (nothing seems to have caught his eye or any of his five or more senses without being for ever ready to serve his vision), was to maintain in art the fierce and jubilant working of life which he perceived even in seemingly static figures of the external world. The form for which he set his course in his great fiction was a rhythmic union of that dramatic immensity of creative restlessness, a background with a fiery and eloquent spirit in it, and of the symbolic ardours and sufferings of human persons perhaps haunted beyond their own actions by strange dynasts. It was a brave attempt, and even Hardy's warmest admirers, even he himself might well admit that his most intense fightings for this form in all its grandeur and choric symmetry never quite achieved the masterpiece which he could foreshadow in the first onset of an idea. He was not capable of giving to his human types, in their talk and outlook, a pervading quality of mystery and eternal presence such as he could suggest in the psychology of things called inanimate. His business was, after all, to entertain the larger class of readers, and they could not have long endured figures of epic cast, even had he been able to people his Wessex with such emanations. His people had to feed the chickens, cook Sunday dinner and catch trains.

When he wrote *Jude the Obscure*, Hardy was less interested in the *King Lear* kind of panorama than he was in some of his other novels. Several great spectacles of the land wherein the characters move are indeed to be found here, but they are bounded and terminated with obvious firmness. The book was, more than any others by him, a protest against the inherited ideas of society, and for all its episodic length and minuteness of array it is a slashing direct attack. It comes nearer to the outline of the " average " successful novel than the others, and could possibly be called one of Hardy's letters to *The Times* extended and backed up with a *dossier*. In the matter of drawing attention to the scarcely tolerable burdens imposed by nineteenth-century opinions upon the exceptional man and woman without " advantages ", this novel must be reckoned a performance of singular urgency and piercing impact. And yet its form, though Hardy was never before so sure in his conduct of the story, is a sign that he had arrived at the last lap of his run in fiction. The unexpected, which had flashed into his former stories with such magnificence, coming like a gale of innumerable messages again and again from the depths of nature, had almost deserted him at the age of fifty ; and yet this might prove a false alarm, if he were freed from the tedious necessity of writing confinedly under the regulations of the novel-buying public.

In *Jude the Obscure*, with all its precision of purpose, announced beforehand in that bleak little motto " The letter killeth ", it is seen that Hardy at the culmination of his prose studies was still liable to have trouble in saying simple things simply. When Jude at last reached Christminster, " his first want being a lodging he scrutinized carefully such localities as seemed to offer on inexpensive terms the modest type of accommodation he demanded ". Many critics have played with these Johnsonian pomposities in Hardy's writings, and a collection of them would be as good as the *Deformities of Dr. Johnson*. Mr. Arthur Symons, who has noticed them, goes further, and turns away from their " lethargy " to the " faultless and uncommon use of words " which the springing of emotion could release in our author. It may be that Hardy's love and exact memory of Carlyle's work was a mixed blessing to him in his own.

The few hundred words in which Arthur Symons (in 1906) paid his tribute to the " genius of Thomas Hardy " are among the best of all the myriads that have been written in answer to the question compelled by the Wessex Novels. " How is it that what at first seem, and may well be, defects, uncouthnesses, bits of formal preaching, grotesque ironies of event and idea, come at last to seem either good in themselves or good where they are, a part of the man if not of the artist ? " Mr. Symons sets out Hardy's chief characteristics as those of " a story-teller of the good old kind ", able to work out a plot so that the attention is held ; of a philosopher, whose commentary may sometimes fight against the pleasure of the narrative ; and next, " the poet, and you need look for nothing beyond ".   But, we may ask, what is this power in whom the gifts of the novelist are said to culminate ? Is it he who enriches and deepens the action with so many beautiful counterfeits of place and moment and mortal lineament—sometimes in the direct course of his tale, often in sidelights, illustrations and quick peculiar compassions ? Certainly few novelists have painted portraits of men and women in words with such fidelity and such resource as well as topographical subjects in lavish variety ; yet this fine art, perhaps, in its detached appearance, is not the force of poetry to which Mr. Symons referred. The poet in Hardy who governs all is still further on : he is a spirit of earth and the other elements, an apprehension of a solitary kind.   " How often, and for how profound a reason, does he not show us to ourselves, not as we or our fellows see us, but out of the continual observation of humanity which goes on in the wary and inquiring eyes of birds, the meditative and indifferent regard of cattle, and the deprecating aloofness and inspection of sheep ? "

XI

" THE DYNASTS "

OCCASION smiled on the story-writer, the philosopher and the poet through the circumstances in which habitual delivery of novels in sections ceased to be his work. In all the world of story, little has been found in any presentation to cast a stronger spell than the annals of Napoleon; and besides their excitements and astonishments, their complexity of what might have been and what was, they have always exercised the enquiring spirit, and called forth the music and memorial of poets. Parts of the story had taken hold of Hardy's mind in boyhood, some through his reading and some through the occasional startling talk of people round about who had seen Napoleon's rise and fall. The rest had grown on him in his manhood, from one cause or another,—his readings in Romantic poetry, his thinkings on the riddle of the individual and the universal, his love of England. To realize, the more he investigated the library of European history or the scenes of actions which had depended on British fortitude and political ideals, that the nation's leadership and tenacity had been so poorly honoured by the world was a challenge. He took it. " The slight regard paid to English influence and action throughout the struggle by so many Continental writers " stirred

him to enlarge his local enthusiasm across all the
borders of Wessex and as far as the ends of the kingdom.

It is remarkable that at the same period two English
poets should have written on Napoleon in the great
style, and with similar insistency on the power, abstraction, doom which appeared to have burst into the
life of men through Napoleon as an embodiment.

> Cannon his name,
> Cannon his voice, he came—

so Meredith spoke in his vision, and again,

> While laurelled over his Imperial form,
> Forth from her bearded tube of lacquey brass,
> Reverberant notes and long blew volant Fame ;

and still,

> The Necessitated came, as comes from out
> Electric ebon lightning's javelin-head,
> Threatening annihilation in the revealed
> Founts of our being.

The terms there used are not far out of the line of
Hardy's main suggestions for the nature of the Napoleonic man, a form, a weapon, a flash of lightning, and
never in the deeper sense more capable of choice than

> the brazen rod that stirs the fire
> Because it must.

However Hardy was moved by his chance to write
the chronicles of his native land in a crowning achievement, to reanimate the heroism of British aristocrat or
common people enduring year upon year of extreme
stress and enigma, a still more acceptable opportunity
called him on when he saw the subject of *The Dynasts*
as his own. In this field he could, indeed he must
deploy a formation of reflections on the underlying
nature of things. For so many years he had watched

the battle of the creeds, the questionings of the natural-
ists, the yearnings of the imaginative ; so long he had
perused his Greek tragedians and their only rivals our
own Elizabethans, with his mind bent on some presid-
ing metaphor to fit the condition of humanity as he
was inclined to view it through history—a wearisome
condition, as Fulke Greville said. Hardy the student
of classical literature, of theological or sceptical mani-
festoes, might now come out into the open much more
than was ever possible in a novel even like *Tess*,—the
events and characters before him being of such actual
and familiar importance to everybody ; the scene, the
world. The momentary hints of crass casualty and
gods that kill us for their sport should now be spun
together into a semblance of a *De rerum natura*, a
stupendous dream (with a method) to explain how our
race had undergone and would still undergo such
apparently capricious typhoons and pestilences and
maimings as the story of *The Dynasts* exemplifies.

Perhaps Hardy would not have written *The Dynasts*
at all in its extant shape, the shape in the main of his
cosmogony, had one or another of the Victorian poets
he honoured gone further in their intellectual disputa-
tion. The matter might be explored at great length,
but a pair of examples will serve. Matthew Arnold
had long since made a fearless and a disturbing comment, at the close of " Resignation " : after depicting
the whole look of things, our own courses, the appearances of nature as a mask of bearing rather than
rejoicing, he wrote,

> Not milder is the general lot
> Because our spirits have forgot,
> In action's dizzying eddy whirl'd,
> The something that infects the world.

What was that Thing Immanent, in Hardyan phrase ?
Robert Browning, in whom Hardy thought he saw a
poet of frighteningly clear thought beguiling the public
towards it with displays of lusty, festive and appetizing
cheer, had in his latest volume attempted " surview of
things " in the poem entitled " Reverie " ; therein,
assuming that he had gathered the evidence of earth's
and heaven's wide show, he

> Could say " Thus much is clear,
> Doubt annulled thus much : I know
>
> " All is effect of cause :
>   As it would, has willed and done
> Power : and my mind's applause
>   Goes passing laws each one
> To Omnipotence lord of laws."
>
> Head praises, but heart refrains
>   From loving's acknowledgement.
> Whole losses outweigh half-gains :
>   Earth's good is with evil blent :
> Good struggles but evil reigns.

And much more, in the way of a new theory of life—
yet, as it emerges, it proves reverie more than insight :
the " loveless Power " is to become Love at last—
" if not on the homely earth, Then yonder, worlds
away ".

Hardy therefore, necessarily striving for a background of fate and creation which should be seen as
the continuous agency of all his many historical beings
and their doings, and heard as a chorus of essential
unity beyond the confusion of voices from a world of
man at war, was aware that he was not unaccompanied
by seers, and equally that they left him on the road
with a good deal to accomplish by himself. He knew
very well that the best in this kind are but shadows,

and yet he agreed strongly with the direction of so
much Victorian thought on the ages ; he therefore
based his *Dynasts* in a First Cause other than that of
the churches, meaning this with all his might if ever
he meant anything.   This Cause,[1] the Immanent Will,
a Power

> Working unconsciously, as heretofore,
> Eternal artistries in Circumstance,

might be known one day as the secret of all our " com-
plicated web of melancholy mirth ".   He refers to the
twentieth century's ideas of God as consonant with
this ; " and the abandonment of the masculine pro-
noun in allusions to the First or Fundamental Energy
seemed a necessary and logical consequence of the long
abandonment by thinkers of the anthropomorphic
conception of the same ".   About this automatic It,
Hardy naturally assembled a number of imaginary
" Intelligences, called Spirits ", through whom according to their different qualities the supernatural debate
on what was happening in consequence or in forecast
of events, might be variously and profoundly carried on.

There is yet another element of sublimity and
mystery in the framework of *The Dynasts* which has
been frequently marked and praised, but which will

---

[1] While *The Dynasts* was in course of publication, Hardy read
McTaggart's *Some Dogmas of Religion*, and sent him a congratulatory letter.   " My own personal connection with the subject
is merely that in . . . *The Dynasts* I have vaguely sketched a
philosophic basis . . . which is not far from what you suggest by
your negative conclusions."   In thanking the same author for *The
Relations of Time and Eternity*, the poet wrote, " I have the
common-place feeling that the Timeless Reality knows no difference between what we call good and what we call evil, which are
only apparent to the consciousness of organic nature generally —
which consciousness is a sort of unanticipated accident."   Hardy
frankly admits that he is no trained philosopher (" though I do read
Mind occasionally.")

always compel fresh admiration. By way of intro-
ducing it once more, let me turn aside from Hardy's
epic drama a moment and find the heroine of *Villette*
crossing the Channel. Before she faltered down into
her cabin, for purely physical reasons, she envisaged
" the continent of Europe, like a wide dreamland, far
away. Sunshine lay on it, making the long coast one
line of gold ; tiniest tracery of clustered town and
snow-gleaming tower, of woods deep massed, of heights
serrated, of smooth pasturage and veiny stream, em-
bossed the metal-bright prospect. For background,
spread a sky, solemn and dark blue, and grand with
imperial promise, soft with tints of enchantment—
strode from north to south a God-bent bow, an arch
of hope." This lovely, living, panoramic vision is
akin to the many aerial views of Europe shown in ivory
brilliance or in sombre mass by Hardy in what are
called the stage directions of *The Dynasts* ; yet those
revelations have something more. Carlyle, revelling
in " The Hero as Divinity ", wrote of the Gods and
the slain Giant Ymer, that they constructed a world
with his corpse. " His blood made the Sea ; his flesh
was the Land, the Rocks his bones ; of his eyebrows
they formed Asgard their Gods'-dwelling ; his skull
was the great blue vault of Immensity, and the brains
of it became the Clouds." This myth of the world
also comes near Hardy's recurring " preternatural
transparency " ; yet that has something more.

For Hardy, concentrating all his matured gifts as
an artist into these marvellous delineations and model-
lings of his European scenes, showing as in the clear
light of the mystic the most beautiful and the most
singular forms of civilization and country, is not only

illustrating the places and the circumstances of the action. He is not merely adding a striking touch of mythology. He is reporting what he feels to be the most convincing idea of the " something " that Arnold mentioned, an unconscious Will expressed in all these works of time, geological or such as shine in a shop-window, and energetic everywhere, in the lovely and the unlovely, in the exquisite and the hideous. So he anatomizes all, with a ray of brief duration but thrilling keenness, and the face of men and things is lost in the recognition of the origin and occupant of them all. " The controlling Immanent Will appears therein, as a brain-like network of currents and ejections, twitching, interpenetrating, entangling and thrusting hither and thither the human forms."

It is not always recollected how large a proportion of *The Dynasts* is written in prose. Considered apart from the philosophical purposes of some of it, this writing alone shows Hardy glorying in his strength and in his liberty to please himself. The restriction which his business called for was excellent for him ; he had to employ that laconic faculty of his which had not been his mainstay in the lengthening out of novels, to engrave his communications as sharply and compulsively into the reader's mind as maps and plans and commands. To some extent, he devised a new style for his introductory and his transitional para-graphs, a style vivid with detail and full of rhythmic attack. Yet this is only one of the means by which he endeavoured to sustain without sameness his " epic drama of the war with Napoleon in three parts, nine-teen acts, and one hundred and thirty scenes ".

From his reading of Shakespeare he had gathered

the methods of technical variety—the prose of the
dumb show or device or interlude of description and
definition ; the prose of dialogue, perhaps in the
mouths of the humbler persons of the drama, perhaps
in contrast to the prominent and public scenes, when
characters withdraw as it were into private delibera-
tion and conspiracy. Blank verse makes the principal
fabric of the rest, and is not always equal to the task,
unless we regard the numerous passages which amble
along and betray the author's uninterested transcrip-
tions of unavoidable historical information as proper
to the full scheme of a chronicler. Hardy knew his
Scott from early days, and Scott's lays of chivalry are
an alternation of the emphatic and energetic with the
jogtrot and conventional. Still, the most stubborn
partisans of *The Dynasts* may concede that Hardy's
blank verse was not so flexible, ample and musical as it
might have been. Now and then he brings in a passage
of ten-syllabled verse in rhyme, as when the semi-
choruses of spirits are to chant forth their eye-witness
accounts of the line of battle. But these again are
often vocal in lyrical stanzas and odes, the movement
of which is quite other than that of the other verse.
" Aerial music ", the words prefixed by Hardy to such
strange intonations, are the best words for the effect
he creates.

For the observer of English poetics the lyrical experiments in *The Dynasts* are particularly interesting,
some of them being adaptations of metres which
Hardy loved in the hands of other men. In the Fore
Scene, the Recording Angel is heard to read from his
book the news of crisis, and the Rumours follow him ;
this they all do in a stanza which is that of William

Barnes in " Woak Hill ", with a modification in the rhyme at the close, though it is still continued on one sound all through.

> Now mellow-eyed Peace is made captive,
>   And vengeance is chartered
> To deal forth its dooms on the Peoples
>   With sword and with spear.
>
> Men's musings are busy with forecasts
>   Of musters and battle,
> And visions of shock and disaster
>   Rise red on the year.

This result is far away from the wistfulness of Barnes's cadences. The same transformation occurs when Hardy plays upon the rondeau form, so much practised by elegant writers in his time, and gives the Chorus of Pities the battle-piece beginning " The skies fling flame on this ancient land." The famous Choruses of the Years, the Pities, the Sinister Spirits on the eve of the battle of Waterloo, in which the incidental havoc of human combat in the humble world of mole, snail, butterfly and bud is announced with so much nervous acuteness, are versified in the pattern of Browning's " The Statue and the Bust " ; but Hardy's theme sounds forth in tones scarcely audible in that piece. From Campbell and Scott, from the hymn-book, from Browning and Swinburne and Tennyson's " Maud " Hardy caught metrical impulses which he knew would be appropriate to his vast argument and which he converted into his own manner of stress and current and shock. It may be suitably added here that he did not try to exclude resemblances of atmosphere or thought or tone to writings which had been long known to him. Shakespeare's way of combining the grandeur

and zeal of heroic characters in action with the odd
realisms of military life, the evocation of the far-
influencing hour amid the trivial and ridiculous, is
reflected in his book ; the matter-of-fact vein of many
speeches in unadorned, unexciting iambics suggests
the translation of *Wallenstein* by Coleridge ; there are
Byronic touches (Byron's Dynasts were " cut-throats "
and as such they sometimes figure in Hardy) ; and
Shelley's poetic dramas are visible in or through
the supernatural commentators on Hardy's stage.
" Hardy ", says Dr. W. R. Rutland, " was indebted,
not directly to Aeschylus and Sophocles, but to the
amplification of the Attic chorus which Shelley introduced into *Prometheus Unbound*, and used again in
Hellas." If the genius of an ancient poet haunts the
composer of *The Dynasts* it is probably that of Lucretius,
who in his fifth book said in plain terms that the constitution of the world was imperfect, and the originative
force answerable for a great wrong, but communicates
the tremendous zest of being in this universe at all.
As for the historical works from which Hardy selected
the personalities, occurrences and conversations necessary to him, it was not required that he should have
appended a bibliography ; he seems to have thought
of doing so. A note or two refers to French authorities ; but the matter is fully inquired into, by Dr.
Rutland, with the evidence of Hardy's collection of
Napoleonic literature. Probably Hardy would wish
that the name of Southey should be associated with his
own venture, not only because Southey's *Life of Nelson*
(and conceivably *History of the Peninsular War*) gave
him materials, but because one or two of this writer's
poems on the wars of his time or before gave him satis-

faction—notably, those seemingly simple lines on the
" Battle of Blenheim ".

Scholars have already paid some attention [1] to the
vocabulary of *The Dynasts*, and indeed it deserves to
be discussed, being a fruit of the inventive energy
which flung up this mighty work. Like Browning and
Meredith, and we now can add Gerard Manley
Hopkins, Hardy was ever aware of the past, present
and future of the language. He had a tireless eye
and ear for the less known word, the less common
significance ; he had a restless determination to make
words embody, carry, illuminate his meaning, even
though, we are told, the " Immanent Will " is not
quite the precise term he wanted for his conception.
He was prepared to develop the dictionary ; and in
this connection we may revive the picture of him
calling on his old friend William Barnes, philologist
(and poet—but Barnes would have thought that much
the same thing).

Whoever opens *The Dynasts* at the Fore Scene,
which is itself such an expression as Barnes might
have approved in some measure, can hardly fail to be
struck by the unusualness of the diction. He reads of
" An automatic sense, Unweeting why or whence ",
of " the pulsion of the Byss ", of deeds being " nulled "
and earth in her labourings " kinged ", of " the Will-
webs " articulating the Prime, " that willed ere ware-
ness was ", of men as " jackaclocks . . . not fugled
by one Will, but function-free ", with many other such
unaccustomed words. If he feels them to be an im-

---

[1] In *The Times Literary Supplement* of February 14th, 1929,
Mr. George G. Loane specified three sorts of striking words used
here by Hardy—words used in a new sense ; new words ; old
words re-invented.

position on the purchaser, for really some of the criticisms occasioned amount to not much more than that, he had better waste no more time on *The Dynasts*. For the whole production is, and it must have been, characterized and completed in its nature by an innovation of word-choice. The two aspects of life which Hardy intends to portray and interpret are the tangible and the spectral, or the real and the phantasmal. The types of word which he wants for his principal utterances are thus the local, graphic, primitive, hard, and the psychological, subtle, abstract —between which two, in the progress of his theme, he may sometimes discover, recreate or compel a surprising relationship.

Intelligences, such as the attendant spirits of Hardy's overworld, are not the easiest beings for even a great poet to call into view and make effective to the audience; by their words only can he truly distribute to them such feigned difference of sense and scope as even the Coleridgean " willing suspension of disbelief " (quoted in his Preface) will count as true. The language of *The Dynasts* is out of the common mainly in consequence of this imaginative enterprise. These speakers are not men in the street. They are elemental and they are angelical. However we approach them, they are another race of beings, with great simplicity and unalterable wisdom ; they, seeing the central mystery as men in its control do not, discourse in a heightened and impassioned sort. For this illusion Hardy relies upon the impacts of Wessex or similar words with an undiminished force in the mention, and on terms with a Grecian or Latin magnitude of thought implicit in them. I do not understand how a poet's excursions beyond general bounds of knowledge or fancy should be reported except by a certain extension and rearrangement of the speech that serves for everyday purposes ; yet Hardy, especially in *The Dynasts*, has been blamed for sending us to our dictionaries. The Spirit of the Years is not likely to voice a judgment drawn from endless watching and accepting in the manner of one just starting up a car ; and when all is said and done, this idiom is not so perplexing as to nonplus our alert attention : or Shakespeare's occupation is gone too.

> Why must ye echo as mechanic mimes
> These mortal minions' bootless cadences,
> Played on the stops of their anatomy
> As is the mewling music on the strings
> Of yonder ship-masts by the unweeting wind,
> Or the frail tune upon this withering sedge
> That holds its papery blades against the gale ?
> —Men pass to dark corruption, at the best,
> Ere I can count five score : these why not now ?—
> The Immanent Shaper builds Its beings so
> Whether ye sigh their sighs with them or no !

Soon after the completed publication of *The Dynasts*, a " Sequelula " to it was delivered to the world by one of the few wits whose topical allusions even retain their zest. This parody by Sir Max Beerbohm includes all the adverse criticism on *The Dynasts* that has been produced in less antic forms elsewhere. Here, the philosophic position of It, and the manner of the phantom conferences upon that and its sublunary consequences, together with the dialect evolved by the poet for his mysteries, and the drudging blank verse into which his informative occasions lapse,— indeed, all the conspicuous phenomena of the epic-drama appear for judgment, except some important ones. As for the Something behind the scenes, the parodist expressed the obvious revolt of plain men against this, or any other fathoming for it : no man could ever get at It. As to its consequences or alleged manifestation in the human universe—" The spirit of Mr. Hardy is visible as a grey transparency swiftly interpenetrating the brain of the Spirit of the Years, and urging him in a particular direction to a particular point ", namely, the County Gaol at Casterbridge, Wessex. It is Christmas Day. But (as " the roof of the gaol becomes transparent, and the whole interior is revealed, like that of a beehive under glass ") the spirits observe a parade of convicts, and their warders, filing mechanically into the chapel. This unseasonable show convinces the Spirit of the Years, among the rest, that

> Automata these animalculae
> Are—puppets, pitiable jackaclocks,

and " he re-trajects himself into Space ". In short, " the sempiternal It " and its designs or attitudes are dismissed, and Hardy reprimanded for presumption in search of his Maker. But Hardy's defence is always that he attempts no formal philosophy, and that all men do receive philosophic and cosmic impressions of which they make some speculative use.

The parody does not deny Hardy's " dark skill in weaving word-patterns of subtle ideographies ", and he is called " a man of genius ". In fact, the cogitations made possible by the leading supposition in *The Dynasts* are not to be valued or avoided on the question whether that datum is the truth about the Will or not ; their excellence is in themselves, as lights thrown on the history of heroic man. But that history in the Napoleonic era, as Hardy tells it anew in his

devoted way, scene upon scene, mood upon mood, is
a not insignificant share of *The Dynasts* which does not
find its token in the " Sequelula ". Separately spoken
of, it is a glorious piece of work, a many-cargoed voyage
through the ocean of time ; where is its rival in our
language, in the way of a chronicle giving us, as in
life, as at our window this very morning or midnight,
the cities, the governments, the personages, speeches,
market-place or downland or shipboard episodes, ghost
stories, terrors, humours, small and great turns of
fortune of the Napoleonic wars ? Elsewhere we may
find one aspect or another opened to us with perhaps
greater knowledge and exacter discrimination, but here
is the epitome, and here especially the whole theatre
of those people and their quarrel is made. The music
of that theatre, besides, is such in its wildness, its
passion, its forlorn or fame-resounding depths as to
make Hardy a historian of the Wars more eloquent
than all—a prophetic bard. Even had the Overworld
and its contesting minstrelsy not been in his plan, there
would have been this lyrical intermission, these
vibrating and throbbing and marching passages by
whose rhythm the detail of so many a scene is gathered
into a higher emotional consonance. Then, truly,
Hardy enables us to discover with some certainty
" what it felt like to be there ".

Let his be the last word of this chapter. Compli-
mented by Edward Clodd on the terribly perceptive,
sympathetic " Chorus of the Years " in Act VI,
Scene VIII of Part Third, Hardy replied, " I must
send a line or two in answer to your letter. What you
remind me of—the lyrical account of the fauna of
Waterloo field on the eve of the battle—is, curiously

enough, the page that struck me, in looking back over
the book, as being the most original in it : though, of
course, a thing may be original without being good.
However, it does happen (so far as I know) in the many
treatments of Waterloo in literature those particular
personages who were present have never been alluded
to before."

XII

THE POEMS

In *Hardy of Wessex* that constant reader of this author, Professor Carl Weber, prints a table of Hardy's eight collections of poems, apart from *The Dynasts*, and arrives at the total number of items in them—918. Such an individual aggregate is not the biggest ever known, but it is sufficient to make any of us pause before producing any concise assertion about Hardy's poetic character. However, glance where we may among all those compositions extending over sixty years and more of experience, one thing makes itself felt. The prevailing attitude of the poet is the criticism of life. It is not so much an attitude as a toil and a pursuit.

For ideal beauty, as the subject of art, Hardy was very far from having any distaste, as many records of his life prove. He, most of all our novelists, alludes to the painters and their serenities, and were we to know how much the National Gallery has meant to individuals it might be that Thomas Hardy's case would be one of the most striking. The same applies to his delight in Palgrave's *Golden Treasury of Songs and Lyrics*, the selective rule of which was to feed the sense of beauty, to give pleasure, to perpetuate the eclectic treatment of one aspect of a subject at one

time. It is familiar also that Hardy had as much
love for the poems of Keats, who so often crystalled
lovely things in his deep calm acceptance, as for those
of Shelley, who was apt to see them frustrated or in
bad company. And in his prose Hardy is sometimes
found viewing one of the shows of life with the loiter-
ing and sweet contemplation which announce the
simple worship of the beautiful ; it need not be the
beautiful which has habitually been called so, but the
appreciation is the same :

" Somerset looked down on the mouth of the tunnel.
The popular commonplace that science, steam and
travel must always be unromantic and hideous, was
not proven at this spot. On either slope of the deep
cutting, green with long grass, grew drooping young
trees of ash, beech, and other flexible varieties, their
foliage almost concealing the actual railway which ran
along the bottom, its thin steel rails gleaming like silver
threads in the depths. The vertical front of the
tunnel, faced with brick that had once been red, was
now weather-stained, lichened, and mossed over in
harmonious rusty-browns, pearly greys, and neutral
greens, at the very base appearing a little blue-black
spot like a mouse-hole—the tunnel's mouth. . . . Mrs.
Goodman broke the silence by saying, ' If it were not
a railway we should call it a lovely dell.' "

As an observer of the beautiful, indeed, Hardy was
extraordinarily quick, and his sense was all the sharper
for his long training in the fine arts. It is of course
present throughout his poems, the visual gift, the
ability to seize with wonderful distinctness just what
makes a moment and a scene—colour, line, contrast,
correspondence, point of light or depth of shade ; no

poems contain more numerous flashes of " the forms
of things ", depicted with profound enjoyment even
when they were concerned in some bitterness of circumstance. But rarely will the poet be found to offer,
as ode or sonnet or elegy, an aesthetic impression con-
tentedly perfected for its own sake, sufficient in itself
without antiphon. He may imply that such poems
would have been a joy to write, as when he responds
" To a Movement in Mozart's E-flat Symphony ", of
which poignant piece these are the first stanza and
the last :

> Show me again the time
> When in the Junetide's prime
> We flew by meads and mountains northerly !—
> Yea, to such freshness, fairness, fulness, fineness, freeness,
> Love lures life on. . . .
>
> Show me again just this :
> The moment of that kiss
> Away from the prancing folk, by the strawberry-tree !—
> Yea, to such rashness, ratheness, rareness, ripeness, richness,
> Love lures life on.

The very metre which may be found recurrent
through Hardy's 918 poems, for all its changefulness,
declares the kind of poetry which it bears along. It is
seldom that which is most easily specified as iambic—
that processional pace which characterizes the best part
of Chaucer's poetry, of Wordsworth's, of Keats's—the
long-approved verse of English contemplative poets.
In such steady measure, the poised study of the beautiful may well receive a sort of static or statuesque
reward, and grace linger without disturbance, wisdom
stand written as over the porch of experience for ever.
We need not plunge into the still vexed questions of
prosody and its diagrams or categories in order to know

how Hardy's verse differs from that kind. His way is
restless, urgent, emphatic,—and was it Mr. Robert
Lynd who likened some of his queerer melodies to the
rattling of a milk-cart ?   In that simile, we may find
the beginnings of the explanation of Hardy's general
lilt or beat : he is, so to speak, ever on the road, working
along, tackling the stony hill rises, catching the notes
of somebody's fiddle or the thumpings of the traction
engine.   Little is he inclined to be static in the actions
of his mind or the wind and rain that swoop about
him.   He is indeed a connoisseur in the voices of
nature, and hears from every kind of tree or plant its
own perpetual music and accent.   In writing most of
his poems, as chance sets them off in his mind, he is
much as one of Nature's sylvan forms, swayed and lifted
and flung back with a sound of energies, reluctances
and pausings.   We may so hear him almost anywhere,

> How it came to an end !
> The meeting afar from the crowd,
> And the love-looks and laughters unpenned.
> The parting when much was avowed,
> How it came to an end ! . . .

> The sparrow dips in his wheel-rut bath,
> The sun grows passionate-eyed,
> And boils the dew to smoke by the paddock-path ;
> As strenuously we stride,—
> Five of us ; dark He, fair He, dark She, fair She, I,
> All beating by.

The surge of strength which such rhythms represent
is not invariably present in the 918 poems (I abide by
Professor Weber's arithmetic), and it is no injustice
to Hardy to think of a great many of these as magazine
verse.   Or perhaps they should be considered as the
occupations of rainy days and noteless interiors, when

something had to be done besides pasting up envelopes
or waiting for the next bundle of printers' proofs ; or
as equivalents of piano practice. The word " Song "
prefixed to an item is to be considered as a warning
that what follows will not be in Hardy's strongest way
of sense or fancy. " In the Street (Song) ", " First
or Last (Song) ", " Vagrant's Song (With an old
Wessex Refrain) ", " I Knew a Lady (Club Song) ",
" Her Apotheosis (Faded Woman's Song) ", " As
'twere To-night (Song) "—these are specimens of the
uninspired Hardy, and rather like the " ballad successes " which he heard from many a piano in his
time but which are heard no more. Of course, there
are exceptions to this idea about his song-titles. " He
Inadvertently Cures his Love-Pains (Song) ", " Dona-
ghadee (Song) ", " The Protean Maiden (Song) ",
" Known had I (Song) ", are not exceptions ; but
" Drinking Song " is. It combines the requirements
of its title with the wittiest of short histories of philosophy ; up come the great ideas, down they go again,
and all ends with a Pickwickian benevolence and social
triumph. Yet even as I confess my unlimited pleasure
in that splendid humorous lyric, recollection of another
Song disturbs it. Hardy called it " A Song of Hope ",
and it has the lugubrious hopelessness of one of those
gentlemen who, having been drinking, beset the
approach to public-houses with renderings of " Abide
with Me ".

Another class of verses by Hardy might as well be
away from the ample mass of his poems. They may
recall to older readers a publication formerly welcome
on railway bookstalls, *Queer Stories from " Truth "*.
They are short stories in rhyme, and as such often

occupy comparatively long tracts among the verse. So greatly did Hardy feel the incidents of life which had anything of the unexpected or peculiar in them, that he believed they would tell very well in some sort of ballad form, without much accompaniment of reflection or choice of phrase. He was too modest in his aims on these occasions. In explanation of the sing-song " Poor Man and a Lady ", he notes, " The foregoing was intended to preserve an episode " in the novel of the same name, which had been destroyed. The method of preservation was rough and ready :

> We met in a Mayfair church, alone :
> (The request was mine, which you yielded to.)
> " But we were not married at all ! " urged you :
> " Why, of course we were ! " I said. Your tone,
> I noted, was world-wise. You went on :
> " 'Twas sweet while it lasted. But you well know
> That law is law. He'll be, anon,
> My husband *really*. You, Dear, weren't so."

This specimen is fair enough for the drifting common-places which Hardy was too ready to drag into metrical form in these tales. They are like rhymes to aid the study of grammar—but are not so useful. They end by being neither one thing nor the other. A good many of them are on some corner of the eternal triangle, and even the facts brought to notice by the novelist on holiday are not nearly so exciting as he intended, nor advantaged by the primitive manner in which he chose to ballad-write them. He had too great faith in the potency of a thing that had happened, to strike us with admiration. " In the Days of Crino-line ", not the worst of these mild scandals, tells of the vicar's lady who went forth to meet her lover in her dowdy tilt-bonnet, but had a brilliant hat concealed

under her skirt, a stratagem which quite baffled her
spouse the vicar. " It was a true story," said Hardy
eagerly. And that was for him full warrant for most
of these anecdotes, brief or lengthy : the titles are often
premonitory if the reader wishes to evade the narrator,
witness a few of them : " A Military Appointment
(Scherzando) ", " The Two Wives (Smoker's Club-
Story) ", " The Mock Wife ", " Her Second Husband
hears her Story ", " The Elopement ", " The Duel ",
" The Contretemps ", " A Woman's Fancy ", " The
Turnip-Hoer ", " The Noble Lady's Tale ". Probably Hardy's habit of writing these verse stories was
at its height in the last part of the nineteenth century,
when he was still so much under the influence of
Browning and his poems of incident and psychological
example, although the fifteen brevities collected under
the title " Satires of Circumstance " prove that he
might fall in love with his simple story at a much later
date. Being short, and considered in rapid succession,
these " Satires " come as near as anything he has left
us to justifying his belief in the bare statement of the
business. A young clergyman has an extraordinary
success with his flock ; he is thereupon seen by chance
doing the acting over again in the vestry which had
seemed like faith's masterpiece in the pulpit. A man
who has left his walking-stick behind turns back for it
—and sees the girl of his choice in a fury with her
mother—he " steals off, leaving his stick unclaimed ".
Such paradoxical pictures with a little more background
are carved out very staringly in the " Satires of Circumstance ", but they would have been less effective
if they had been spun out like so many of Hardy's
points of misery.

While the monotonous and inferior in Hardy's poetry are being noticed, we may complain to his shade that he has often given us the unwelcome chance of knowing a long time ahead what he was going to say. He reveals his genuineness as a poet, it is true, by having a continuity in his world of observation and reasoning, and by being haunted through the years by his daemons ; we know that he is not writing, in the long run, for any other reason than the imparting of his profoundest recognitions. But there is a formula of Hardy's which is not of his deepest thinking, and which overcomes his freedom at times when a pleasant-looking subject attracts him. The reader is compelled to expect a melancholy close. " Julie-Jane " opens merrily enough,

> Sing ; how 'a would sing !
> How 'a would raise the tune
> When we rode in the waggon from harvesting
> By the light o' the moon ;

but the odds always are that before the last line we shall be informed,

> Yes, that's her burial bell.

On the same lines are the poems which say that there used to be such doings, such happy days, such marvellous people at such and such a place or house, but now there are only ghosts ; times change. Hardy himself has commented on this tendency to wander back into the past and protest that it *is* the past, in the stanzas " Life Laughs Onward ".

> Life laughed and moved on unsubdued,
> I saw that Old succumbed to Young :
> 'Twas well. My too regretful mood
> Died on my tongue.

Were the Collected Poems to be reduced to a fifth
of their number, or a tenth, the remaining pieces would
exhibit an impressive variety as well as an organic excellence. Passing thus from the duller pages to those
that are bright with Hardy's true and harmonizing
powers, each taste will prefer some special example,
and opinions on the classes of theme wherein the poet
achieves most permanence may still vary. But by
common consent there is a body of poetry by Hardy
which, having already stood many years among the best
that England has yielded, looks certain to keep its
place and to contribute to the thought and character
of coming generations.

Hardy's own arrangement of his poems in one
volume is like that of many poets—he does not feel
able to sort them out beyond a certain point ; nor will
any of us feel that the dividing lines between group
and group can be drawn with rigidity, if that were
desired. The selection made in 1940 by Mr. G. M.
Young is in two parts, the excerpts from *The Dynasts*
being duly given their own additional section : this
accomplished critic gathers first Poems of Place and
Incident (where some of those " queer stories " are
included, whatever the rebellious may say against
them), and then takes Poems of Memory and Reflection. From Hardy himself we get suggestions for
a grouping of rather different character, though nothing
systematic,—still, indicative of his general notions
about his field of action, depicted in the title-page
" Human Shows, Far Phantasies, Songs, and Trifles ".
To stretch out the large landscape of his poetry in
something like that manner may have its uses, if it
brings to mind more thoroughly the determination,

the range, the unorthodoxy and the originality of his work.

The poems which are especially due to contemplating time and change, and have the signs mostly of autobiography, are many and various. Some are undisguised statements, some are humorous in a way that suggests the Middle Ages, some are illusions of ghostliness, some tender and steady in acceptance. Everyone is capable of saying " How it came to an end ! " but few can make that kind of daily observation the foundation of an unforgettable poem as Hardy has done. Everyone gets to know that the bright scene and the great occasion are apt to be gone for ever when they are gone, and Hardy realizes that this knowledge has its own sad and notable music, as in " Middle-Age Enthusiasms ". He is an Ecclesiastes of the field path, the passing carriage, and the party on the lawn. In " Reminiscences of a Dancing Man " the Hardy of the grim jest appears, begins his song with loveliness and high spirits, ends suddenly with the enormous dance of death ; in " Voices from Things Growing in a Churchyard " he plays with strange versatility upon the common saw of " pushing up daisies ", finding also a new turn for " made one with nature ". And there is no melancholy in this lyric.

> These flowers are I, poor Fanny Hurd,
>   Sir or Madam,
> A little girl here sepultured.
> Once I flit-fluttered like a bird
> Above the grass, as now I wave
> In daisy shapes above my grave,
>   All day cheerily,
>   All night eerily !

The spirits sing one after another through the tangled

luxuriance of their place apart, and the poet presently
offers chorus for all :

> And so these maskers breathe to each
>   Sir or Madam
> Who lingers there, and their lively speech
> Affords an interpreter much to teach,
> As their murmurous accents seem to come
> Thence hitheraround in a radiant hum,
>   All day cheerily,
>   All night eerily !

Such pieces as " The Garden Seat " tell us of ghosts
not so well attuned with the flowing strength of Nature,
and these apparitions are children of sorrow ; but again,
as in the long and justly beloved " Friends Beyond ",
Hardy expresses a serenity of the grave such as seems
to complete all his studies of human endeavour and
desire—when

>   ignoring all that haps beneath the moon,
> William Dewy, Tranter Reuben, Farmer Ledlow late at
>   plough,
>   Robert's kin, and John's, and Ned's,
> And the Squire, and Lady Susan, murmur mildly to me
>   now.

To see how the same feeling might revisit Hardy with
quite another melody, another memory, it is only necessary to turn to the chiming stanzas " Regret not Me ".

Often enough Hardy's poems are chiefly of the
mœurs de province kind, though his instinct for looking
into the further bearings of a theme does not vanish
from these. But as an artist of country life and
occasion he has not many superiors among English
poets. Even the celebrated Christmas piece " The
Oxen " with its universal significance is primarily a
picture of Wessex worthies. " A Sheep Fair " is a
mercilessly true record, a " picture of misery " not

escapable, nor much reflected upon, in an agricultural community ; " Bags of Meat ", no doubt meant incidentally to speak to the humane, is in almost every word a still more biting registration, indeed an etching on the senses, of something which happens—has happened for ages—at every beast-market in the land. Then Hardy gives us, like a French short-story-writer, a Daudet rather than de Maupassant, some little group of rustic people, pathetic maybe, as in " The Ruined Maid ", or in " Unrealized " (which, under the title of " Orphaned : a Point of View ", Hardy so strangely thought suitable for Queen Alexandra's gift-book) ; else comical, as in " The Curate's Kindness ". And even when his own life was most closely bound up with the topic, he has often worked his poem in the plainest manner of a thing that you might have seen once in Wessex—of which " A Church Romance," already mentioned, is a delightful and kindly example. It may be less gracious than that, yet the artist still trusts to the virtue of the real faithfully presented as acceptable to the world, where few have leisure or chance to observe such remote and unsophisticated things for themselves ; " The Homecoming " is a ballad with a Teniers picture in every stanza :

" Now don't ye rub your eyes so red ; we're home and have
    no cares ;
Here's a skimmer-cake for supper, peckled onions, and some
    pears ;
I've got a little keg of summat strong, too, under stairs :
—What, slight your husband's victuals ? Other brides can
    tackle theirs ! "

The wind of winter mooed and mouthed their chimney like a
    horn,
And round the house and past the house 'twas leafless and
    lorn. . . .

" I didn't think such furniture as this was all you'd own,
And great black beams for ceiling, and a floor o' wretched
     stone,
And nasty pewter platters, horrid forks of steel and bone,
And a monstrous crock in chimney. 'Twas to me quite
     unbeknown."

In a land which has ever been prolific in men and
women who seek to know the world of wild nature
well, Hardy will be remembered, and that for his
poems as much as his prose. " Look how our
partner's rapt " : Hardy is found at many a turn of
the road peering into the miracles of the life of " the
others ". In that little poem of 1899, " An August
Midnight ", he explains his feelings simply, though in
his own knotty idiom : there are present as he writes
" a longlegs, a moth and a dumbledore . . . a sleepy
fly that rubs its hands. . . ."

" God's humblest, they ! " I muse. Yet why ?
They know Earth-secrets that know not I.

Not their knowledge alone stirs his admiration. His
" Darkling Thrush ", his " Blinded Bird " are to him
marvellous in their natures, their virtues, and these
songs in honour of such " corages " have been among
his best enjoyed verse. The desire that man should at
length be found in harmony with these moved him
to poetry, and he did not invariably utter so grave a
view on what is happening in the world to the " others "
through man's development as is presented in that
magnificent epicedium " The Mother Mourns ". In
imaginative presages like that, he was of course not
alone among his contemporaries, the earlier ones like
Browning, the later ones like Mr. Ralph Hodgson
and Mr. Walter de la Mare. The problem which

haunted him, the process of disregard for the balance of nature, has not grown less, and his words may be of some value to those who are thinking of the rescue of all that matters from the gross haste of human power.

Another part of Hardy's poetry describes in richly changing forms his gratitude to men of genius. Perhaps he had been led this way by his early reading of Carlyle, but even more he had the spirit of hero-worship in himself. He felt a personal indebtedness to those who by word or deed had lit up the general travel of mankind, he loved the magic of the destined being. So we have his extraordinarily precise recallings of Gibbon in his garden, of Keats at Hampstead and Lulworth Cove, of the anonymous Abbey Mason who (it might have been his old master John Hicks) had the fortune and wisdom to invent " the ' Perpendicular ' Style of Gothic Architecture " ; in a few stanzas brimming with light and faith he summons up Shelley inspired with the song of a skylark, Barthélémon the Vauxhall Gardens violinist answering Bishop Ken's " Awake my Soul " with a stately strain, Shakespeare as he came and went among the townspeople of Stratford-on-Avon. Who but he in modern times would have attempted a song in honour, as in vision, of " Xenophanes, the Monist of Colophon ", making that long dead free-thinker seem as near as a Dorset neighbour ?

From the sympathetic call through fifteen centuries to the enquiring Monist, it is possible to go directly to the most insistent and profound endeavour of Hardy the lyrical poet,—a large series of poems written on impulse all through his life almost, and as plentifully

supplied with fresh means of symbol or allegory as
they are aimed at one object.   First and last, Hardy as
poet recurs to the riddle of the universe, and to his
solitary notions on the apparent contradictions in the
nature of things.   Again and again, from one angle and
another, he seems to observe where the truth rests,
and hazards a solution, such as he interweaves with
the outward and human shows of *The Dynasts* ;   the
titles of these strange philosophical rhythms and fables
speedily say what he was trying to get into focus,
" Hap " for example, " Nature's Questioning ",
" Doom and She ", " The Sleep-Worker ", " Heredity ", " God's Funeral ", " The Clock of the Years ",
" The Absolute Explains ".   Even when the topic
might not seem at first likely to lead his meditation that
way, Hardy often produces a fresh instance of this
consuming passion for a ray of enlightenment from
" the Byss ".   That poem of his old age, " On the
Portrait of a Woman About to be Hanged ", which
was remarked as one more sign of his " keeping in
touch " with the events of the day, ends in fact as one
more sign of his search through all the days for a
reasonable explanation.

> Would that your Causer, ere knoll your knell
> For this riot of passion, might deign to tell
>   Why, since It made you
>   Sound in the germ,
>   It sent a worm
> To madden Its handiwork, when It might well
>   Not have assayed you.

If the fantasies which arise in him on the question of a
First Great Cause are generally melancholy, yet they
include an element of melioration, of submission and
goodwill which is too easily forgotten in discussion of

his creed. In the imaginary conversation with Time
called " The Lacking Sense ", which is set in " a sad-
coloured landscape, Waddon Vale ", the conclusion is
as generous and benevolent as it is immense in its
speculative force. Time imparts the tragedy of the
Mother who brings confusion to her finest creations
thus :

—"Ah ! knowest thou not her secret yet, her vainly veiled
     deficience,
   Whence it comes that all unwittingly she wounds the lives
     she loves ?
That sightless are those orbs of hers ?—which bar to her
     omniscience
   Brings those fearful unfulfilments, that red ravage through
     her zones
         Whereat all creation groans.

" She whispers it in each pathetic strenuous slow endeavour,
   When in mothering she unwittingly sets wounds on what
     she loves ;
Yet her primal doom pursues her, faultful, fatal is she ever ;
   Though so deft and nigh to vision is her facile finger-
     touch
         That the seers marvel much.

" Deal, then, her groping skill no scorn, no note of male-
     diction ;
   Not long on thee will press the hand that hurts the lives
     it loves ;
And while she plods dead-reckoning on, in darkness of
     affliction,
   Assist her where thy creaturely dependence can or may,
         For thou art of her clay."

Out of all the injuries to Nature's excellence multi-
plied through the ages by some " lacking sense ", that
of war troubled Hardy most. War drew from him
many poems, and some of his best, though war poems
are not the best beloved. He could regard the details

of this ever returning monster's prowess with the same
eye, ear and touch that all incident and scene found
ready in him, and so his picture got from tradition of
" Valenciennes " is among the masterpieces of our battle-
poetry, his " And There Was a Great Calm " founded
in immediate perceptions is one of the writings that
catch the peculiar life of the war of 1914–1918 as in an
eternal transparency. His spirit, however, was not
able to dwell too long on the aspect of war which the
Othellos of all generations are content to face, and he
lamented that this especial calamity should be so be-
wilderingly likely to rush down upon the multitudes
of every race. At one time he believed that the forces
of peace and altruism would put an end to it, and then
he wrote (with some recollections of Leigh Hunt's
" Captain Sword and Captain Pen ", I surmise) that
splendid vision " The Sick Battle-God ", great in its
portraiture of *la gloire*, and in its counterstrokes of
modern conscience and reason. This was forty years
ago. Before his death Hardy, with something like the
additional sense of a master mariner in a fog, was con-
strained to think that he had been dreaming ; he knew
in his own way that there was a fresh and appalling
disaster ahead.

No classification would quite fit all of Hardy's
poems, and some of them that have given pleasure to
the greatest number evade such a register as has just
been outlined. " Waiting Both " is just an imaginary
conversation, mainly in monosyllables :

> A star looks down at me,
> And says : " Here I and you
> Stand, each in our degree :
> What do you mean to do,—
> Mean to do ? "

I say : " For all I know,
Wait, and let Time go by,
Till my change come."—" Just so,"
The star says : " So mean I :—
So mean I."

Only that. It does not ask for much in the margin.
It confronts us like a lonely bridge in a fen, or the
eye of a bird on a nest. It is a biography of all that is
made, and yet it is Thomas Hardy, his alone. The
question of the beautiful or the significant hardly
seems to arise. Hardy, merely reporting a moment
at night, with nothing " happening ", is there for ever,
a distinct, separate, seared but unconquerable handi-
work of—whom ? No hurry this time to answer.
These are the occasions in poetry which baffle almost
every commentator, like Shakespeare's ballad of the
rain that raineth every day, and Scott's " Proud
Maisie ", but which haunt the race. Yet all the more
intricate and circumstantial parts of Hardy's poetry
will necessarily be borne in mind, in some such fashion
as I have represented them, if we are to judge him in
comparison with others who have built up a far-looking
temple of idea through many years of shifting light
and shade rather than sung and danced as caprice
delightfully invited. There was a master plan.

By way of pointing out some probable fields of
enquiry in Hardy's poetry in its manner and technical
affinities, some few thoughts about a piece here and
there may be sufficient now. In the first of his volumes
of poetry, the first offering is called ' The Temporary
the All (Sapphics) ". Thus he instantly announced,
in his new disclosure of himself, not only his zeal for
discerning what is truly difficult in the scheme of experience, but also his enthusiasm for the classics. How

oddly unhappy some of these sapphics are ! No wonder
that T. S. Omond in his chronicles of prosody insisted
on mentioning the poem only to dismiss it. But more
could be said. Hardy's theory of verse was that it
should be strong, symmetrical, bright ; but that it
should express a considerable amount of working
thought. He may have had in mind, he would surely
have agreed with Gautier's miraculous doctrine
demonstrated :

> Oui, l'œuvre sort plus belle
> D'une forme au travail
>   Rebelle,
> Vers, marbre, onyx, émail. . . .
>
> Sculpte, lime, cisèle ;
> Que ton rêve flottant
>   Se scelle
> Dans le bloc résistant !

The faults of Hardy's verse are seldom those of the
mediocre man, with his apparently easy measures,
never quite full measure ; they are those of a zealous
experimenter, whose materials do not always obey the
purpose or yield a restful completeness. We may grow
accustomed to some of Hardy's peculiarities in their
places, constructions of sentence that have no reason
for being so awkward, archaisms which are not at all
useful in poems of modern consciousness and among
terms of newest thought :

> 'Thwart my wistful way did a damsel saunter. . . .
> Bettered not has Fate or my hand's achievement ;

but such as they are they repel the general reader.

In this first poem some words reflect Hardy's faith
in William Barnes's Wessex poems : " forthcome ",
" a breath-while ", " earth-track ". He makes use of

Barnes's " Woak Hill " stanza, with modifications, in
a number of poems on a wide range of subjects. But,
on the whole, he feels the broader volume of his verse
music in a way which keeps him from trying to follow
up the intricacies of Barnes (had he been inclined to
such ingenious minor complexity). It is not often
that a poem by Hardy can be regarded as closely
modelled on a poem by another, and if anything does
reveal such an obligation it is probably the tune.
" Friends Beyond " is apparently a metrical aftermath
of Hardy's listening to " Locksley Hall ", though he
has obtained a new effect by working in a short line in
recurrence. Underneath the emphases of the charming " Ditty " to E. L. G. in 1870, we catch those so
magnificently sounded by Thomas Campbell on quite
another theme, " Of Nelson and the North ".

> And Devotion droops her glance
> To recall
> What bond-servants of Chance
> We are all.

Many notes have been made on similarities between
Hardy's verse and Browning's. The love of lyrical
meditation, and lyrical portraiture, is common to them
both, and here and there one may catch with some
confidence the elder man's rhythms and rhymings
in his admirer's utterance, even where the topic is not
the same. The imitation is never inert ; Hardy is in-
capable of mere borrowing, even of repeating unconsciously. But when Browning depicts " A Pretty
Woman " in this form,

> To think men cannot take you, Sweet,
> And enfold you,
> Ay, and hold you,
> And so keep you what they make you, Sweet,

and Hardy calls " To Outer Nature ",

> Why not sempiternal
> Thou and I ?   Our vernal
> Brightness keeping,
> Time outleaping ;
> Passed the hodiernal !

the resemblance, the metrical discipleship can hardly
be denied.   And perhaps it was from an admiring
familiarity with Browning's poems that Hardy had a
liking for an occasional parade of rhyming skill.   It
does not always contribute to the true worth of the
poem.   It is well enough in such a merry complaint
as that on the continued refusal of a memorial in
Westminster Abbey to Byron :

> " 'Twill next be expected
> That I get erected
> To Shelley a tablet
> In some niche or gablet.
> Then—what makes my skin burn,
> Yea, forehead to chin burn—
> That I ensconce Swinburne."

It is charming in the loving fancy-sketch of Liddell
and Scott talking over the completion of their Greek
Lexicon :

> " O that first morning, smiling bland,
> With sheets of foolscap, quills in hand,
> To write ἀάατος and ἀαγής
> Followed by fifteen hundred pages,
>   What nerve was ours
>   So to back our powers,
> Assured that we should reach ᾠώδης
> While there was breath left in our bodies ! "

But when he is exploring his life and spiritual performance gravely, as he does in the poem " After
Reading Psalms XXXIX, XL., Etc.," it is a disturbing

thing to have him forcing his verse for the difficult
rhyme :

> When I failed at fervid rhymes,
>   " Shall," I said, " persist I ? "
> " *Dies* " (I would add at times)
>   " *Meos posuisti !* "
>
> So I have fared through many suns ;
>   Sadly little grist I
> Bring my mill, or any one's,
>   *Domine, Tu scisti !*

This perverse trick is exposed at once by the following
poem, in something of the same mood, called " Surview " (the word is Browning's), a very noble and unaffected confession, with no clamour, no disarranged
English :

> " *You taught not that which you set about,*"
>   Said my own voice talking to me ;
> " *That the greatest of things is Charity.* . . ."
> —And the sticks burnt low, and the fire went out,
>   And my voice ceased talking to me.

The painter-poet insists on being very much in the
middle of things time and again in Hardy's verse,—
perhaps the black-and-white artist would be more
usually his definition. Even in studies of severe distress of mind, this quality may stand forth, as it does
in " Neutral Tones " dated 1867, with its fiercely
caught and impressed details of the pond, the white
sun, the few grey leaves from a single ash on the
starved ground, the woman's tired face with the dead
smile and unshining eyes. Touch upon touch, this
draughtsmanship invigorates poems of his beyond
counting now, as his life proceeds : he can hardly
discuss the abstract without his exact picture of the
sensuous. Celebrating the jubilee of the *Cornhill*

Magazine, he notices and builds his meaning on a pictorial feature, which most would have failed to see out of sheer familiarity :

> —Here, on your cover, never tires
> The sower, reaper, thresher, while
> As through the seasons of our sires
>
> Each wills to work in ancient style
> With seedlip, sickle, share and flail,
> Though modes have since moved many a mile !
>
> The steel-roped plough now rips the vale,
> With cog and tooth the sheaves are won,
> Wired wheels drum out the wheat like hail. . . .

In his latest days, Hardy often contents himself with a metrical description, of course implying some part of a view of life, but much in the way that the woodcuts of Thomas Bewick do. "An Unkindly May" is a concentrated impression of foul weather, sour, ragged, bloodless ; in the midst of all, there is the reason for the sketch, but still in terms of description :

> A shepherd stands by a gate in a white smock-frock :
> He holds the gate ajar, intently counting his flock.

This way of his, this graphic poetry, is seen to have been present to his mind quite easily and naturally in the stanzas " Lying Awake ",

> You, Morningtide Star, now are steady-eyed, over the east,
>   I know it as if I saw you ;
> You, Beeches, engrave on the sky your thin twigs, even the
>   least ;
>   Had I paper and pencil I'd draw you.
> You, Meadow, are white with your counterpane cover of
>   dew,
>   I see it as if I were there ;
> You, Churchyard, are lightening faint from the shade of the
>   yew,
>   The names creeping out everywhere.

The parodist may fairly indulge his humour on some prevalent weaknesses of the Muse of Hardy, who doubtless lives too much in the frown, and whose churchyard exultations are like Dickens's " Sundays are our happiest days " ; the style, like the substance, has its oddities, tempting to the cheerful lover of a little burlesque. Hardy's poetic language is sometimes a peculiar compound of the high-flown and the dull. If he means " I asked " he is liable to say " I queried " or rather " Queried I " ; he is liable to " opine " instead of think, and if it be a crime to exclaim " God wot " he commits it more than once. No admirer of the Wordsworthian

> Spade, with which Wilkinson hath tilled his lands

can go far unrewarded in Hardy's poems ; they have their share of stuffed-owl simplicities, such as the observation in the railway waiting-room,

> The table bore a Testament
> For travellers' reading, if suchwise bent.

But Hardy risks all that. He goes his road in the matter of expression, unworried about grinning faces, and in this spirit he arrives at numberless decisive ways of putting things, offered him and accepted from an open love of life.

> The lamps, just lit, begin to outloom
> Like dandelion-globes in the gloom. . . .

> Cries still are heard in secret nooks,
> Till hushed with gag or slit or thud. . . .

> Down here in shade we hear the painters shift
> Against the bollards with a drowsy lift,
> As moved by the incoming stealthy tide.
> High up across the bridge the burghers glide

As cut black-paper portraits hastening on
In conversation none knows what upon :
Their sharp-edged lips move quickly word by word
    To speech that is not heard. . . .

On the frigid face of the heath-hemmed pond
    There shaped the half-grown moon :
Winged whiffs from the north with a husky croon
    Blew over and beyond.

And the wind flapped the moon in its float on the pool,
    And stretched it to oval form ;
Then corkscrewed it like a wriggling worm ;
    Then wanned it weariful.

Such is his independence in saying what he means
in his verse, such his strength founded in a constant
principle of doing the work thoroughly. The result
is to be a translation of the actual, and the terms must
therefore have as much of the shrewdness and par-
ticularity of life, according to our senses' report, as
words can have ; it does not matter to Hardy whether
others would have given these words a ticket of
admission or not. So long as they are words that
strike, bite in, caress, disturb, unveil the truth, quicken
the curiosity, they will suit him. In this aspect, he
may be considered as the son of his province, just as
he is in so many of his mind's workings ; he is bringing to poetry a speech, a manner of making others
feel with all their powers, not derived from the dialect
of his native place—that he left to William Barnes—
but characteristically like that kind of language.
Hardy's respect for and reliance upon the intellectual
resources of the fully developed English tongue are
obvious ; he was entirely receptive of that eloquence
also, and can employ it ; yet in many of his poems
the immediate, physical, substantial effect of local

experience, the word formed with primitive intensity upon the thing indicated, is his mark and his command.

Two printed versions of Hardy's *in memoriam* poem on Sir Frederic Treves are added here to show the craftsmanship which interested him, and induced him to make numerous minor changes, adjustments and strengthenings : even the third version, in his collected poems, has its own variants. " In the Evening " appeared thus in *The Times* of January 5th, 1924 :

> In the evening, shortly after he was dead,
>   He lay amidst the dust and hoar
> Of ages, and to a spirit attending said
>   " This chalky bed ?
> I seem to have been here before ? "
>
> " O yes. You *have* been here. You know the place,"
>   The sprite replied, " long ere your call !
> And if you cared to do so you might trace
>   In this white space
> Your quality, your substance, and your all."
>
> Thereat he said : " Why was I called away ?
>   I felt no trouble or discontent.
> Why did I not prolong my ancient stay
>   Herein for aye ? "
> The sprite looked vague. " None knows ! You went.
>
> " True, Time has not as yet revealed to you
>   Your need to go. But, some men tell,
> A marvellous Deftness called you forth—to do
>   Much that was due.
> Good. You have returned. And all is well."

The second version occurs in the *Year Book of the Society of Dorset Men in London* for 1924, one of a series which preserves many things for the curious lover of Hardy's life-work :

In the evening, when the world knew he was dead,
    He lay amid the dust and hoar
Of ages ; and to a spirit attending said,
    " This chalky bed ?—
I surely seem to have been here before ? "

" O yes. You have been here. You know the place,
    Substanced as you, long ere your call ;
And if you cared to do so you might trace
    In this gray space
Your being, and the being of men all."

Thereto said he : " Then why was I called away ?
    I knew no trouble or discontent.
Why did I not prolong my ancient stay
    Herein for aye ? "
The spirit shook its head.   " None knows : you went."

" And though, perhaps, Time did not show to you
    Your need to go, dream-vision sees
How Æsculapius' phantom hither flew
    With Galen's too,
And his of Cos—plague-proof Hippocrates,

And touched you forth, whose skill had read as theirs,
    Maybe, had Science chanced to excel
In their day with its scope to stem despairs
    That mankind bears ! . . .
Enough.   You have returned.   And all is well."

XIII

FROM the first, the man whose literary career has been briefly reconsidered in this book was a student. He went youthfully into the world not as one who would there find glittering prizes or anything which would make a difference to himself in the way of practical gains and key positions, but as one with his powers all bent on the advancement of learning—more light in himself, and in others through him, if that turned out right. Learning, indeed, but not in a limited sense, summoned him from the byroads and benches of his forefathers, and changed the region in which he perfected his own skill, though, happily, the move was not made before he had practised more than a little in their many-centuried knowledges and craftsman-ships. As for any egotistical satisfaction in the fame which Thomas Hardy's study of universal things brought him, from every part of the world, it would be hard to find signs of it in anything he said or wrote when he was being idolized. An old contemporary remarked that he " was getting vain ", but there was nothing to support this. Hardy liked to be liked, and was pleased if any goodness were found in anything that had come out of his workshop, and that was all. He was not so preternaturally simple as to be ignorant

of his sway as a writer, and the reward of his judgment
in seeking his living by the pen ; but in contemplating
those facts he might have been contemplating the case
of another man with the same name.

All that has been written upon the writings of
Hardy, and all that can be written, leads to one general
fact : they coalesce into one work, and it is that which
he had in view from the time when he conned *Walkingame's Arithmetic* " with the bent of a bee " in his
first village school.   It is a vast work of study in the
school of our planetary life, comprising a multitude of
memoranda and of imaginative or meditative exercises
upon them, varying widely not only in the forms in
which they are embodied and the apparent importance,
seriousness, diligence which attaches to them, but still
forming one extraordinary continuous volume of inspired industry in this ancient scene of enquiry.   " Unadjusted impressions have their value, and the road
to a true philosophy of life seems to lie in humbly
recording diverse readings of its phenomena as they
are forced upon us by chance and change."   So he
wrote, but one may extend the sense of his words,
if they suggest that he was at all a passive recorder.
His habit was to be uncommonly wide-awake in case
chance and change were producing something of
interest, and not much force was necessary for getting
him to comment on the phenomenon of the human
or any other organism.   His impressions were unadjusted, that is, impartial and direct, except where
he was engaged in a narrative with the usual artistic
boundaries and coherent dispositions of character and
incident within them—unadjusted, in so far as they
were achieved by new contacts with circumstance, not

preceded by a desire to work up any favourite theme of others or even of himself, though he had as everyone knows some tendency to detect the death of the beautiful, and salute the glorious rather by contrast than in its noontide of strength.

> In nature's infinite book of secrecy
> A little can I read.

As he drew from that encyclopaedia the elements of his own quite ample portfolio, Hardy certainly began to read a continuous meaning in his numerous points of information, and to paraphrase it in several forms of literature. He claimed " a little ", or a very little, of true and unassailable interpretation as his, and few would ask from him or anyone else of mortal clay a central and sufficient theory of this transitory life. Most of the sages have resorted to one version or another of the golden age as a way out of its labyrinth of roses and thorns. Perhaps Hardy was no abler thinker than these, and an age of gold did not seem to him immoral ; but he did not finally call off the pursuit of a workable conjecture on the nature of things and mask the move in a kind of gaudy day, presided over by pleasant desire and reverie. He at any rate stuck to his evidence, and made something of it, a deduction which was easily damned by any scribe as pessimism. His defence was as easy : he was an explorer of reality, knowledge of one's situation is essential to any improvement attempted in or from it, " amendment and not madness lies that way ". In a single term, he called the result of all his studies a creed of " evolutionary meliorism ". Was he wrong when he thought of the Immanent Will as having an imperfect consciousness, and as being on the way towards a better ? Was that a gloomy, and therefore retrograde conjecture ? At least nothing of greater power, or more worthy of discussion, or likely to yield some comfort and some sense of prospect to those who see their world in violent and seemingly illogical confusion, was enunciated by the novelists, dramatists and poets of Hardy's long day.

Crudities, lapses, monotonies, inconsequences and other faults are discoverable in his writings ; some tastes, though it hardly need be said of any one writer more than another, are utterly unable to accept them. The mention of George Moore is instance enough, though his pleasantries at the expense of " the author of these absurd words " are found to refer to a limited number of them. It can be admitted by almost any Hardyan that the poor passages in his work are an offering to the wanton or the unsympathetic critic. Those dragging sentences, those stuffy wordings ! " One evening of late summer, before the present century had reached its thirtieth year, a young man and woman, the latter carrying a child, were approaching the large village of Weydon Priors on foot. They were plainly but not ill clad, though the thick hoar of dust which had accumulated on their shoes and clothing from an obviously long journey lent a disadvantageous shabbiness to their appearance just now that did not belong to it in ordinary times." It cannot be called a heaven-sent opening for a novel ; yet it is the first paragraph of no less a novel than *The Mayor of Casterbridge*. And to many, Hardy's novels have been like the works of Nature, the persons and voices and occurrences have come of that kind which passes in the feelings into the plane of the historical; to many, the faults of style and sentiment are not present, their appearance being merged into the urgency of the life-story which Hardy brings forth.

There are signs enough that Hardy himself not only ceased to write novels but was inclined to decry those he had written. This turn was not in its first nature a resentment aroused by the attacks on the latest of them, even if he did one day [1] point to a sample of hostile and one-sided criticism and remark that this sort of thing would stop his career in fiction. It is much more likely to have been an awareness that he could not for all his concentration and " faith and fire " achieve a mastery over the conditions of writing serials and at the same time deliver the most effective and intense figures of truth. Even as he thanks Coventry Patmore in 1886 for a handsome allusion in the *Fortnightly Review*, he reveals his own discontent with what he was producing : " It is what I might have deserved if my novels had been exact transcripts of their original irradiated conception, before any attempt at working out that glorious dream had been made— and the impossibility of getting it on paper had been brought home to me ". In spite of that, the Wessex Novels form a large part of his vast register of the world he knew, and though we may regret with him that they suffer to a greater or less degree from the artificial restraints imposed on him in the writing, they contain much of his most unexpected knowledge and enlivening intuition. They are a lasting tribute to private virtue.

[1] Rider Haggard mentions an instance, when he and Hardy were by themselves in the little writing-room of the Savile Club.

I could almost wish that Hardy had been an ancient classic, and that chance and change, his old favourites, had managed to overwhelm some of his novels and tales and even some of his poems, leaving us a volume of stately dimensions still,—all that was extant,—a mighty book of the old folio order. As it is, his entire works may be regarded as something like that, among the classics, a treasure-house of things for the mind in many of its appetites and needs ; perhaps to be set not far from *The Anatomy of Melancholy*, or the works of John Webster, or even of Francis Bacon. Or it might not be foppery to let them occupy the space between Gibbon and Samuel Taylor Coleridge ; to each of these studious and eloquent men, he bears much likeness in his amplitude of observed fact, and his anxious investigation through the immense phantasm of time ; with some hope comparable to theirs that confusion, though of persistent growth, might be reduced by honest thought. Truth was worth an expedition.

To the end of his life Hardy kept some quality of childhood, which caused Mr. H. M. Tomlinson to write, " Sometimes when talking to him you felt this child was as old as humanity and knew all about us, but that he did not attach importance to his knowledge because he did not know that he had it. Just by chance, in the drift of the talk, there would be a word by Hardy, not only wide of the mark, but apparently not directed to it. Why did he say it ? On the way home, or some weeks later, his comment would be recalled, and with the revealing light on it." This excellent recollection might be borne in mind, and possibly should have been at one or two points in this

volume more than it was, when Hardy's reader is re-
flecting on some pages of his prose and verse with a
desire that they might be excised, as unguided, irre-
levant or empty. Almost any habitué of literature
could apparently lend him a hand and improve the
appeal of his genius by judicious retrenchments. Much
might be done, but some caution would be required
lest the editorial treatment did not always remove only
what was otiose. The reasons for some of Hardy's
words being included in his book, when they appear
at the outset not to be valuable to it, are apt to occur to
the mind on a reconsideration. He did not go into
the matter very " clearly ", nor make an attempt to
exhibit his poems in particular as they might look
most orderly in a surface view, or resemble a prize
essay.

That he was a lover of precise work and system is
of course true ; it was an inherited and practical thing
with him, the builder's son, the architect's pupil, the
man of measurements, elevations and proportions.
Close observers of his work find that he laid out a
great deal of it, and the fiction especially, with the
same firmness as he brought to the building of Max
Gate and the arrangement of his trees, lawns, flower-
plots and approaches. It is discovered that not only
are the Wessex Novels based upon a map of the old
kingdom but that each of them is mainly related to a
subdivision of that region ; and in the matter of the
chronology which they rest upon, they are subject to
a plan of time keeping each tale as distinct as possible.
This preliminary charting is discussed and illustrated
in Professor Carl J. Weber's biography of Hardy, not
merely for the sake of a curious scholarship but because

Hardy's orderly distinctness of design is connected
with " a different geographical atmosphere—a different
literary climate " for at least ten of the novels.   But, in
reading, we can scarcely feel that the author is working
to a schedule ; the precise lines have been overgrown
with a fertility of Nature, the landscape of passions and
sympathies is wide and multitudinous, and Hardy
seldom seems to enquire into the exact relations of his
work again, being content with the principles of underlying form and outward freedom, colour and fruitful-
ness.   That is ever the way of the man of genius, the
eloquence of the original mind ; and, if no comparison
with others truly fits this Wessex worthy, yet to those
names which have been introduced by way of suggestion only one more can be added.   It could hardly
be omitted.   It is John Milton.

Hardy the student on the great scale was often indebted to his splendid predecessor for an idea, to which
he was himself coming, uttered in masterly sentences.
Dr. W. R. Rutland puts his finger on a token or two
of this, when he traces a quotation in Hardy's vision
of Gibbon at Lausanne to " Milton's *Doctrine and
Discipline of Divorce*, which is also quoted for the
chapter heading to the fourth part of *Jude* ".   The
critic concludes, " We may add some of Milton's more
daring prose works to Hardy's philosophical studies."
In his preface to *The Dynasts* we find Hardy explicitly
" excluding the celestial machinery of *Paradise Lost*, as
peremptorily as that of the *Iliad* or the *Eddas* " ; but
the reference shows where his consultations had been
held.   Yet the naming of Milton which I have ventured
upon in this place is due to another aspect of both
him and our later composer of epic drama, as also

severe critic of marriage and of prelates. In *Paradise
Lost*, as well as in many of Milton's prose pamphlets,
while the argument in the author's mindsight was noted
down in a sharply clear epitome, almost as methodical
as a sermon by Hardy's friend Parson Thirdly, God's
plenty breaks forth with invincible animation, and the
poem is crowded with the richness of thought and
sensation, prolific, and sinuous, and of every form and
hue. No wonder that when the topic itself is one of
teeming creation the poet's nature rises to it and the
verse rolls forth an extraordinary luxuriance of " phenomena ",—as notably in the triumph-song for the Days
of Creation. Thus far of Milton, and a similar impassioned and carefree exuberance, if not in quite the
same tropical panoply, characterizes Hardy when he
has got his design into full swing. Such passages of
his as show his great spirit, informed by long and
bright-eyed observation, remind me of another poet's
Pillars of Wisdom :

> Eta with living sculpture breathes,
> With verdant carvings, flowery wreaths
> 　　Of never-wasting bloom ;
> In strong relief his goodly base
> All instruments of labour grace,
> 　　The trowel, spade, and loom.

There are figures of tragedy, frustration, pain, stupidity,
malignancy on Hardy's pillar ; but we shall trace in
the unifying style of this master, to quote from
Christopher Smart again, a

> Wish of infinite conceit
> For man, beast, mute, the small and great,
> 　　And prostrate dust to dust.

His stories are more likely than not to illustrate the

bitter experience, the want of wisdom, the failure of
the possible correspondence between the deserving and
the occasion ; but I cannot agree with the Chester-
tonian attacks upon him as one with a soured and
dangerous mind, gloating over the bad. For one thing,
his vision did not stop at the human scene, but traversed
the far wider universe about us with the feeling that
our particular lot is not the only thing that counts ;
for another, it is only his infinite wish to see a world
of harmonious relationships and intelligent joy that
makes him dwell upon examples of the chaotic.

C. E. Montague, serving on the Western Front
during the first World War, turned to Hardy's books
again, and was more than ever impressed by the big-
ness of the author in comparison with his contemporaries; but he demurred at a passage or two of the
Wessex Novels in which Hardy summed up human
experience as getting worse and worse. He noted that
Hardy's own work included the answer to such a
verdict, in those other passages which treated of life
with a rich confidence and the pride of expressing the
beautiful and flourishing in a fine way. Among the
recently published letters of Florence Hardy to Sir
Sydney Cockerell—letters which are worthy of a place
in any collection of modern examples of this immemorial art—there is one which can be associated
with C. E. Montague's comment as a reader of Hardy.
Mrs. Hardy sends word of Hardy's being in high
spirits, and explains that he has just been writing a
poem—of course a very dismal poem. Her humorous
instance is indeed a piece of profound understanding.
Hardy, even while he is wrestling with his *agnostos
theos*, his impersonal Cause, and all the misshapes of

mortal multiplicity, provides the best conceivable defence of his and of everybody's being here at all.

> There is delight in singing, though none hear
> Beyond the singer.

Action is famous, accomplishment is happy, and the
privilege of doing a thing well and intently is a salve
for a myriad injuries.

It is true that his last printed poem, figured out
with all the precision of a lifetime, and necessarily to
be considered with great attention since Hardy conceived poetry to be his first and last secret of power,
declares that he has discerned something taking place
in our world which overwhelms all other interest.
The nature of this irremediable thing seen is concealed
—that is the way in which the poem is conceived,
" tell it not ",—but we can conjecture it from the third
stanza, stenographic though it is :

> Let Time roll backward if it will ;
> (Magians who drive the midnight quill
> With brain aglow
> Can see it so,)
> What I have learnt no man shall know.

At an earlier date (1922), in his " Apology " for a new
volume, Hardy had uttered some thought that troubled
him in somewhat the same way : " Whether owing to
the barbarizing of taste in the younger minds by the
dark madness of the late war, the unabashed cultivation
of selfishness in all classes, the plethoric growth of
knowledge simultaneously with the stunting of wisdom,
' a degrading thirst after outrageous stimulation ' (to
quote Wordsworth again), or from any other cause,
we seem threatened with a new Dark Age ".   But that
would imply a condition from which there could and

would be recovery. The vision which he concealed in " He Resolves to Say No More " appears to be of some mathematically determined regression in the scheme of things which quite makes futile all our progress of the past and best and noblest aspiration of the present.

Then, if he was assured that our race was doomed to this disappointment, and that the retreat from our furthest point of civilised intelligence and spiritual pilgrimage was imminent because the world was so made, as the mortal span is for individuals, it was not pessimism in him to admit the fact. If in some vigil, there at Max Gate with his old writing equipment and lamp and the land he knew out in the dark, he had a kind of vision with prelude of the war that was only a dozen years ahead, and following dreadfully hard upon the last grimacings of its forerunner, it was not possible for him to unsee it. Many of those with whom he passed a little of his later years will not easily treat the question of his being unusually sentient, even presentient as a sheer fancy. He had grown in simple receptivity more like one of those non-human beings whose powers of detecting the supernatural he was always observing—he did not look on Wessex the dog without musing on several strange things that dog was aware of but men were not. " It may be true that as a man thinks so he is, and that may be why Hardy's head was satisfying with expected beauty. . . . When Hardy was in repose his face was that of a seer." So, as the sum of all his study of the mystery of things, he claimed at last to " have learnt " one particular and to all appearances catastrophic certainty ; and for once, he declined to be a disciplined student and to record the phenomenon in his book. Therein he had set down for any to share that would, for ultimate mastery of circumstance and contribution to the strength and success of human life, so many things in so many forms of plain view or enchanting parable ; but this last thing, this narrowing necessity he could not set down there, and it was not that his immense honesty or personal keenness with pen and pencil had failed him. It was his longing to be a voice of gladness to his fellow-men, to be on the side of free happiness and bloom, which at last was compelled to be the opponent of his clear love of knowledge ; and even where he felt convinced that he had chanced upon a key to the future of unequalled importance, the thought that the workings of it would darken and burden us already burdened people caused him in his eighty-eighth year to leave a blank page after all.

Nevertheless, he had often selected from others as well as worded for himself such thoughts as counteract apprehension of this sort. If one of these inscriptions in his book would be found as epilogue, it might be this :

" This is the chief thing : Be not perturbed, for all things are according to the nature of the universal."—(Long's) *M. Aurelius Antoninus.*

" The foregoing is one passage, among others, that I have had much in mind."

INDEX

Printed in Great Britain by Richard Clay (The Chaucer Press), Ltd., Bungay, Suffolk